# COMPARATIVE POLITICS

*Revised and Enlarged Edition*

VIDYA BHUSHAN

ATLANTIC

PUBLISHERS & DISTRIBUTORS (P) LTD

**ATLANTIC**
PUBLISHERS & DISTRIBUTORS (P) LTD

7/22, Ansari Road, Darya Ganj, New Delhi
Tel.: +91-11-4077 5252, 2327 3880
E-mail: orders@atlanticbooks.com
Web: www.atlanticbooks.com

Published by Atlantic Publishers & Distributors (P) Ltd. 2025

Reprinted in 2000, 2006, 2011, 2014, 2018, 2019, 2020, 2021, 2022, 2023, 2024, 2025



Printed & bound in India by Atlantic Print Services

# Preface to the Second Edition

A wide scale induction of the new concepts, approaches, theoretical frameworks, paradigms, and orientations in the discipline of 'political science' in general and in the field of 'Comparative Politics' in particular has been witnessed since the mid-fifties. These new developments not only provide an overview of the major transformations in the field of 'Comparative Politics' in recent times, categories and concepts appropriate for the comparison of political systems differing radically in culture and structures but also equip it with new and enlarged capacities to comprehend and analyse the political realities being faced by the contemporary developing and the underdeveloped nation states *i.e.*, the non-western political systems. The quest is that 'Comparative Politics' should be non-parochial, non-formalistic, non-legalistic, analytic and genuinely comparative. The trend is, therefore, towards taking the study of politics to the level of a scientific enquiry into the phenomenon of power.

In spite of all these developments, not many broad-ranged books on the subject are easily available to the Indian students. The present work is, therefore, intended primarily to explain in simple and clear language the new concepts, approaches, paradigms to the Indian readers. Moreover, the first edition of this book was very well received by the students. It has, thus, encouraged me to bring out a complete textbook to cater well to the requirements of the students of 'Comparative Politics' at the graduate and post-graduate levels studying in Indian Universities. It will also be equally useful to those who are interested in acquiring a core knowledge of the fast expanding discipline of Political Science.

I may, however, once again point out that the various topics included in this book are based on the findings and observations of many eminent Western and Indian authors on the subject, to whom I express my deep sense of gratitude.

I hope that the teachers and students will find this revised and enlarged edition of the book worthwhile and will be kind enough to oblige me by sending their comments and suggestions in the light of which necessary changes may be made in the next edition or print of this book.

**VIDYA BHUSHAN**

# Preface to the First Edition

In the twentieth century, particularly since World War Second, "Comparative Politics" has witnessed not only development on a scale never reached so far but it has become more and more popular. The reason is that till the middle of this century, its area was limited largely to those countries in Europe and English-speaking world which were either highly developed or had long lived political institutions. But since then efforts have been made to include the new nation states — developing and underdeveloped — within the scope of universal or broad generalizations and, thus, in the discipline of 'Comparative Politics'.

Moreover, the field of 'Comparative Politics' has been greatly affected by the extension of investigations into the emerging states of Asia, Africa, South East Asia, Latin America and Middle East. By providing fresh and exciting new laboratories for the analysis of political development, these countries have, therefore, significantly expanded the universe of 'Comparative Politics'.

In spite of all these developments, not many broad-ranged books on this discipline are available to Indian students.

The author has been teaching 'Comparative Politics' at the Postgraduate level in the University of Jammu, Jammu-Tawi (J & K) since 1983, and all the time has been reminded by his students, of the need for a book with simplified description on the subject by an Indian Scholar.

In order to introduce the students to the subject of 'Comparative Politics', the present Volume though rich in material, written in simple language and handy in size, is designed to present a simplified description of different aspects of 'Comparative Politics'.

I may further point out that the various topics included in this book are based on the findings and observations of many eminent Western and Indian writers, to whom I express my sense of gratitude.

In the end, I hope that it will cater well to the requirements of those engaged in the study of 'Comparative Politics' for their Post-graduate degree in Indian Universities. It will also be equally useful to those interested in acquiring a core knowledge of this fast expanding discipline of Political Science.

**VIDYA BHUSHAN**

# Contents

# 1

# The Study of Comparative Politics

## 1.1. COMPARATIVE POLITICS—MEANING, NATURE AND THEORY

'Comparison' is man's instinctive tendency which impels him to appraise his own conduct *vis-a-vis* those of others. He is ever keen to know how people around him live, behave and act. This comparative interest, according to a thinker, arises out of the following fundamental urges of a man :

"(i) To know how others live and act;

(ii) to discover similarities and dissimilarities between oneself and others and, thus, gain an enriched perception of one's own self; and

(iii) to accept what is perceived to be the best in others. In other words a reformist motivation."[1]

Comparative politics is one of the results of these human urges.

Moreover, scientific investigations in these days involve systematic analysis and study of various problems and objects which include political institutions and organisations also. The necessity of rigorous research subjects various parameters to strict scrutiny through quantitative as well as qualitative measurements and systematisation. Each political problem of today is, therefore, being subjected to various processes, keen observations and systematic investigations before it is finally adopted or discarded by the society. The horizon of political science is, thus, ever expanding and the comparative politics on the other hand helps in the study of increasing political problems in a scientific and systematic way.

The study of Comparative Politics is at the heart of contemporary Political Science. Comparative Politics has, therefore become a field of growing importance in all the countries.[2]

More recently, modern Social Science has increased our power to observe and compare systematically empirical world of facts around us and to subject many of these facts and processes to qualitative measurement and logical and mathematical analysis. At the same time, the behavioural Sciences have given us a good deal of new and partly verified information as to how people think, feel, perceive and act individually and in a group.[3]

In other words due to the discovery of more and more sophisticated tools for understanding and explaining political realities and inter-disciplinary focus on the matters of political significance, by and large, responsible for expanding the frontiers of political Science particularly in the empirical studies of several uncultivated regions considered as non-state areas. As a result traditional approaches to the study of Politics resting primarily on the foundations of History, Ethics and Law are being replaced by new approaches drawn from discipline of Sociology, Economics, Psychology, Biology etc. and the study of Comparative Politics becoming more popular.[4]

### 1.1.1. Meaning of Comparative

Before we attempt to define 'Comparative' Politics' we should first define the term Comparative and then Politics.

***Comparative :*** By Comparison, one can see patterns of activity, taken by different regimes, analyse differing ideologies and processes and decision-making and examine propositions about both importance of certain characteristics under study and the relationship between classes of data. Comparison allows systematic empirical testing of generalization used to order diverse data. By comparison one may observe patterns, similarities and differences.

Comparisons can be made across space as well as over time. For example, we may study the voting behaviour or law making processes in a number of countries. We can also study these phenomena over the dimensions of time *e.g.* Voting Behaviours in first General Election (1952) and 1980 General Election and pinpoint similarities and differences. Comparison may be of both entire States or Political Systems and Political Systems or particular processes or institutional activity. Comparison aids understanding of a particular system or activity.

### 1.1.2. Meaning of Politics

The story of the world 'Politics' began with the 'Polis' the City-State community of ancient Greece. Plato, Aristotle and many of their contemporaries regarded Politics as the affairs of the Polis.[5]

Politics is, therefore, only one of the several Social activities of man. The essence of it said to lie in fundamental freedom of man in society to master his own fate by political means.[6] Politics is, thus, "the process through which man orders the society in which he lives according to his political ideas about the ends of man". According to Harold D. Lasswell Politics means "who gets what, when and how".[7] Karl Marx and his followers saw politics "as nothing more than a reflection of prevailing economic conditions, especially of economic technology and the distribution of the ownership of capital".[8] According to Peter Merkl "at its best, Politics is a noble quest for a good order and justice, at its worst, a selfish grab for power, glory and riches".[9]

In short, Politics is an organised dispute about powers and its use, involving choice among competing values, ideas of persons, interests and demands. The study of politics is concerned with the description and analysis of the manner in which power is obtained, exercised and controlled, the purpose for which it is used, the manner in which decisions are made and the context in which those decisions take place.[10] Politics also means striving to share power or striving to influence the distribution of power, either among states or among groups within a state.[11] We may conclude by saying that Politics deals with power, rule or authority.

Thus, Politics is a continuous and timeless process but an ever-changing one. The purpose, the context, the manners, the personnel, the arena of politics are always in flux and changes. Since the selection of the significant and relevant subject-matter of politics depends on changing goals and interests, the proper subjects for its study—whether institutions, behaviour, power, decisions or interests—always require personal interpretation.[12]

In the field of Comparative Politics, the term Politics, however, has three connotations—Political Activity, Political Process and Political Power.

#### *1.1.2.1. Political Activity*

It consists of the efforts by which conditions of conflicts are created and resolved in a way pertaining to the interests of the people, as far as possible, who play their part in the struggle for power. If politics means the authoritative allocation of values, some measures of conflicts is bound to arise between values as desired by the people and the values as held by the men in power. Arising conflicts, demands for their solution and the efforts in this regards constitute political activity.

It is the government that has to resolve these conflicts by whatever means are at its disposal. The only limitation being that in doing so it must prevent the breakup of the polity. According to Blondel "Politics ceases where secession and indeed civil war begins".[13]

### *1.1.2.2. Political Process*

It comes after Political Activity and it is wider and covers all those who are included in decision-making process. In the process of decision-making not only state but state agencies are also included. According to Finer, "Set of procedures whereby the private associations within the state seek to influence the government, is or to participate of policy formation by the government or to become the government is the Political Process".[14]

### *1.1.2.3. Political Power*

It is key concept in the study of Politics. It is still remained undefined. However, "Political Power is the capacity of effecting the behaviour of another person by the threat of some form of sanction[15] "Greater the sanction, or the more numerous the sanction, the greater will be the political power".[16]

## 1.1.3. Meaning of Comparative Politics

Comparative Politics is concerned with behaviour, institutions, processes, ideas and values present in more than one country. It searches for those regularities and patterns, those similarities and differences between more than one nation state that help clarify the basic nature, working and beliefs of regimes.[17]

Comparative Politics studies a broader range of Political activity, including governments and their institution as well as other forms of organisations not directly related to national government; for example, tribes, communities, associations, Unions etc.[18]

Comparative Politics, like Political Science, relates both to Theory and Methods. "Theory refers to sets of systematically related generalizations and Method is a procedure or process that involves the techniques and tools utilised in inquiring and for examining, teaching, testing and evaluating theory".[19]

Comparative Politics is also concerned with the norms, basic beliefs and values underlying political activity.[20] The field of Comparative politics involves the systematic and comparative study of nations and their political systems.[21]

The study of Comparative Politics, thus, involves Political Activity, Political Process and Political Power.

## 1.2. COMPARATIVE GOVERNMENT AND COMPARATIVE POLITICS

### 1.2.1. Comparative Government and Comparative Politics—Closely Linked with Each Other

The study of Comparative Government and the Comparative Politics are closely linked with each other. Finer, however, points out four meanings of the term government—it denotes activity or process of governing and the extent to which it exercises control over others; indicates the state of affairs in which that activity or process is to be found; tells about the people who are charged with the duty of governing and denotes the manners, method or system by which a particular society is governed.[22] Government is, thus, a standardised arrangement for taking decisions which affect the whole group".[23] And the need of government arises as it is essential for territorial associations to adopt a common policy and as in many cases rival bodies of members advocate mutually exclusive policies.

Alan Ball has tried to establish a link between the Government and the Politics.[24] There is now a, great stress in both on informal political process than political institutions of the state. That is why Freeman points out that Comparative Politics is nothing else but comparative analysis of various forms of government and diverse political institutions.[25] Jean Blondel also agrees with the view and says the "Comparative Government can be defined as the study of patterns of national governments in the contemporary world".[26]

### 1.2.2. Comparative Government—Distinct from Comparative Politics

But still host of scholars make a distinction between the Comparative Government and Comparative Politics. They believe that the scope of the study of comparative government is much limited than that of Comparative Politics. Comparative Government comprises the study of states, their institutions and functions. It does not take into account of the non-governmental institutions and is also not concerned with their functions. But Comparative Politics is concerned with politics *i.e.*, power relationship—wherever they occur. Hence its jurisdiction is not limited to the State only. Comparative Politics is, therefore, not concerned only with the comparative study of the state and its institutions and processes but it also deals with non-state Political context such as leadership, political socialisation, resolution of political conflict, bargaining, communication, decision-making etc.[27]

While making a distinction between the two Michael Curtis points out that, "Comparative Politics is concerned with behaviour, institutions, processes, ideas, and values present in more than one country. It searches for those regularities and patterns, those similarities and differences between more than one nation-state that help clarify the basic nature, working and beliefs of regimes.[28] The study of Comparative Politics, thus, involves "Comparison of both entire nation-state or political systems and partial systems or particular processes or institutional activity".[29]

By drawing distinction between Comparative Government and Comparative Politics, Ronald Chilcote writes, "Comparative Government usually refers to the study of countries or nation-states in Europe, and the focus of the study is on the institutions and functions of those countries, with attention to their executive, legislatures, and judiciaries as well as supplementary organisations as political parties and pressure groups. Comparative Politics, in contrast, studies a broader range of political activity, including governments and their institutions as well as other forms of organisations not directly related to national governments; for example, tribes, communities, associations, unions".[30]

Jean Blondel, is however, of the view that Comparative Government can become Comparative Politics when both the vertical and horizontal aspects of comparison are taken into account.[31]

## 1.3. LANDMARKS AND RECENT TRENDS IN COMPARATIVE POLITICS

Comparative Politics has a long history and its father was no other than Aristotle—the father of Political Science. But its systematic study begain with an historical theoretical examination of legal institutions of the democracies of the Western Europe and North America.[32] In twentieth century, particularly since post-World War Second, Comparative Politics has witnessed not only development on a scale never reached so far but it has become more and more popular.

### 1.3.1. Comparative Politics in Pre-World War Second Era

Since Aristotle, however, the scholar of Comparative Politics "has analysed the nature and quality of Political regimes, the behaviour of rulers and their relationship with the ruled, the manner in which the rules are determined, made and executed, the way in which conflicts are decided or arbitrated, the conditions of political stability and the causes of change, the factors affecting political decisions, and the values held by the political communities".[33] But very little attention was given to the informal arrangements of the society and their role in the exercise of political power and decision-making, political processes and political behaviour of the individual and groups.

### 1.3.2. Comparative Politics in Post-World War Second Era

Moreover, till the middle of the 20th century the area of Comparative Politics was limited largely to those countries in Europe and English speaking world which were either highly developed or had long lived political institutions.[34] But after that efforts have been made to include the new nation states *i.e.* developing and under-developed within the scope of universal or broad generalisations[36] and thus in the discipline of Comparative Politics.

The traditional approach to the study of Western Political systems, being focused on the formal constitutional aspects such as chief executive, Parliaments, Civil Services and electoral systems, was mainly a matter of abstract and formal speculation upon the broads conceiveable questions with little regards for the empirical content of speculation.[37] But in their attempt to embrace a larger geographical area and a wider spectrum of human experience and to be more truly comparative and realistic, the theorists have borrowed concepts from other disciplines such as from Law, Philosophy, Political Sociology, Economics, Psychology, Anthropology, Biology, Science of Cybernetics, Mathematics etc. They also used varieties of techniques and approaches. Departing from the legal framework and method, scholars began to probe into non-legal levels and processes of politics. They, therefore, turned away from purely formal and constitutional approach to a consideration of political dynamics and the processes of decision-making.[38]

Data for comparative inquiry has now been collected from a wide variety of sources *i.e.* from the study of elites, mass opinion polls, voting statistics, content analysis, aggregate data such as Economics, Demographic, or census material, history and other Social Sciences yielding information about political behaviour.[39]

World War Second has another effect on the field of Comparative politics. It has been greatly affected by the extension of inquiry into Asia, Africa, South-East Asia, Latin America and Middle East. By providing fresh and exciting new laboratories for the analysis of political development, these countries significantly expanded the universe of Comparative Politics. Moreover, inquiry into the changing politics of these Non-Western World has pointed out the inadequacy of traditional approaches which did not take into account critically important social and cultural factors.[40] Thus, in studying Non-Western Political Systems, the scholars began to deal not only with strange societies but also with ideas and values often incomparable with those of the West.[41] In their quest to find out categories and concepts appropriate for the comparison of political systems differing radically in culture and structures the scholars of Comparative Politics listed some of the new concepts such as Role Structure, Political Culture, Political System, Consensus, Actors, Socialization, Rationality, Structural-Functional Analysis[42] etc. All these provided the scholars of Comparative Politics convenient sets of tools for analysis.

Many approaches are, therefore, being used by the political Scientists such as System Approach, Structural. Functional Approach, Communication Approach, David Apter's Structural and Behavioural Approach, Inter-disciplinary Approach, Developmental Approach, Cultural Approach etc.

These new approaches have provided a diversity to the field of Comparative Politics.

The field of Comparative Politics had also been undergone another fundamental transformation. In the SSRC's (Social Sciences Research Council) Inter-University Research Seminar on Comparative Politics 1952, the participants stressed that the focus of Comparative Politics was parochial (studying exclusively the nations of Western Europe) descriptive rather than analytic, formulative and legalistic rather than concentrating on more dynamic processes, case study oriented rather than geniunely comparative. The view was that Comparative Politics should be non-parochial, non-formalistic, non-legalistic, analytic and genuinely comparative. They, therefore, called for more emphasis on the study of inter-group behaviour as well as informal aspects of Political behaviour.[43]

Gabriel A. Almond then became the Chairman of the Committee on Comparative Politics and he soon emerged as leading theoretician of Political Development. He stressed that development should not be treated just as a phenomenon to be analysed in a scientific sense but also as a moral ethical, and political 'Good' among the developing nations.[44]

In the late fiftees and early sixtees David Easton had begun to publish his general work on the political system which has given further impetus to the study of flow, process, informal actors and input-output analysis that was also incorporated into Comparative Politics.[45] A parallel work on development and nation building was being done by Karl Deutsch during the same period. Lipest published his Political Man (1959) showing the inter-relations between social modernisation and political democracy.[46]

A variety of more alternative approaches also began to emerge in the field of Comparative Politics in late 1960s and early 1970s. The two of them—Corporatist Approach and Marxist Approach—have given new life to the failure of the Liberal-developmentalist Approach. There also emerged a renewed interest in the Phenomenon of state-society relations and mathematical modelling.[47]

Political Scientists, afterwards rediscovered the state as a major variable, as distinct from the 'Black Box' on neutral reference of system theory. There also emerged a renewed interest in the phenomenon of state-society relations, Mathematical modelling of Comparative Politics and in Political Economy. Public Policy Analysis—a new field in the discipline of Comparative Politics has also been emerged.[48]

## 1.4 APPROACHES TO THE STUDY OF COMPARATIVE POLITICS—TRADITIONAL AND NEW

Approaches are tools by which the scholars of Politics arrive at greater political understanding. These contain certain criteria for selecting problems and relevant data for intensive analysis. Approaches aid in defining the kinds of facts which are relevant.[49] The diversity of approaches are, therefore, used by political scientists to attack the complexity of political systems and behaviour.[50]

The different approaches in comparative politics however, started from the recognition that society and political system consist of individuals. At the same time individuals could not be understood apart from their society or system. Political analysts have, therefore, varied between macroanalysis, focusing on the whole society of political system as a unit of analysis and microanalysis, focusing on the individual parts to a greater degree.[51]

### 1.4.1. Traditional Approaches

The traditional approach is an amalgam of views on the nature and functions of the state in human society expressed generally in philosophical and ethical terms. Since the days of Plato and Aristotle, the great issues of politics have revolved around the organization and operations of the state and its relationships with the society.

But before the advent of the present century, the study of Political Science remained largely dominated by History, Ethics, Philosophy and Law that ascribed to it the lable of having traditional approaches.

That is why Comparative Politics was also studied with the help of traditional approaches. According to Chilcote the traditional approach historically had inter-related fact and value in the study of Comparative politics.[52] Even during the early 20th century when its orientation shifted to the study of the institutions of individual countries, it became non-comparative, descriptive, parochial and static.[53] Traditional approaches then focused on the study of only Western (*i.e.*, G.B. France, Germany, Switzerland, U.S.A., U.S.S.R. etc.) governmental structures; formal state institutional organizations, systems, political institutions, like Cabinet, Legislative bodies, Executive, Courts, Electoral system, Political parties, bureaucracies and the like in historical or legalistic manner.[54] The basis for the whole study used to be the legal and written documents.[55] It tended to describe Political institutions without comparing them, other than to identify types such as Parliamentary in contrast to Presidential. The principles of the Political Theory were, therefore, laid with the help of History, Law, Ethics and Philosophy.[56]

These approaches continued to remain in operation for a very long time and examined every political institution with the help of available evidences.

It may, thus, be pointed out that the study of government was philosophical, historical, legalistic and institutional.

#### *1.4.1.1. Philosophical Approach*

Being one of the oldest approach its first features is that it made thinker to fly in the heights of imaginations to find out the truth and knowledge. Some of the topics of its interests are justice, liberty, equality and idea of good. It is normative in character and believes in building norms or ideal in prescribing a certain standards. For Example Plato prescribed certain standard of ideas such as philosopher king; Communism of property and family; and plan of education. It is ideological in nature also. All thinkers who study a thing from philosophical point of view, tried to weave norms into theory, which they thought could be realised in practice. Plato became philosopher of the Ideal State, Hobbes of Absolute Monarchy, Locke of Constitutionalism, Marx of Communism. For quite some time, therefore, this approach was called ideological approach. It followed the deductive method where researcher has his own values and predetermined notions.

It, however, got set back in the days of behavioural revolution. It has also influenced some of the twentieth century thinkers like Laski and Barkar who developed the concept like equality, liberty, rights, duties, justice, political obligations etc.[57]

### *1.4.1.2. Historical Approach*

This approach emerged towards the last quarter of the 19th century. A number of Political Scientists pleaded that only through the study of historical background, they could have a better and close insight into the working of those institutions and forces that condition political phenomena. Sabine, like others, attached supreme importance to this approach. "A Political Theory", according to him, "is always advanced in reference to a petty specific situation." It is therefore, essential to understand the time, place and circumstances in which it was produced. Moreover, political theories of far reaching importance have generally been evolved during periods of social and political crisis.

There had been two periods of about 50 years each in two places where political philosophy have thrived most—in Athens in the 2nd & 3rd quarters of the 4th century B.C. when Plato and Aristotle wrote their great works, in England between 1640 to 1690 when Hobbes and Locke and others evolved their political theories. Thus, in order to understand political theory, we must bear in mind the time, the place and circumstances in which it evolved. We study the origin and growth of certain political institutions in historical perspectives *e.g.*, tracing the origin of the British Parliamentary system to Magna Carta and study its development through successive historical stages. It is assumed that parallel historical accounts of evolution of the French Parliament or the German representative assemblies will indicate similarities and differences.[58]

### *1.4.1.3. Institutional Approach*

It was most prominent in the first quarter of the present century. It is, however, dated back to the times of Aristotle who had analysed 158 constitutions of the World. In modern age it has been stressed By Utilitarian writers who wanted to reform institutions in order to reform the society. It concentrates the study of institutions ranging from constitution and other basic document on which government is supposed to rest. For example structure of Legislature, Courts, Executive, Rules by which Political parties are run, registration and election laws, intricacies of different forms of municipal governments. It, therefore, focuses only on institutions which have been formally and legally established by the society.

This approach does not take any notice of the individuals who run those institutions. That is why Easton says that institutionalists treat individuals as Wooden automation. They regard individuals as faithful executors of the decisions. They have no role of their own or will of their own that counts in it.

Under the impact of this approach the constitutional position of British Monarch, Prime Minister, Parliament or Cabinet was analysed in detail. The study was extended to the structure of the court, rule of law, representative laws, the election laws, and relation between different branches of government. In case of federalism, it studies the relations between centre and federating units. More often these studies were conducted on comparative basis. Some of the important studies are Herman Finer's "The Theory and Practice of the Modern Government"; Dicey's "Law of the Constitution"; Mancro's "European Governments" and Jenning's "Cabinet Government".

#### *1.4.1.4. Legalistic Approach*

Here the students are exposed primarily to the study of the powers of the various branches of governmental agencies with reference to the legal and constitutional provisions.

### 1.4.2. Characteristics of Traditional Approaches

The traditional approaches, however, bear the following characteristics :

1. There is an emphasis on the study of formal institutions and the neglect of political processes.
2. It is focused on the Western European political systems and thus, the non-Western political systems are neglected. It is, therefore, cultural bound.
3. The traditional comparative politics adopts country-by-country approach with no serious attempt to identify similarities and dissimilarities between the countries.
4. There is emphasis on description of existing institutions with little attention given to the analysis and development of systematic generalisations about the political phenomena.
5. There is lack of concern for the development of theories through collection and analysis of data in order to test specific hypothesis.
6. There is a neglect of the findings of other social sciences having bearing on the political phenomena.
7. The traditional approaches have showed insensitiveness to non-political determinants of political behaviours and thus to the non-political bases of governmental institutions.
8. Comparative politics is therefore, dominated by a reformist zeal and entails value judgements indicating what ought to be nature of political structure and institution. In other words comparative politics is normative in nature.

### 1.4.3. New Approaches to the Study of Comparative Politics

"A great deal of experimentation is now going on with new approaches, new definitions, new research tools, perhaps the main reason for the present intellectual ferment is a widespread feeling of disappointment and dissatisfaction with the traditional descriptive approaches........"[60]

—*Bernard E. Brown*

The publication of Graham Walla's 'Human Nature in Politics' and Arthur Bentley's 'The Process of Government' in the first decade of the 20th century symbolised a change in political studies.[61] As host of political scientists, then started thinking to lay greater stress on the informal processes of politics and less on state political institutions in isolation.[62] They, therefore, began free borrowing from other social disciplines and to give the new empirical orientation to the political studies which ultimately led to an examination of such political concepts as power, authority and political elites.[63]

Since the end of World War Second, the American writers on contemporary political science also began to borrow something from other sciences—natural and exact, in order to enrich their findings. Political power has, therefore, become one of the key concepts of political scientists. Political scientists have been borrowed from the discipline of biology, the idea of cybernetics—communication and control system and tried to fit their equilibrium and communication and control system.[64] At the hands of leading writers like David Easton, Gabriel A. Almond, Karl Deutsch, David Apter and a host of others the field of comparative politics has been widened so much as more and more attention is now being paid to non-governmental and social groups, to the political process and the politically oriented behaviour of individuals and groups.[65]

The very definition of the term 'Political Science' has, thus, changed. It is no longer regarded as the study which begins and ends with the state[66] or a branch of social sciences dealing with the theory, organisation, government and practice of the state.[67] It is now "regarded as struggle to gain or retain power, to exercise power as influence over others, or to resist that exercise" (Robson).[68]

The Social Science Research Council of the United States has, however, constituted a committee on comparative politics. This committee began to support researches in the field and thus, encouraged new theoretical and methodological approaches to the study of comparative politics. The widespread but vague desire for change in comparative politics as was, thus, given a definite direction and coherence as a result of finding of this committee.[69]

Similar support also began to come from the Ford Foundation, the Rockefeller Foundation, the Carnegie Foundation, etc. These foundations also provided funds, for studies in comparative politics including training in research methodology.[70] U.S.A. has, therefore, provided leadership, environment as well as finances for effecting a breakthrough in comparative politics. As a result, the discipline of comparative politics became empirical and its study began to be pursued to promote theory building.

A host of writers are of the view that the emergence of new states in Asia, Africa, the Middle East and in Latin America in the post-World War Second, signified the end of the traditional approaches as these were incapable of comprehending these new political realities. As the traditional approaches had addressed themselves to those western political system, which have highly developed or long lived political institutions, these proved to be untenable when applied to the newly emerged/emerging states. Perter A. Merkl rightly points out "the most momentous single factor for the current transformation of the study of comparative politics was the rising importance of the politics of the developing areas...with...their increasing importance in world politics, they could no longer be ignored".[71]

While reporting on its activities from 1954 to 1970, the Committee on Comparative Politics of the Social Science Research Council of the United States has also confirmed this fact and observed :

> "From the outset the committee undertake to bring to the centre of comparative politics the study of the non-western world and the problems of political development of the new states that emerged with the end of colonialism."[72]

The World War Second can, therefore, easily be said as the watershed dividing the traditional and the modern comparative politics.

However, as already pointed out, many new approaches are now being used by the political scientists to study intergroup behaviour as well as the informal aspects of political behaviour. These are Behavioural Approach; Inter-disciplinery Approach; Post-Behavioural Approach; System (or Input-Output) Approach; Structural-Funcational Approach, Communication (or Cybernetics) Approach; David Apter's Structural and Behavioural Approach; Developmental Approach; Cultural Approach; Decision-making Approach; Corporalist Approach; Marxist Approach; Harold Lasswell's Distributive Approach etc.

## 1.5. THEORY BUILDING IN COMPARATIVE POLITICS

There has been now a shift of emphasis on description to theory building in comparative politics. In other words, we may say that the development of theory is among the foremost concerns of modern comparative politics. In fact, comparison carries meaning only if it seeks to interpret political data in the terms of theories and hypothesis. If comparative politics is to acquire the status of a science, it must lay emphasis on theory building.

The concepts used earlier in political science have, therefore, been found to be inadequate in terms of the need to develop theories in the comparative politics. The need of modern comparative politics is, thus, to develop concepts when go beyond institutional structures and legal processes and which would be useful in discussing the political phenomena wherever they occur. "Thus, instead of the concept of the 'State', limited as it is by legal and institutional meanings, we prefer, 'political system'; instead of 'powers; which again is a legal concept in connotation, we are, beginning to prefer 'functions'; instead of 'office' (legal again), we prefer 'roles'; instead of institutions, which again directs us towards formal norms, 'Structures'; instead of 'public opinion' and citizenship training, 'formal and rational in meaning, we prefer 'political culture' and 'Political socialisation'.[73]

In short comparative politics has been evolving a language which can be used to evaluate similar pattern of action and behaviour in different countries and over different periods of time.

Theory building in comparative politics would, therefore, become possible only when such a language evolves.

While summing up we may say that "modern comparative politics is markedly different from the traditional. It has broadened its scope of study, refined its tools of analysis and shown sensitivities to a large number of variables. It has assimilated a lot from other social sciences and is indeed interdisciplinary in nature."[74]

## REFERENCES

1. Maheshwari, S.R., *Comparative Government and Politics*, Lakshmi Narain Agarwal Educational Publisher, Hospital Road, Agra-3, 1985, p. 1.
2. Hans Raj, *Comparative Politics*, Surjeet Publications, 7-K, Kolhapur Road, Kamala Nagar, Delhi, 1985, p. 1.
3. Deutsch, Karl; *Nation and World*, Contemporary Political Science, Towards Empirical Theory, McGraw Hill Co, New York, 1967, p. 207.
4. Johari, J.C., *Comparative Politics*, Sterling Publishers Pvt. Ltd, New Delhi, 1980, preface.

5. Merkl, Peter H., *Political Continuity and Change*, Harper & Row, Evansten, London, 1967, p. 7.
6. *Ibid.*, p. 10.
7. *Ibid.*
8. *Ibid.*, p. 9.
9. *Ibid.* p. 13.
10. Curtis, Michael, *Comparative Government and Politics*, Harper & Row Publishers, New York, 1978, p. 3.
11. Maheshwari, S.R., *Comparative Government and Politics, op. cit.*, p. 3.
12. Curtis, Michael, *Comparative Government and Politics, op. cit.*, p. 3.
13. Blondel, Jean, *An Introduction to Comparative Government*, Weidenfeld and Nicolson, London, 1969, p. 7.
14. Finer, S.E., *Comparative Government*, Allen Lane the Penguin Press, London, 1970, p. 7.
15. Lasswell, H.D. & Kaplan A., *Power and Society*, London, 1952, p. 76.
16. Bali, Alan R., *Modern Politics and Government*, The Macmillan Press Ltd. London, 1971, p. 26.
17. Curtis, Michael, *Comparative Government and Politics, op. cit.*, p. 1.
18. Chilcote, Ronald H., *Theories of Comparative Politics*, West-View Press, USA.
19. *Ibid.*, p. 4.
20. Lasswell, H.D. & Kaplan A., *Power and Society, op. cit.*, p. 1.
21. Wiarda, Howard J., *New Direction in Comparative Politics*, West-View Press, Boulder, London, 1985, p-preface.
22. Finer, S.E., *Comparative Government, op. cit.*, p. 7.
23. *Ibid.*
24. Ball, Alan R., *Modern Politics and Government, op. cit.*, p. 27.
25. Hansraj, *Comparative Politics, op. cit.*, p. 7.
26. Blondel, Jean, *An Introduction to Comparative Government, op. cit.*, p. 6.
27. Maheshwari, Sriram, *Comparative Government and Politics, op. cit.*, p. 6.
28. Curtis, Michael, *Comparative Government and Politics op. cit.*, p. 1.
29. *Ibid.*
30. Chilcote, Ronald H, *Theories of Comparative Politics*, West-View Press, USA, p. 3.
31. Blondel, Jeans, *An Introduction to Comparative Government, op. cit.*, p. 7.
32. Larson, Allan L., *Comparative Political Analysis*, Nelson-Hall, Chicago, 1980, p. 141.
33. Curits, Michael, *Comparative Govt. and Politics, op. cit.*, p. 3.
34. Larson, Allan L., *Comparative Political Analysis, op. cit.*, p. 141.

35. Courtis, Michael, *Comparative Government and Politics, op. cit.*, pp. 3-4.
36. *Ibid.*
37. Larson, Allan L., *Comparative Political Analysis, op. cit.*, p. 141.
38. Welsh, William A., *Studying Politics*, Praeger, New York, 1973, pp. 39-40.
39. Curtis Michael, *Comparative Government and Politics, op. cit.*, p. 4.
40. Larson, Allan L., *Comparative Political Analysis, op. cit.*, p. 142.
41. *Ibid.*, p.143.
42. *Comparative Politics*, vol. II, No. 1, 1968, p. 1 (Journal).
43. Wiarda, Howard J., *New Direction in Comparative Politics, op. cit.*, p. 13.
44. *Ibid.*, p. 14.
45. *Ibid.*, pp. 14-15.
46. *Ibid.*, pp. 19-20.
47. *Ibid.*, p. 19.
48. *Ibid.*, p. 20.
49. Larson, Allan L., *Comparative Political Analysis, op. cit.*, p. 15.
50. *Ibid., op. cit.*, p. 16.
51. Curtis, Michael, *Comparative Government and Politics, op. cit.*, p. 5.
52. Ray, Amal; Bhattacharya, Mohit, *Political Theory* : The World Press Private Ltd., Calcutta 1983, pp. 14-15.
53. Chilcote, Ronald H., *Theories of Comparative Politics, op. cit.*, pp. 19-20.
54. Maheshwari, Sriram, *Comparative Government and Politics, op. cit.*, p. 18.
55. Larson, Allan L., *Comparative Political Analysis, op. cit.*, p. 16.
56. Hans Raj, *Comparative Politics*, op. cit., p. 13.
57. *Ibid.*
58. For details see S.P. Verma's Book '*Modern Political Theory*', Vikas Publishing House Pvt. Ltd., New Delhi, 1975, pp. 11-13.
59. *Ibid.*, pp. 13-15.
60. Brown, Bernard E., *New Direction in Comparative Politics*, Asia Publishing House, New Delhi, 1962, p. 1.
61. Ball, Alan R., *Modern Politics and Government, op. cit.*, 1979, p. 9.
62. Johari, J.C., *Comparative Politics, op. cit.*, p. 20.
63. Ball, Alan R., *Modern Government and Politics*, op. cit., p. 9.
64. Johari, J.C., *Comparative Politics, op. cit.*, p. 20.
65. Curtis, Michael, *Comparative Government and Politics, op. cit.*, p. 7.
66. Garner, J.W. and Row, *Political Science and Government*, World Press, 1952, p. 9.
67. Rodee, Carlton Clymer, Anderson Tolton James, Chistol Carl Quimby; Greene, Thomas H., *Introduction to Political Science*, McGraw Hill, 1957, p. 4.
68. Robson, W.A., *The University Teaching of Political Science*, Political Science (Paris, UNESCO, 1954), pp. 17-18.

69. Maheshwari, Sri Ram, *Comparative Government and Politics,* op. cit., p. 14.
70. *Ibid.*, p. 14.
71. Merkl, Peter H., *Modern Comparative Politics, op. cit.*, p. 10.
72. Lucian, W. Pye and Kay Ryland, *Committee on Comparative Politics,* A Report on the Activities of the Committee, 1954-70, Social Science Research Council, New York, 1971, p. 1-2.
73. Almond; Garbriel A. and Coleman, James S (ed.), *Politics of Developing Areas*, Princeton University Press, Princeton 1970, p. 4.
74. Maheshwari, Shriram, *Comparative Government and Politics, op. cit.*, p. 17.

# 2

# Models of Political System's Analysis

## 2.1. DAVID EASTON'S INPUT-OUTPUT ANALYSIS

David Easton is the first political scientist to have developed a systematic framework for the study of politics on the basis of the systems analysis approach. It is he who had introduced the concept of system to politics, together with a vocabulary of inputs and outputs, demands and supports and feedback during the early 1950's.[1] He has selected the political system as the basic unit of analysis and concentrated on the intra-system behaviour of various systems as principal areas of research.

### 2.1.1. Definition of Political System

He has defined political system as 'a set of interaction' and politics as 'making authoritative allocation of values'.[2]

David Easton's system analysis is also known as input-output analysis or conversion process. The most important feature of input-output analysis is, the conversion of inputs into outputs by the system. For him the political system absorbs inputs in the form of demands on authorities and supports from institutions and the political community and produces outputs in the form of policies and decisions.[3]

Input-output analysis treats all political systems as both open and adoptive systems. The central focus of the approach is on the nature of the exchange and transaction that take place between a political system and its environment.[4] Political activities constitute "a system of behaviour embeded in an environment to the influences of which the political system itself is exposed and in turn reacts".[5] Input-output analysis, therefore, systematizes the study of relationships between a system and its total environment.

### 2.1.2. Environment—Intra-Societal and Extra-Societal

The environment may be divided into two parts—the intra-societal and extra-societal. The intra-societal environment consists of those systems in the same society as the political system but excluded from pol. system for the reason of not being engaged in authoritative allocation of values. The intra-societal system includes economy, culture, social structure or personalities. These are segments of the society of which the political system is itself a part. The extra-societal environment, on the other hand, includes all those systems which lie outside a given society. Such as the International Political systems, the International Economic systems. They too have their impact on a given pol. system. The political system is linked with its environment through the process of inputs and outputs.[6]

### 2.1.3. Input Functions

In elaborating his input-output Analysis, David Easton has chosen to deal with inputs from various environments in the form of demands and supports; conversion processes; outputs and feedback mechanisms that inject the effects and consequences of output back into a system as inputs. He calls them as summary variable.[7]

Inputs which give political system its dynamic character and furnish it both with the raw material or information that the system called upon to process and the energy to keep it going are of two kinds—demands and supports.[8]

#### *2.1.3.1. Demand and their Kinds*

"A demand may be defined as an expression of opinion that an authoritative allocation with regard to a particular subject matter should or should not be made by those responsible for doing so".[9] Demand is, thus, "the raw material out of which finished products called decisions are manufactured".

Demands have their birth either in the environment of a system or within the system itself. David Easton calls them external and internal demands respectively.[10] In the environment these exist systems such as the ecology, economy, culture, personality, social structure and demography. In other words there exist social environment, cultural environment, economic environment, physical environment, ecological environment etc. Each of these systems constitutes a major set of variables in the setting that help to shape the kind of demands entering a political system. These are external demands. But all demands do not originate or have their major locus in the environment. Important types of demands may also stem from situations within a political system itself. These are internal demands. Such demands are like demand for alteration in the political relationship of the members themselves as the result of dissatisfaction emerging from these relationships, demands for changes in the process of recruitment of formal political leaders, demands for modification of the way in which constitutions are amended.[11]

The demands may be of the following four types :

(i) Demands for allocation of goods and services such as wage, hour laws, educational opportunities, housing and medical facilities etc.,

(ii) Demands for regulation of behaviour such as control over markets; provisions for public safety; rules relating to marriage, health and sanitation etc.,

(iii) Demands for participation in the political system such as right to seek election, to hold office to organise processions, to petition public officials etc., and

(iv) Demands for communication and information such as communication of policy intent from political elites or display of the power of the political system in periods of threats or on ceremonial occasions".[12]

There are several major types of stress inherit in the demand segment of the political cycle. In other words if we regard demands as message units calling for authoritative action, the problem of overload emerges as central to demand stress. Overload of this kind can arise either from excess quantities of demands (volume stress) or from some qualitative elements in the nature of particular demands (content stress).[13]

### *2.1.3.2. Regulatory Mechanisms to Regulate the Pace of Entry of Demands into System or Prevent the Demands from Entering the System*

All demands whether internal or external do not automatically converted into political issues. Many demands die at birth or linger on with the support of an insignificant fraction of the society and are never raised to the level of possible political decisions. Others become issues that the members of political system are prepared to deal with. In other words many demands come and get articulated into the input system but all these do not get converted into output and got lost in the conversion process. In the input system several times too many demands are put and the channels, thus, very much get loaded and need arises to ensure that there is minimum of overloading. Every political system, therefore, possesses regulatory mechanisms of its own to prevent the demands from entering the system or regulates the pace of their entry as well as for handling difficulties relating to want conversion and demand stress.[14] In other words in order to transform demands into issues and to determine whether a demand should become a matter for serious political discussion or remain to be resolved privately among the members of society, there are regulatory mechanisms in every political system.[15]

According to Easton, such regulatory mechanisms are of the following four types :[16]

*2.1.3.2.1. Structural Mechanism*

(i) *Structural Mechanisms :* There are informal political structures which serve as gatekeepers at the boundary of the political system. They regulate the flow of wants entering the system and becoming articulated demands. All political systems develop gatekeeping roles and operating rules to be followed by them. For example political parties and pressure groups which screen the demands flowing from environment and decide which of them should be acted upon.

*2.1.3.2.2. Cultural Mechanism*

(ii) Every society has certain cultural mechanisms and socio-cultural norms. The demands which are not in harmony with them remain unacceptable and are not articulated.

*2.1.3.2.3. Communicational Channels*

(iii) A political system can develop a third mode of demand regulation centres *i.e.*, a number of communicational channels through which demands may get scattered widely and thus get diluted.

*2.1.3.2.4. Reduction Processes*

(iv) Demands can be regulated by various reduction processes during the conversion phases of the political cycle. Through them demands may be converted into specific issues for purposes of political processing or without which they would not be fed the conversion process of the political system. For example legislators, executive and administrative bodies etc.

### *2.1.3.3. Supports and their Types*

Supports are those structures or processes which give the political system the capacity to cope with the demands made upon it. Support means giving obedience and showing loyalty to a political system. It refers to the expression of willingness to accept particular value allocations or the processes by which the allocations are made. In other words it refers to remaining input transaction between a system and its environment after demands have been substracted.[17] Easton, however, defines support by saying that 'A' supports 'B' either when A acts on behalf of B or when he orients himself favourably towards B. B may be a person or group, it may be a goal, idea or institution".[18]

Supports may be classified as Overt support and Covert support. Overt support refers to actions that are clearly and manifestly supportive while covert support refers to supportive attitude or sentiments.

A political system receives considerable support from the environment without which it cannot survive. Supports are of the following four types :

(i) "material supports, such as the payment of taxes or other levies, and the provisions of services such as labour on public works or military service;

(ii) obedience to law and regulation;

(iii) participatory support, such as voting, political discussion, and other forms of political activities;

(iv) attention paid to governmental communication and manifestation of deference or respect to public authority, symbols and ceremonials".[19]

### *2.1.3.4. Support is Fed into Political System in relation to*

Support is fed into political system in relation to the following objectives :

#### *2.1.3.4.1. The Political Community*

Political community consists of members of the system seen as a group of persons bound together by a political division of labour. When a group of people get together and show willingness to co-operate in solving the system's problems, a political community emerges. In other words a political community comes into existence when the people living together come close to each other in a bid to solve their political problems.[20]

The political community is however, an important component of the political system and the latter gets subjected to stress when there is a decline in support for it. Moreover, political community does not come to an end with mere change in regime or authority.[21]

#### *2.1.3.4.2. The Regime or Basic Values, Political Structures and Norms*[22]

Regime means the constitutional order *i.e.* the constitution of the country and its written or unwritten rules, regulations, conventions, even sentiments. In other words it consists of all those arrangements that regulate the way in which demands put into the system are settled and the way in which decisions are put into effect.[23] Constitution determines the structure of political organisation and norms on which organisation of government is based. To this Easton calls as regime.[24]

*2.1.3.4.3. Political Authority*

The political authority means who holds power at any given time. It refers to the group of individuals who run the government for the prescribed period of time.

The support may be to one or two or all of these various components of the political system. According to Easton the systematic persistence depends upon, "the maintenance of a minimal level of attachment for each of the three identified political objects. When the input of support falls below the minimum, the persistence of any kind of system will be endangered".[25]

The political support may decline or get eroded due to one reason or the other. But this happens mainly on account of the failure of the political system to deliver the goods *i.e.*, output failure.[26] In other words a political system is subject to support stress at some time. This means that a system may suffer a loss of support given to it by the members of the system. Such a situation occurs in the event of cleavages among members within a system; a failure of the system to produce outputs in response to the demands made on it or it produces outputs satisfactory to its members or a structural failure of the system itself.[27]

A political system can adopt itself to the support stress in several ways. One of which can be the change of its structural elements, representative system, party system etc. The political system may also try to counter-balance the lack of specific support by generating diffuse support through a sense of legitimacy and the feeling that there is common or public interest furthered by the persistence of the political system.[28] Building up diffuse support for the political system refers primarily to various processes for developing and spreading a sense of community among its members.[29]

### 2.1.4. Outputs of Political System

A political system, therefore, maintains itself partly through its own regulatory mechanisms and partly through the support, specific as well as defused, which it can generate in the society. The main test of its effectiveness lies in what it does for society. Here comes in Easton's concept of outputs.[30]

An output of a political system is a political decision or policy.[31]

Easton points out that outputs "not only help to influence events in the broader society of which the system is a part, but also, in doing so, they help to determine each succeeding round of inputs that finds its way into the political system".[32]

### 2.1.5. Feedback

This process is described as a feedback loop. It is an important type of response to support stress in a political system. The feedback is, thus, a dynamic process through which information about the performance of the system is communicated back to the system in such a way as to affect the subsequent behaviour of the system.[33] Young rightly points out ". . . . outputs play a crucial role in generating specific support for a political system because of the existence of feedback loops that complete the cycle of a political system and make it a dynamic and regenerative operation".[34] Easton believes that whole political system is basically input-output mechanism. It is always concerned with political decisions making process and activities. It has its own place in our social structure. It concentrates to study the process influences which environments throw into the political system and as to what is their response to these influences.[35] Easton analysis is also free from many of the shortcomings of structural functional Analysis. It goes beyond the equilibrium analysis, and takes note of change in the political system. He talks of system persistence rather than system maintenance and makes a clear distinction between the two. His conceptual frame-work consists of standardised set of concepts and categories, which make it easier to have broad overview of political system.[36] Moreover, his input-output analysis can be used for studying all kinds of political systems—democratic and otherwise.[37]

### 2.1.6. Criticism

However, David Easton's model of Input-Output Analysis has been subjected to the following criticism :

1. It is said to be too abstract and too far from empirical reality. His analysis confines to the question of location and distribution of power in the political system. But its capacity to deal with a wide variety of political phenomena is severely restricted. Oran Young, thus, rightly points out that "system approach does not have much to offer for studies dealing with the political aspects of such matters as perception, expectation, formation or cognition". Even Eugene Meehan points out that "Like Parson, Easton does not think of a theory in terms of explanation but in terms of the creation of conceptual framework. The result is

highly abstract structure that is logically suspect, conceptually fuzzy and empirically almost useless". Easton's political system, therefore, "turns out to be an abstraction whose relation to empirical politics is virtually impossible to establish".[38] Because of high level of abstraction in Input-Output Analysis the realities of political life may not always be neatly placed in system model.[39]

2. As Easton's Input-Output Analysis attaches importance to the questions concerning persistence and adaptation of the political system and the regulation of stress, stability and systems equilibrium, it has also charged from time to time with harbouring *a status quo bias.*[40]
3. It is also said to have been developed as a conscious alternative to Marxism and is an anti-Marxist approach because Marxism generates a philosophy of revolutionary change and disequilibrium. In other words revolutionary change is hardly mentioned and even the possibilities of evolution of new system forms are not covered in detail in Input-Output Analysis.[41]
4. Moreover, Easton's analysis contains comparatively little material concerning goals and values beyond the question of persistence.[42]
5. Young points out that Easton's "Input-Output Analysis has little to say about the politics of decline, disruption and breakdown in political system".[43]
6. While criticising the Input-Output Analysis, Maheshwari points out that it discusses little the conversion function of political system. "The reader does not know about what happens to demands when these come out in the form of rules, laws and decisions. The conversion function *i.e.*, the governmental institutions were the dominant concern of the traditional comparative politics".[44]
7. Input-Output Analysis has been said to be designed for macro-level studies and not for micro-level studies. Even at macro level it is not applicable to the study of third world countries of Asia, Affrica, and Latin America. It is applicable only to North America and Western world. Then third world countries, which owe their existence in the face of external threats to keep internal conflicts within bounds, passionately seeking revolutionary changes in all sphere of life— economic, social, cultural, etc. Easton model, however, cannot comprehend the pace, scale and

nature of changes in them. And, thus, inapplicable and unsuited to such a fast changing unstable societies.

8. Easton's model has also been criticised for his empty vision of politics, because it has shown very little interest in the individual. Paul F. Kress, while discussing the shortcoming of Easton's theory points out that in it "there is lack of substance, articulate nature of system as its members, replacement of actor by container and disappearance of boundries as limits of possibility".[46]
9. As Easton's Input-Output model is concerned with the present and has no perspective of future and no sound study of the past, it is called as anti-historical. It has, therefore, completely ignorant of the complexities of social conflicts and class relationship.[47]

## 2.2. GABRIEL A. ALMOND : STRUCTURAL FUNCTIONALISM

Closely related to the system analysis is that of Structural Functionalism. This approach is also concerned with the definition of particular functions as well as with the roles played by political structures and processes in the maintenance and adaptability of political systems.[48] In other words structural functionalism seeks to discover the functions which an organism or system must perform in order to exist or remain in operation. It was first applied in 1960 by Gabriel A. Almond and James S. Coleman to the study of non-western politics. They developed structural functionalism in the introduction of their book "politics of developing areas."[49]

### 2.2.1. Political System

Almond examined the 'universe of political system and concluded that all political systems have a structure *i.e.*, legitimate patterns of human interactions by which order is maintained ; all political structures perform many functions, though in different degrees in different systems; that the same functions are performed in all political systems, though with different frequencies and by different kinds of structures and in different style; and that none are either completely 'modern' or completely primitive. All political systems are, therefore, mixed ones containing the elements of both modern and primitive cultures.[50]

### 2.2.2. Almond's Seven-fold Classification of Functions Performed by a Political System

Thus applying structural-functionalism, Almond has formulated a sevenfold classification of functions performed by a political system.[51] He divides them into four inputs (political) and three output (governmental) functions :

These are :

**A.** *Input functions (Political)*

1. Political socialization and recruitment;
2. Interest articulation;
3. Interest aggregation;
4. Political communication.

**B.** *Output functions (Governmental)*

1. Rule making;
2. Rule application;
3. Rule adjudication.

### *2.2.2.1.* *Input (or political) functions*

The first four of them are input functions. They are performed by the non-governmental sub-systems including the general environment. The last three are output functions. These are performed by the government. These are the three well known traditional functions—Legislative, Executive and Judicial. Gabriel A. Almond's contribution primarily lies in enunciating the four input functions. He further asserts that the input functions are more important in the political systems of the developing countries. While mentioning that the various functions are universal *i.e.* they are common to traditional, transitional and modern systems, Almond believes that the mode, manner or style of their performance differs. This style is measured by him on four dimensions *i.e.* (i) manifest-latent, (ii) specific-diffuse, (iii) general (or universal)—particular, and (iv) instrumental (or effectively neutral)—affective. The modern style is characterised by manifestness, specificity, universalism and affective whereas the traditional style has just the opposite attributes, tending to be latent, diffuse, particularistic and affective.

#### *2.2.2.1.1. Political Socialisation and Recruitment*

Political socialisation is psychological concept. All political systems tend to perpetuate their cultures and structures through time, and that they do this mainly by means of the socializing influences of the primary and secondary structures through which the young of the society pass in the process of maturation.[52] According to Almond and Verba, it is, thus, a process by which political cultures are maintained and changed.[53] It is concerned with the orientation of individuals towards political objects. In other words political socialization is the process of induction into political culture and it promotes a set of attitudes among the members of the system. Political systems tend to perpetuate their cultures and structures through times and all this is done by the socialising influences. Political socialization is, thus, transmitting of the political values and norms of the society.[54] In political socialisation, Almond includes values, norms and patterns of behaviour suited to the political system. Its end product is, therefore, a set of attitudes—cognitions, value standards and feelings—-towards the political system, its various roles, and role incumbents". "It also includes knowledge of values affecting, and feelings towards the inputs of demands and claims into the system, and its authoritative outputs."[55] If attitudes, orientations and values change through times they bring about change in the political culture also.

Since the individual is continually being influenced in the shaping of his political attitudes, orientations and values, the process of socialisation goes throughout his life.[56] As the process of political socialization is going on all the time, there is a possibility of its getting accelerated through major crisis. The family, the church, the school, the peer groups, voluntary associations, experiences during employment, mass media, political parties and direct contacts with the political systems, however, serve a major agents in the process of political socialisation.

The process of socialisation may be latent or manifest, specific or disfuse, particular or general (universal) and affective or instrumental. It is latent when it is in the form of transmission of information, values or feelings *vis-a-vis* the role, input or output of other social systems such as the family which affect attitudes towards role, input or output of the political system. It is manifest when it takes the form of explicit transmission of information, values, feelings *vis-a-vis* the roles, inputs and outputs of the political systems. The process of political socialisation is diffuse, particularistic and ascriptive in a traditional society but as it modernises itself the process becomes specific, universalistic and instrumental.

The political recruitment function takes up where the general political socialisation functions leaves off.[57] Political recruitment means the obtaining of political leaders.[58] In other words the method through and by which citizens are recruited for specialised role of the political system is known as political recruitment. It refers to the recruitment of the members of the society out of particular sub-cultures—religious communities, statuses, classes, ethnic communities, and like and inducting them into the specialized roles of the political system, training them in the appropriate skills, providing them with the political cognitive maps, values experiences, and affects.

"Style of Political recruitment may be compared according to the way in which ascriptive and particularistic criteria with performance and universalistic criteria. Thus, in a modern western political system, recruitment is affected both by ascriptive and by performance criteria. Kinship, friendship, school ties, religious affiliation and status qualities affect recruitment in various important ways, but the more thorough going the political modernisation, the more these ascriptive criteria are contained within or limited by achievement criteria—educational levels, performance levels on examinations, formal records of achievement in poltical roles, and the like. The recruitment, pattern is, thus, both structurally and culturally dualistic. In the primitive or traditional political system the recruitment function is also dualistic. But the achievement or performance criterion is less explicitly and generally applied"[60]

*2.2.2.1.2. Interest articulation*

Interest articulation means the voicing of political demands to the decision-makers.[61] It is concerned with the formulation and expression of interest, claims and demands for political action. In other words the process by which individuals and groups make demands on political decision-makers is called interest articulation. It is the first step in political conversion process and occurs at the boundary of political system. "The particular structures which perform the articulation function and the style of their performance determine the character of the boundary between polity and society."[62]

Almond distinguishes the following four main types of structures involved in the interest articulation :

(i) Institutional interest groups, (ii) non-associational interest groups, (iii) anomic interest groups, and (iv) associational interest groups.

In institutional interest groups, he has included legislatures, political executives, bureaucracies, armies, churches and the like. In the category of non-associational groups he has included kinship lineage, ethnic, regional, religious, status and class groups These often perform the articulation function intermittently and informally through individuals, cliques, family and religious heads etc. The third category is concerned with spontaneous break throughs into the political system from society such as riots, demonstrations and the like. Although anomic groups articulate interests, "they may end up performing a recruitment function (*i.e.* transferring power from one group to another), rule-making function (*i.e.* changing the constitution, enacting, revising, or rescinding statutes), a rule application function (*i.e.* freeing prisoners, rescinding a bureaucratic decision) or rule adjudication function (*i.e.* tryping and lynching), an aggregative or a communicative function (*i.e.* drawing other interest groups to it or publicizing a protest)".[63] The last category of associational interest groups includes specialized structures like trade unions, businessmen or industrialists, ethnic associations, associations organised by religious denomination, civic groups and the like. They are formed to represent explicitly the interests of a group to formulate procedures for expressing demands and channelling them to the other political structures, parties, legislature and bureaucracies.

Interest articulation is diffuse, particularistic and ascriptive in the traditional society but it becomes specific, universalitic and instrumental in modern one.

According to Almond even the performance of the interest articulation function may be manifest or latent, specific or diffuse, general or particular, instrumental or affective in style. A manifest interest articulation is an explicit formulation of a claim or a demand. It is latent when it takes the form of behavioural or mood cues which may be read and transmitted into the political system. It is instrumental when it takes the form of a bargain with consequences realistically spelled out. It is affective when it takes the form of a simple expression of gratitude, anger, disappointment and the like.[64] The demand or claim may also be specific or defuse in general or particular. It is specific when it takes the form of a request for a particular piece of legislation or a subsidy; it is diffuse when it takes the form of a general statement of dissatisfaction or preference (*i.e.* we need a change, the political system is rotten, we need socialism, and the like). Demands and claims are general when they are couched in class or professional groups terms (*i.e.* the rich ought to be taxed more; The big estates should be divided). They are particular when they are couched in individual or family terms (*i.e.* I will give you my vote or something of value if you lower my taxes).[65]

*2.2.2.1.3. Interest Aggregation*

Interest aggregation means the managing of political demands by bodies such as parties and interest groups.[66]

Every political system has some way of aggregating the interests, claims and demands which have been articulated by the interest groups of the polity. Interest aggregation is achieved "either by the formulation of general policies in which interests which have been articulated may be combined, accommodated and compromised or by the recruitment of political personnel who are more or less committed to a particular pattern of policy".[67]

The function of Articulation and aggregation overlap just as do those of aggregation recruitment and rule making. The distinction between interest articulation and interest aggregation is a fluid one. But aggregation refers to the more inclusive levels of the 'combinatory process' pressure groups and political parties in developed modern political system have distinctive regulative functions, the first for articulation, the second for aggregation. In some systems, however, the aggregative function may be performed by the legislative bodies, the political executive (cabinet, presidencies, kingships and chieftainships). The bureaucracy, the media of communications, the interest group of the various types, parties, factions, blocs in legislatures, cliques or faction in political executives and bureaucracies, individual parties or party coalitions outside the legislature, individual interest groups or *ad hoc* coalitions of interest groups also perform an aggregative functions, either by formulating alternative public policies or by supporting or advocating changes in political personnel.[68]

Party system is, however, the distinctively modern structure of political aggregation and in the modern, developed and democratic political system it regulates or gives order to the performance of the aggregative function by the other structures.[69]

Almond classifies party system into (i) authoritarian systems, (ii) dominant non-authoritarian systems, (iii) competitive two party systems, and (iv) competitive multiparty systems. From the point of view of the aggregative function is performed; political parties fall into the three categories (i) secular, pragmatic, bargaining parties, (ii) absolute value-oriented or ideological parties; and (iii) particularistic or traditional parties.

*2.2.2.1.4. Political Communication*

Political communication means the sending of messages within the political system and between the system and the outside.[70]

All the functions of political socialization and recruitment, interest articulation, interest aggregation, rule making, rule application and rule adjudication are performed by means of communication. It is, therefore, the medium through which all other functions of the political system have necessarily to be performed.

According to Almond political communication, "is the crucial boundary maintenance function. Autonomy is the media which makes for a free flow of information from society to polity and from one political structure to another, as well as an open feedback from output to input again". It can communicate "the articulation of interest emananting from political parties, legislatures and bureaucracies which themselves can correct the actions of interest groups". He compares it with blood circulation.

In modern political system differentiated media of communication have arisen which have developed a vocational ethics of neutral or objective communication. Primitive political systems, however, "have their drummers and runners, medievial town had their criers, noblemen and kings their heralds."[71]

#### 2.2.2.2. *Output (or Governmental) Functions*

Along with the input functions, there are three output functions. These are (a) Rule Making (b) Rule Application and (c) Rule Adjudication.

As already pointed out that these are three well known traditional governmental functions *i.e.*, legislative, executive and judicial.

##### *2.2.2.2.1. Rule Making*

According to Almond in traditional or primitive societies "rule-making tends to be either charismatic process or slow process of accumulation of traditions which are in part a derivative of the day-to-day rule enforcement and rule adjudication of the system". There is no political system in which rule making process in some form or the other does not exist. In simple political systems the structures or institutions which are involved in the making of rules may be groups of adult males whereas in partrimonial kingdoms by political rulers such as Kings or Council of Officials. In developed political systems this task is performed by parliaments, representing the people.

##### *2.2.2.2.2. Rule Application*

Rule application means the enforcement of rules which have been made available to the society in one form or the other. In other words it means enforcement of rules once enacted. The major problem involved is how to ensure that the rules are properly enforced. In modern times it is closely linked with administrative capability and increased role of bureaucracy. Moreover, rule application also means search for goals and policies on the one hand and their interaction on the other. It is of course difficult to set new rational goals, but still more difficult is together pre-requisites for such goals.

##### *2.2.2.2.3. Rule Adjudication*

It means to ensure that rules once enacted are not violated. If violated, the penalities must be specified and imposed. Rule adjudication should be capable of resolving conflicting situations within the political system and without putting any extra pressure on the rule makers to make new laws.

Each input and output has inter-relationship with the system as a whole.

The input and output functions have a meaning in relations to the system and the structure of an ongoing system. These represent a certain ordering of determinate relationship by means of which they contribute to the equilibrium of the system. The system receives input from the environments, which undergo process of conversion and are given back as outputs. The outputs have again their impact upon the environment which lead to a new flow of inputs into the political system. This process of interaction and exchange is what he terms as feedback. In other words if environments are input then output have their effect on environments, which in turn lead to new inputs in the system and thus are feedback of the system as a whole. This inter-relatedness of the structures and functions gives to the structural functional analysis of Almond the systematic character.

### 2.2.3. Criticism

S.P. Varma has summed up the criticism of Almond's Structural-Functional analysis in the following points :[72]

1. "First of all, Almond talks of functions without referring to a system in which functions have a meaning. A system, according to him, is a set of interaction but he does not care to define what a system actually means or what the full connotation of an interaction is".
2. "Secondly, his definition of political system is not very sound. He has defined political system as that system of interactions to be found in all independent societies which performs the functions of integration and adaptation (both internally and *vis-a-vis* other societies) by means of the employment or threat of employment of more or less legitimate physical compulsions. It is not clear what he means by 'independent societies' or how are they related to, and what the role of territory is in regard to them. Similarly the definition of a system in spite of its being comprehensive, inter-dependent and having boundaries separating it from other systems leaves out of consideration a number of other problems associated with the systems approach."

3. "Thirdly, when we come to a statement of the characteristics of political system we find that they all belong to the western political system, mainly to the American political system". So his analysis is not applicable to non-Western societies. Moreover, there are unique patterns of development for each society. Structural-functionalism is, therefore, weak and unhelpful when applied to most of the third world, which are still in a process of evaling the necessary network of institutions and structures, to make them ongoing system.
4. Fourthly, "the seven variables list of categories of functions also has its shortcomings. Between various interest groups mentioned, it becomes difficult to draw a boundary between the political and non-political".
5. "Fifthly, Almond has not attached enough importance to the output functions, and has failed to emphasise the importance of the feedback process in aggravating or minimising the challenges to the existence, or even the survival of the political system".
6. About his functionalism, Mechan says "Almond has not produced a theory of course, nor even well articulated classification scheme. The Taxonomy is incomplete and ambiguous".
7. Lastly S.P. Varma says, "when he moves on to more important tasks of political analysis, namely explanation and evaluation, we find that they are not best served by a comparative approach."

A phenomenon can best be explained in the context in which it appears.[73]

In addition to, we may mention few more points of criticism :

1. The whole thrust of structural-functionalism is on the survival capacity of the political system. Indeed, the emphasis on the maintenance of the system is so deep that the structural-functional approach has become in fact conservative and even *status-quoist* in its nature.[74]
2. Although the structural-functionalism is claimed as a theory of political development, it would be more appropriate to consider it as an explanatory theory of democratisation in western liberal democratic setting. Holt and Turner argue that Almonds framework "appears to have several limitations which prevent it from being completely effective as a basis for developing more general theory of political modernisation. It is difficult to apply

on a broad basis to include both historical and contemporary cases . . . ."[75]

3. Almond's analysis cannot be applied to the study of political development in communist countries.

   According to Almond's definition communist Russia does not have a modern political system. It is undifferentiated and does not have autonomous structures to regulate the rule making, rule application and rule adjudication function. It is, thus, to be equated with the traditional system.

   But the style of performance of input functions in the Soviet Union does not justify such a labelling. Holt and Turner rightly point out that "In the Soviet Union after Stalin's death more interests were apparently articulated than had previously been the case, and the style in which they are articulated reveals a curious combination of modern and non-modern features .. ."[76]

4. Almond's analysis is really a highly complicated one which threatens to defeat the very purpose it seeks to fulfil. Almond has devised 17 to 20 separate criteria or dimensions to differentiate a modern political system from the traditional. This has actually created a problem.[77]

5. The structural-functional brings about a separation between function and structure. While commenting on this G. Sartori says, "the structural functional analyst is a lame scholar. He claims to walk on two feet, but actually on one foot—and a bad foot at that. He cannot really visualise the inter-play between 'structure' and 'function' because the two terms are seldom, if even, neatly, disjointed, the structure remains throughout a twin brother of its imputed functional purposes"[78]

6. Structural-Functionalism is virtually a thorn in the Marxian flesh. A belief in the inevitability of class war is the basic Marxian philosophy, but it is not recognised in structural-functionalism. This approach has, thus, a counterpoise to Marxist Social Science.[79]

   In spite of all the above points of criticism, and limitations structural-functionalism has introduced new conceptual tools in political science and enriched the discipline. It has provided new insights into political realities. It has, therefore, broad-based and enriched comparative politics.

## 2.3. THE COMMUNICATION ANALYSIS OF KARL DEUTSCH

The Communication Analysis is chiefly attributed to the formulation of Karl Deutsch. He developed the communication framework for political analysis in his book 'Nerves of Government'. Like Easton, he also believed that the differences between the behaviour of living things and that of social organisations have greatly narrowed down because of the new development in the communication science.[80] Both of them regard communication or cybernetics models as contributing to a linking of science of living things to self-regulating machines and social systems. All the systems involved can be seen as networks of inter-connected parts, the patterns of the network being, in fact, patterns of information flows.[81]

### 2.3.1. Science of Cybernetics

The concepts which Karl Deutsch use to describe political phenomena are drawn from cybernetics—a new science dealing with control of information flows[82] or a theory of information, self-regulating system, and the physiology of the nervous system originally formulated by the Harvard Scientist Norbert Weiner.[83] According to Davies and Lewis, "Deutsch is able to perceive similarities in processes and functional requirements between living things, electronic machines and social organizations, and having rejected the other models of analysis, suggests that cybernetics analysis is relevant to the understanding of social systems, since they do in their processes resemble other types of organizations. The brain, the computer, the society all have characteristics which make them organizations. They have the capacity to transmit and react to information".[84] Communications or cybernetics analysis is, therefore, concerned with ways in which certain kinds of apparatus are maintained through feedback *i.e.*, devices by which the entropy of a system is counter-acted by returning some of output into input.[85] Deutsch points out that "communication or cybernetics model can replace the classic analogues or models of mechanism, organization and process which so long have dominated much of scientific thinking".[86] He is led to analyse the amount of variety of information network, the structure of sub-systems, the feedback system, the organization of system's memory mechanisms; and the rules which determine the behaviour of the system.[87] The Communication Approach looks at the task of government and politics as processes of steering and co-ordinating human efforts towards the attainment of some set of goals. Within this framework the basic mechanism through which these processes manifest themselves is the decision. The communication approach is more interested in process of making decisions as contrasted with the actual consequences of the decisions. The communications or cybernetics approach focuses on decision-making as process rather than on the results of decisions.[88]

## 2.3.2. The Concepts of the Communication Theory

The communication theory has two types of concepts :

(a) Concepts relating to operating structures, and

(b) Concepts focusing on various flows and processes.

### *2.3.2.1. Concepts Relating to Operating Structures*

Such as Reception systems; Memory; Value complexes and Decisions-making centres.

So far as first Deutsch tries to evolve a model of the way in which the operating structures function. These are receptors or reception systems, which deal and receive (or intake) information from the environments-domestic as well as foreign (or external).[89] The notion of reception covers several functions. In addition to the simple intake-like scanning operations, selection of information, data processing etc. most systems develop a set of fairly specific operating rules for processing the flow of incoming information.[90] Within the decision making apparatus, information is handled and acted upon by structures representing memory, value complexes and actual decisions-making centres. Memory relates incoming information to relevant past experiences concerning both processes and consequences. Value complexes perform the normative task relating possibilities to preferences. Finally, there are structures that operate to implement completed decisions and to feed information concerning performances back into the apparatus as a new or fresh input.[91] This is how the entire systemic process is started all over again.

### *2.3.2.2. Concepts Focusing on various Flows and Processes*

Such as Channels; Loads; Load capacity; Responsiveness; Fidelity; Recall and Combinatorial capacity.

The second category of concepts concern with flows and processes. It is a communication network and consists of a patterned set of information flows which involve several kinds of other concepts, particularly channels, loads and load capacity. Out of them, load capacity is determined by the number and type of channel available for information flow. Load relates to the over-all intake of information at any given time. In other words the total amount of information which a system may possess at a particular time. In a political system loads tend to vary substantially over times as well as show significant differences in quality. Deutsch mentions a number of other factors to which load capacity is very intimately related. These are responsiveness, fidelity, background, noise and distortion. If the apparatus is capable of handling incoming information with deftness, it can be considered as responsive. The notion of fidelity, refers to the accuracy with which information is transmitted in the various processes of perception, selection and handling.[92]

He further holds that the communication system is capable of associating, locating and bringing forward past experiences that are relevant to the analysis of the incoming information. This is the notion of recall. In other words the term recall means the ability of the communication system to associate, locate, and bring forth past experience that is relevant to the analysis of incoming information.[93] Moreover, the capability of the system to deal with a wide range of information inputs in such a way as to make and implement decisions with positive consequences for the attainment of goals, has been termed as 'combinatorial capacity'. In other words combinatorial capacity is a measure of ability to deal with a wide range of information inputs in such a way as to make and implement decisions with positive consequences for the attainment of the goals of a political system.[94]

So far as qualitative aspects of the communication system is concerned, the first condition of a good system should remain in a highly unstable state of equilibrium. Otherwise it cannot effectively react to the information flowing into it from the environment.[95] Much also would depend on the selectivity of the receiver. The receiving system can also be simple as well as complex.

### 2.3.3. Feedback Mechanism—Such as Negative Feedback Load; Lag; Gain and Lead

A key concept which, according to Deutsch, distinguishes his approach from the equilibrium approach is that of "feedback". The term 'feedback' (or a servo-mechanism as it is called) is a communication network that produces action in response to an input of information; and includes the results of its own action in the information by which it modifies its subsequent behaviour.[96] "The feedback mechanism allows the organization to change its state if necessary in reaction to information. But equilibrium systems simply react in such a manner as to attempt to return to its original state. The feedback concept has therefore introduced the element of dynamism in communication analysis".[97]

Deutsch also introduces sub-concepts of the feedback concept such as negative feedback, load lag, gain and lead.[98] Negative feedback refers to process through which information about the consequences of decisions and implementing action is put back into the system. In other words "a negative feedback is one which transmits back to itself information which is the result of decisions and actions taken by the system and which leads the system to change its behaviour in pursuit of the goals which it has set itself".[99] Load, as already pointed out refers to the total amount of information which a system may possess at a particular time. It also indicates to the extensiveness of the systems activities in relation to the capacity of the channels of communication. In other words, it means the extent and speed of changes in the position of the target in relation to the goal seeking system.[100] Lag refers to the amount of delay which the system experiences between reporting the consequences of decisions and acting on the information received.[101] In other words it refers to slowness in the response of the system to information regarding the consequences of decisions and actions, assuming that it has reached the system in time and in good shape.[102] Lead, on the other hand, illustrates the extent to which a system has the capacity to react to predictions about the future consequences of decisions and actions.[103] The interaction of these variables determine the consequences of the feedback processes.[104]

Political system, according to Deutsch, are goal-seeking entities. He points out "the chances of success in goal-seeking are . . . always related to the amount of load and lag. Upto a point they may be positively related to the amount of gain, although, at high rates of gain, this relationship, maybe reversed, and they are always positively related to the amount of lead".[105] A system may over-respond to information received and it is likely that above a certain rate of gain, any increase would be dysfunctional to the realization of the system's goals. Deutsch's major focus is on the attainment of goals. He refers to the similarity of the processes of steering and goal seeking in living thing and political systems. He says that "perhaps it is possible to set goals with respect to foreign affairs and they may also try to maintain some state of affairs they deem desirable, such as prosperity in economics or transquility in politics".[106]

### 2.3.4. Other Concepts : Such as Learning; Innovation; Growth and Self-Transformation

Deutsch also introduces the concepts of learning, innovation, growth and self-transformation. "Learning is the ability of the political system to adopt its modes of action in response to the information it receives through bringing about necessary changes and readjustment in the elements of its internal structure and process".[107] A political system goes through the process of innovation, growth and self-transformation when it moves beyond mere adaption to drastic change. It may lead not only to change in its goals, structure or process—which may be described as adaptive changes—but to changes of a fundamental nature, growth in completely new direction and even to a complete transformation, the last one involving changes of such a fundamental and far reaching character as to bring about qualitative transformation in the functioning of the political system.[108] Self-transformation, "thus, is the ability to generate sustaining processes of change internally and is so doing ultimately to produce qualitative changes".[109]

## 2.3.5. Criticism

Karl Deutsch's communication Analysis has been criticised on several grounds. The main points of the criticism are as under :

1. Communication analysis has attached for greater importance to the area of pattern maintenance *i.e.* stability and equilibrium. But in matter of revolutionary change, this approach does not very far.
2. It is far too mechanistic in nature and has tried to give an essentially engineering orientation to human behaviour. It appears that something bodily has been lifted from the field of engineering to that of the social sciences, which is not conducive for the study of human behaviour.
3. In communication analysis there is not only the difficulty of applying models picked up from engineering to political science but in addition, the "model-building does not serve the purpose for which it is being increasingly used in social sciences." Models are built in simple terms. But in the case of Deutsch, the model itself has become so complex that instead of helping in the understanding of the phenomena, it has a tendency of confusing it.
4. Moreover, the terms which have been used for the study of communication model have been lifted from engineering but have not been clarified. In fact, it is alleged that these have been carelessly used.
5. Deutsch's model however, raises a number of interesting questions about the performance of governments but offers very little help in answering them.[110]

6. Communication analysis of Deutsch lays more stress on decision-making processes rather than studying the consequences of those decisions.
7. Critics point out that this analysis provides excellent tools for studying information itself, but the study of politics is very complicated affairs and these tools help only in locating power in political system and do not in any way assist in studying the behaviour of various elite groups in handling the power.[111]

## REFERENCES

1. Verma, S.P., *Modern Political Theory*, Vikas Publishing House Pvt. Ltd., New Delhi 1975, p. 175.
2. *Ibid.*
3. Curtis Michael, *Comparative Government and Politics, op. cit.*, p. 7.
4. Larson, Allan L., *Comparative Politics Analysis*, Nelson-Hall (nk), Chicago 1980, p. 76.
5. Easton, David, *A System Analysis of Political Life*. The University of Chicago Press, Chicago, New York, 1965.
6. Maheshwari, Sriram, *Comparative Government and Politics*, Lakshmi Narain Agarwal Educational Publishers, Hospital Road, Agra-3, 1985, p. 47.
7. Young, Oran R., *System of Political Science*, Prentice-Hall Inc., Englewood, Cliffs, New Jersey, 1968, p. 39.
8. Kebschull, Harvey G., *Politics in Transitional Societies*, Appleton-Cantury-Crafis Educational Division, Meredith Corporation, New York, 1968, p. 22.
9. Easton, David, *A System Analysis of Political Life*, op. cit., p. 7.
10. Kebschull, Harvey G., *Politics in Trasitional Societies, op. cit.*, p. 22.
11. *Ibid.*, p. 23.
12. Almond, Gabriel A. and Powell, G. Bingham Jr., *Comparative Politics—A Developmental Approach*. Oxford and IBH Publishing Co., New Delhi, 1978, pp. 25, 26.
13. Young, Oran R., *System of Political Science, op. cit.*, p. 40.
14. *Ibid.*, p. 40.
15. Kebschull, Harvey G., *Politics In Transitional Societies, op. cit.*, p. 23.
16. Young, Oran R., *System of Political Science, op. cit.*, pp. 40-41.
17. *Ibid.*, p. 41.
18. Easton, David, *A system Analysis of Political Life, op. cit.*, p. 159.
19. Almond, Gabriel A. and Powell, G. Bringham Jr., *Comparative Politics—A Developmental Approach, op. cit.*, p. 26.

20. Hans Raj, *Comparative Politics*, Surjeet Publications, 7-K, Kolhapur Road, Kamla Nagar, Delhi, 1985, p. 21.
21. *Ibid.*, p. 22.
22. Young Oran R., *System of Political Science, op. cit.*, p. 41.
23. Kebschull, Harvey G., *Politics in Transitional Societies, op. cit.*, p. 25.
24. Hans Raj, *Comparative Politics, op. cit.*, p. 22.
25. Easton, David, *A System Analysis of Political Life, op. cit.*, p. 220.
26. *Ibid.*, p. 230.
27. Maheshwari, Sriram, *Comparative Government And Politics, op. cit.*, p. 50.
28. Young Oran R., *System of Political Science, op. cit.*, p. 42.
29. Verma, S.P., *Modern Political Theory, op. cit.*, p. 181.
30. *Ibid.*
31. Kebschull, Harvey G., *Politics In Transitional Societies, op. cit.*, p. 26.
32. Verma, S.P., *Modern Political Theory, op. cit.*, p. 181.
33. *Ibid.*
34. Young, Oran R., *System of Political Science, op. cit.*, p. 43.
35. Hans Raj, *Comparative Politics, op. cit.*, p. 22.
36. Maheshwari, Sriram, *Comparative government and Politics, op. cit.*, p. 52.
37. *Ibid.*
38. Verma. S P., *Modern Political Theory, op. cit.*, p. 185.
39. Ray, Amal and Bhattacharya, Mohit, *Political Theory*, World Press Private Ltd., Calcutta, 1983, p. 26.
40. Young, Oran R., *System of Political Science, op. cit.*, p. 48.
41. Puri, S., *Modern Political Analysis*, New Academic Publishing Company, Jullunder, 1977, p. 84.
42. Young, Oran R., *System of Political Science, op. cit.*, p. 45.
43. *Ibid.*
40. Maheswari, Sriram, *Comparative Government and Politics, op. cit.*, p. 52.
45. Hans Raj, *Comparative Politics, op. cit.*, p. 23.
46. *Ibid.*
47. *Ibid.*
48. Curits, Michael: *Comparative Government and Politics, op. cit.*, p. 7.
49. Almond, Gabriel A., Coleman, James, S., *The Policies of Developing Areas*, Princeton University Press, 1960, pp-Introduction.
50. *Ibid.*
51. *Ibid.*, p. 17.
52. Kebschull, Harvey G., *Politics in Transitional Societies, op. cit.*, pp. 35-36.
53. Verma, S.P., *Modern Political Theory, op. cit.*, p. 297.
54. Curtis, Michael, *Comparative Govt. and Politics, op. cit.*, p. 7.
55. Kebschull, Harvey G., *Politics in Transitional Societies, op. cit.*, p. 36.

56. Verma, S.P., *Modern Political Theory, op. cit.*, p. 297.
57. Kebschull, Harvey G., *Politics in Transitional Societies, op. cit.*, p. 36.
58. Curtis, Michael, *Comparative Government and Politics, op. cit.*, p. 7.
59. Kebschull, Harvey G., *Politics in Transitional Societies, op. cit.*, p. 37.
60. *Ibid.*
61. Curtis, Michael, *Comparative Government and Politics, op. cit.*, p. 7.
62. Kebschull, Harvey G., *Politics in Transitional Societies, op. cit.*, p. 38.
63. *Ibid.*, pp. 38-39.
64. Almond, Gabriel A. and Coleman James S., *Politics of Developing Areas*, op. cit., pp. 34-35.
65. Kebschull, Harvey G., *Politics in Transitional Societies, op. cit.*, p. 38-39.
66. Curtis, Michael, *Comparative Government and Politics*, p. 7.
67. Kebschuil, Harvey G., *Politics in Transitional Societies, op. cit.*, p. 40.
68. *Ibid.*, p. 41,
69. *Ibid.*
70. Curtis, Michael, *Comparative Government and Politics, op. cit.*, p. 7.
71. Kebschull, Harvey G., *Politics in Transitional Societies, op. cit.*, p. 43.
72. Verma, S.P., *Modern Political Theory, op. cit.*, p 173.
73. *Ibid.*, p. 175.
74. Maheshwari, Sriram, *Comparative Government and Politics, op. cit.*, p. 40.
75. *Ibid.*, p. 41.
76. Halt, Robert and Turner, John E., *The Political Basis of Economic Development*, East-West Press, New Delhi, 1970, pp. 12-13.
77. *Ibid.*, p. 13.
78. Sartori, G., *Concept Misformation on Comparative Politics*, American Political Science Review, Vol. 54, 1970, p. 1049.
79. Maheshwari, Sriram, *Comparative Government and Polities, op. cit.*, p. 42.
80. Ray, Amal, Bhattachatya, Mohit, *Political Theory, op. cit.*, p. 27.
81. Gandhi, Madan G., *Modern Political Analysis*, E-16, Rohtak University, Rohtak, 1976, p. 87.
82. *Ibid.*
83. Ray, Amal, Rhattacharya, Mohit, *Political Theory, op. cit.*, p. 27.
84. Davies, Morton R., Lewis Vaugham A., *Models of Political System*, Vikas Publications, Delhi 1971, p. 75.
85. Gandhi, Madan G., *Modern Political Analysis, op. cit.*, p. 87.
86. *Ibid.*
87. Davies, Morton R.; Lewis, Vaughan A., *Models of Political System, op. cit.*, p. 75.
88. Young Oran R., *Systems of Political Science, op. cit.*, p. 50
89. *Ibid.*, p. 51.
90. Verma, S.P., *Modern Political theory, op. cit.*, pp. 317-318.
91. Young, Oran R., *Systems of Political Science, op. cit.*, p. 52.
92. *Ibid.*,

93. *Ibid.*,
94. *Ibid.*
95. Gandhi, Madan G., *Modern Political Analysis, op. cit.*, p. 89.
96. Davies, Morton R., Lewis, Vaughan A., *Models of Political System, op. cit.*, p. 76.
97. *Ibid.*
98. *Ibid.*, p. 77.
99. *Ibid.*
100. Verma, S.P., *Modern Political Theory, op. cit.* p. 321.
101. Davies, Morton R., Lewis, Vaughan A., *Models of Political Systems, op. cit.*, p. 77.
102. Verma, S.P., *Modern Political Theory, op. cit.*, p. 321.
103. Davies, Morton R., Lewis, Vaughan A., *Models of Political Systems, op. cit.*, p. 77.
104. Young, Oran R., *Systems of Political Science, op. cit.*, p. 53.
105. *Ibid.*
106. Davies, Morton R., Lewis, Vaughan A., *Models of Political Systems, op. cit.*, p. 77.
107. Verma, S.P., *Modern Political Theory, op. cit.*, p. 325.
108. *Ibid.*
109. *Ibid.*
110. Gandhi, Madan G., *Modern Political Analysis, op. cit.*, p. 100.
111. Dr. Hans Raj., *Comparative Politics, op. cit.*, p. 233.

# 3

# The Classification of Political Systems

"A classification of regimes or political systems 'highlights similarities and dissimilarities between them and by doing so it deepens our understanding of them."

There is no end to the classification of political system. Since every regime is at once unique and, in flux, all classifications are, therefore, at best partial and temporary. As regimes exist in continuuam, somewhere between total reliance on either persuasion or coercion differing in the amount of power exercised and the way it is distributed, they do not fit nearly in rigid categories. Nevertheless classification serves to highlight the major politically meaningful similarities and dissimilarities between regimes.[1]

## 3.1. THE CLASSICAL DIVISION

### 3.1.1. Plato's Classification of Political Systems

The history of the classification of political systems dates back to the days of ancient Greeks. Plato had presented a classification of his own in his 'Politicus' or 'Statesman'.[2]

Plato's six-fold classification can be put in the form of following table:

**TABLE 1**

| Number of rulers | Law abiding states | Lawless states |
|---|---|---|
| One | Monarchy | Tyranny |
| A few | Aristocracy | Oligarchy |
| The many | Moderate Democracy | Extreme Democracy |

Plato, thus distinguishes law-abiding from lawless state and under each type he mentioned three forms *i.e.* rule of one, rule of a few and rule of the many.[3] The rule of one, he called, as Monarchy, when the state was law-abiding. When it was lawless he called it as tyranny. The rule of a few was termed by him as Aristocracy, when it was law-abiding and oligarchy when lawless. The rule of many was termed as moderate democracy if it was law-abiding and extreme democracy if it was lawless. Plato further pointed out "since a law abiding state is always better than a lawless one, moderate democracy, which is law-abiding, must always be ranked superior to oligarchy which is lawless.[4] So far as lawless forms, extreme democracy was ranked superior to oligarchy. According to Plato the democracy was the worst of law-abiding but the best of lawless forms and in either case it stood higher than oligarchy."[5]

It was, however, much different from what he had given in his Republic. Plato, therefore, seemed to be much confused on the subject.[6]

### 3.1.2. Aristotle's Classification of Political Systems

Aristotle, who was regarded not only the father of Comparative Political Analysis but the classification of political systems also, followed the Platonic classification of political systems according to rule by the one, the few or the many."[7] He, however, analysed the purposes of the good society and its relationship to individual happiness. He, therefore, considered alternative forms of regimes in the context of the ends of both the polity and individual.[8] In other words, his six fold classification of regimes was based "on the number of people who participated in governing, on the ethical quality of their rule depending on whether it was in their personal or the general interest, and on their socio-economic status."[9] Those regimes that served the interests of the ruling group only were perversions (or perverted form) of the true constitutional forms. He believed that all states went through a cycle of revolutions, thus a state began with the finest possible type of government—the rule of one man, who from the point of view of political authority, was the supremely virtuous one.[10] According to Aristotle one man would so excel all others in virtues that he would obviously be the one whom all should obey.[11] This was the Monarchy or Royalty. But after a time such a virtuous man could no longer be produced; yet the rule of one man remained, and his power was maintained by force. This type of regime was called the tyranny or Despotism.[12] Aritsotle define tyranny as "Just that arbitrary power of an individual, which is responsible to no one, and governs all alike, whether equals or better, with a view to its own advantage, not to that of its subjects, and therefore, against their will."[13] The tyrant would one day meet the opposition of a body of upright men who would overthrow him and rule in his stead. It was Aristocracy.[14] According to Aristotle, "When the few well equipped rule for the public interest, through law and the public interest historically can be attained only through law, which is reason unaffected by desire, one has an aristocracy."[15] The spirit of the aristocracy, however, would after a time begin to degenerate, "though the rule of the few would continue, it would cease to stand on the basis of political virtue and maintain itself by the use of force or corruption. This corrupt form of aristocracy is called oligarchy."[16] In an oligarchy, the standard of merit would come to be wealth alone, and distributive justice therefore, was informed by this criterion.[17] Against this hateful rule there would break out a popular uprising and the oligarchy would be superseded by the rule of the many. It is called polity.[18] Polity means a kind of mixed rule, in which the claims of many and the propertied are blended under law.[19] Michael Curtis refers to it as Democracy.[20] Polity would soon degenerate and become licence and anarchy and the rule of the mob. Aristotle called it as Democracy. Michael Curtis, on the other hand, refers it as Ochlocracy.[21] It would be nothing but negation of the rule. "Out of the darkness, then, again would arise a supremely virtuous man i.e. some Caesar, who alone could restore order and reason. The cycle would, thus, completed and would begin all over again.[22]

On the whole, "Aristotle thinks that democracy is the 'least bad' of the perverted forms, just as tyranny is the worst of the three."[23]

Aristotle's sixfold classification of regimes (Political Systems) has been presented in the following Table 2 :[24]

**Table 2**

| Number of rulers | Rule in the general interest | Self-interest rule | Social group |
|---|---|---|---|
| One | Monarchy | Tyranny | King |
| Few | Aristocracy | Oligarchy | The Wealthy |
| Many | Polity or Democracy | Ochlocracy | The Poor |

(Table adopted from Michael Curtis's book Comparative Government and Politics", Harper & Row Publishers, London, 1978, p. 55).

Aristotle's classification has been useful as it indicates the number and nature of governing groups in a regime and whose interest were likely to be taken into account.

Modern elitists have suggested that Aristotalian classification on Classical division is limited in its utility. They are of the view that as all political systems and organizations are oligarchic, the majority of people are in fact, therefore, ruled by small minorities (*i.e.* Delites) in all the regimes. For example "an elite is as observable in the Soviet Union, with its daches and personal privileges, and in Sri Lanka, where two families—the Senanayake and Bandaranaike, have alternated in the primership, as it is in the Western world."[24]

### 3.1.3. Polybius, Classification

Another classical classification of political systems was given by Polybius—an historian, a world traveller, a politician, a military strategist, an adviser to Roman Generals and a confident of Roman Statesman.[25] Polybius took over from Plato and Aristotle their six-fold classification of regimes as well as the theory that governments pass through a cycle of changes.[26] He also learnt from the study of history two inevitable laws—of growth and decay. He had applied these laws to the classification of regimes given by Plato and Aristotle. Moreover, though the idea that unmixed forms or regimes degenerate more quickly than mixed one's was first mooted by Plato and Aristotle, it received great emphasis at the hands of Polybius.[27]

Polybius was interested in determing the reasons of the success of the Repulic. By success he meant "the ability to conquer most of the world within a relatively short period of time and of equal importance, the stability supposedly achieved in Roman institutions."[28] He found the key to that success in the balance of the constitution. Moreover, he ascribed in the great stability of the Roman government to its mixed character. According to him Roman polity did not rest on one species of power.[29] It was a happy blend : the monarchic, aristocratic and democratic elements.[30] According to Polybius the Roman polity had a monarchic and a despotic aspect in the consuls, an aristocratic element in the Senate, and a popular one in the Commitias—an Assembly of the people.[31] He, however, sought to combine in his mixed constitution the elements of the different forms of governments. He divided the powers of government into different organs—each representing one form of government. The supreme military power belonged to the consuls who represented the monarchic elements in the state, the judicial and financial power assigned to the Senate which constituted the aristocratic element, while some deliberative functions were given to the popular[32] assemblies which formed the democratic element. He further pointed out that the real stability of the Roman system was because the three powers—the consuls, the senate and the comitias—used to check each other from becoming too powerful.[33] If the consul, which was ostensibly supreme in its command of the army, tried to assert its authority too much, it could be checked by the senate which had the power of the purse *i.e.*, power for the voting of the supplies. Polybius pointed out the senate had important prerogatives which could limit and condition the consuls, as well as the other magistrates.[34] They could also, by its actions, emphasize or de-emphasize the merits and demerits of respective generals and thus make or break them in their careers. Likewise, the senate and people (*i.e.* popular assemblies) were also mutually interdependent. The senate must get the consent of the people (popular assemblies) for decrees which punished offences with death. Moreover, people were final in passage or rejection of new laws. In other words Tribunes (magistrates elected by the Roman plebeians to defend their rights) had a veto on acts of the senate. Tribunes in peculiar sense were the agents of the people. Popular assemblies thus exercised control over the other organs through their power of bestowing offices and passing and repealing laws. The people were, on the other hand, too very much dependent on the consuls "For men do not rashly resist the wishes of the consuls, because one and all may become subject to their absolute authority on compain."[35] In Roman system each organ was, therefore, set off against the others. In short the Roman system was based on the principle of checks and balances.

### 3.1.4. Cicero's Classification of Political Systems

Cicero, who was born in 106 B.C. only fifteen years after the death of Polybius[36] when the republican constitution was crumbling due to the civil war between two powerful factions in Rome, was not a political philosopher or a leader of any school but a lawyer-statesman. His political treaties—the Republic and the Laws—were the best index of political thought at Roman, especially in conservative and aristocratic circles, during the last days of the Republic.[37]

He was of the view that the constitution of the perfect state was the product of a long course of evolution to which several minds working under different circumstances, contributed. It could not be established through the genius of one man but required many ages to come up. According to him the constitution of Rome was the most stable and perfect form of government that political experience had evolved.[38] He pointed out that by tracing its development and analyzing its parts in relation to one another it should be possible to arrive at a theory of the state in which mere speculation was reduced to minimum.[39]

There was nothing new in Cicero's classification of political system. He distinguished three primary forms of regimes— monarchy, aristocracy and democracy. He emphasised that each of them would tend to degenerate into its corresponding corrupt form. This tendency according to him, could be kept in check only when the elements of the three were combined in a mixed form.[40] He seemed to have accepted Polybius view of the Roman constitution as a balance of social, economic and political power.[41] He, like Polybius, also regarded the Roman constitution as the best example of mixed constitution.[42] He, thus, believed in the excellence of the mixed constitution and praised its advantages.

He thought of a society held together by an ancient tradition which assigned to each part of the polity its due bound.[43] But he did not tell us how that regime (constitution) came to be, whether by reason or by trial and error.[44] He simply accepted it as the norm by which all good Romans should live. He tended to reject all drastic proposal for change, whether covering from the aristocracy or from the populus as these would likely to disturb the balance.[45]

Cicero further pointed out that the Polybian cycle theory—the orderly alternation of good and bad constitutions, from monarchy to tyranny, from tyranny to aristocracy, from aristocracy to oligarchy, from oligarchy to moderate democracy to mob-rule—did not fit idea of Roman history.[46]

### 3.1.5. Niccolo Machiavelli's Classification of Political System

Niccolo Machiavelli, who was born in 1469[47], did not think of political society as natural in the classical Greek sense. But accounted of the origin of the State, which attributed the first government to chance.[48] He was of the view "that mankind were at first scattered, but as they became more numerous, they began, rather unconsciously, to submit themselves to the stronger for self protection."[49] The government, thus, had its origin in physical force. He believed that in the beginning, presumably, the ruler "selected" himself through his sheer ability to dominte. Later, when men became more aware of the reason for rulership, they began to elect their sovereigns for their wisdom and justice.[50] Non-elective sovereignty, however, emerged, since men concluded that the children, of those who had proved wise and just ruler, must inherited their father's virtues.[51] When it proved otherwise the degenerated governors found themselves objects of jealousy and hatred by their subjects. The prince reacted to this hatred by becoming himself fearful, by developing tyrannical habits to check possible conspiracies. Thus they used naked force.[52]

Meanwhile, those who possessed virtues lead many plots against the tyrant and eventually succeeded to overthrow him and capture power. Thus aristocracy was established.[53] He further pointed out that in the long run aristocracy would also become lawless and transmitted into an oligarchy. The oligarchy would also provoke rebellion and as a result masses of energetic men pushed forward to control affairs. Thus, the popular government would establish.[54]

While summing up Machiavelli observed that all forms of Government were defective. The good governments were defective, because they usually flourished for relatively short periods of time and the bad because by their very nature they subverted the preservation of the State.[55]

Like Aristotle, he also believed that mixed government would provide the relatively best scheme. Though it had less good than pure monarchy, aristocracy or popular government, yet it had a tendency to persist longer. It had neither the inherent virtuousness of the bad forms nor the brief life of the good ones.[56]

### 3.1.6. Jean Bodin's Classification of Political Systems

Jean Bodin, being one of the greatest men and most notable French Political Philosopher of 16th century also classified political system on the bases of location of sovereignty in them.[57] In other words her classification of government depended upon the manner and system in which soverngnty was exercised. He pointed out, "If the sovereign authority resides in one individual, the State is said to be a monarchy, if it is possessed by a small number of individuals, it is known as aristocratic, and if it vests in the mass of citizens as a whole, the state is called democratic."[58] He further stressed that in an aristocratic political systems the honours and offices were bestowed upon members of small and narrow class and the masses excluded from the benefits thereof. In a democratic state on the other hand honours and offices were to be conferred upon all alike on the basis of merit irrespective of class distinction.[59] Out of three forms of State—monarchy, aristocracy and democracy Bodin regarded monarchy of French type which enlisted the cooperation of all sections of the people worked for larger social happiness and provided political stability to the society, was the best. He said that the vesting of the Supreme power of the state in a minority of citizens or in the whole body of citizens would lead to anarchy and the ruin of the subjects.[60] According to him the monarchy would have three sub-divisions *i.e.,* Despotisim, Royal Monarchy and Tyranny.[61]

Since sovereignty cannot be divided between various elements, he did not plead for the mixed form of the government.[62]

### 3.1.7. Montesquiue's Classification *i.e.,* Republican Monarchies and Despotic Political Systems

The eighteenth century French philosopher Montesquieu had classified political systems into republican, monarchic, and despotic.[63] His classification was different from that of Aristotle in the sense that his republican form of regime covered aristocracy and democracy identified by Aristotle.[64] In other respect it is reminiscent of the Aristotelian one because the type of government depends upon the number of persons holding power.[65] According to him when political power is shared between the few or the many, the regime is republican one[66]. In other words, republics can be either aristocratic or democratic and which are more likely to be endowed with charity and patriotism than monarchies.[67] Monarchy regimes are those in which the rules are subject to restrains of custom, local privileges or his own law.[68] In other words, where power rests in the hands of a single person motivated by wide social interests it is monarchy.[69] The despostic regimes are those in which the sovereign was unrestrained.[70] In other words, it is the worst form of government for in it power vests in one individual who acts arbitrarily and in his own interest.[71] Moreover, Montesquieu, in his classification of regimes recognises the relation between the form of government and the type of society.[72] He further points out that education, morals, patriotism, level of economic equality etc. effect the form of government existing in the society.[73] He also emphasises the relationship between a country's size and its form of government. He stresses that large empire breeds despotic authority, a monarchy is suitable for a moderate territory and a small territory lends itself admirably to a republic.[74]

While criticising Montesquieu's classification of political systems, Curtis points out his classification as more appropriate for eighteenth century than for contemporary conditions.[75]

We may conclude that the Aristotles classification of political systems made in the 4th century B.C. had influenced not only the thinking of subsequent political scholars but also the theories of the classifical divisions of the political systems. However, the steady proliferation of independent states and increasing diversity in styles and patterns of governance, the earlier classifications of political systems have become inadequate and even outdated. Moreover, modern elitists suggest that the classical division of political systems is limited in its usefulness as all political systems and organisations are oligarchic in nature.

## 3.2. LIBERAL CLASSIFICATION—BRITISH AND AMERICAN MODELS

Liberal Democracy is an English export.[76] A liberal democratic political system is one which believes in democracy and has faith in the democratic way of living and behaving. There is rule of people and each action taken by the government is supposed to have the support and approval of the people; the government is run by the elected representatives of the people and in ultimate analysis, they are responsible to them for their policies and programmes; elections are periodically held and electorates are given full freedom to express their opinion in the way they like; the representatives claim to be working in the collective interests of the people. Sovereignty is supposed to be vested in the people; the political system is to look after the interests of all—not only of majority but also of the minority, there is a freedom of conscience and morality, the political system has no religious ideology of its own and has to keep communal forces in check so that they do not challenge the secular character of the state; the executive is the combination of political and permanent executives; both are not only jointly try to run the govt, but also try to interfere in legitimate sphere of the other organs; the civil servants are political non-commital, faithfully implement the political programmes of the party in power and try to cooperate the political bosses and ensure the success of the govt. 'Liberal democratic political system is also based on the principal of limited government; powers are not allowed to be concentrated and each organ of the government has allotted sphere of activity; social, economic, religious and industrial groups are not suppressed; personality of groups and associations not only accepted but also recognised; maximum participation of the people in political activities and processes; political parties are allowed to be organised and there is freedom to compete with other for capturing political powers.[77]

Some political systems have maintained this form of government for well over a century *e.g.*, U.K., U.S.A., Canada, Australia, New Zealand, Belgium, Holland, Switzerland and Scandinavian countries. Countries like France, Germany (west), Italy and Japan, which adopted it later have by now fully assimilated. Liberal democratic form of government in India, Sri Lanka, Malayasia and in many other countries of third world is at experimental stage. However, nearly one-third of the world's population today lives under liberal democratic system.[78]

The Liberal classification of the British and American Models is presented as under :

**TABLE 3**

Liberal classification of political system of British and American Models

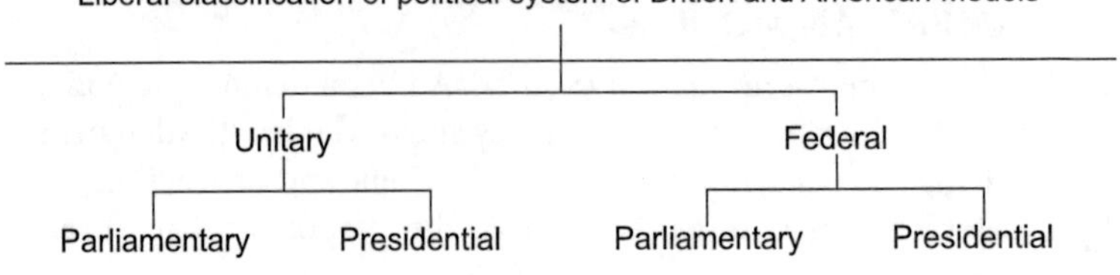

### 3.2.1. Unitary and Federal form of Political Systems

"The Political systems be classified into 'Unitary and Federal Types' *i.e.*, in terms of the method by which the powers of government are distributed between the government of the whole country and any local govern-ments which exercise authority over parts of the country."[79]

#### *3.2.1.1. Unitary form of Political System*

A Unitary political system is one in which the central or national government is the supreme—possessing complete governmental power. "No spheres of governmental action are assigned by the constitution to smaller unit of government, such as States or provinces."[80] The national government may, and usually does, delegate many duties to local or regional units, by an ordinary statute enacted by the national legislature, but not by the constitution. These duties may be withdrawn with equal facility. In other words, a unitary political system is one in which the central set of political institutions exercise legitimate authority, as in England or France or Sweden. Local authorities obtain their powers from the Central authority which can amend those powers if it so desires.[81] While discussing the political implications of unitarianism Prof. Dicey says that there is "the habitual exercise of supreme legislative authority by one central power" that is the supremacy of the central legislature is the essence of a unitary type of government. The unitary constitution, therefore, does not preclude the exercise of subsidiary law-making bodies like local councils or corporations, and the powers which are exercised by these local bodies are at the discretion of the central government.[82] A political system with a unitary constitution, "thus, exhibits the two essential characteristics[83] 1. The supremacy of the central parliament, and 2. the absence of subsidiary sovereign bodies." While discussing the supremacy of British parliament Prof. Dicey points out :

(a) "Parliament has the right to make or unmake any law whatever.

(b) No person or body is recognised by the law of England as having a right to override or set aside the legislation of parliament.

(c) the right or power of parliament extends to every part of the King's dominions."[84]

But the supremacy of legislature here does not preclude the supremacy of the constitution itself. For example, the constitution of the Irish Republic prohibits the central legislature from making laws permitting divorce which involves the special process of referendum to the people.

Thus, it means the absence of subsidiary sovereign bodies. There may be local bodies created by a statute of the central legislature to function as subsidiary law-making bodies, but not to act as subsidiary sovereign bodies. For example in G.B. the London county council is a subsidiary law-making body and is a creature of the parliament and not of the constitution. It is not at all a subsidiary sovereign body.[85] Whereas in U.S.A. (a federal system) the regional units *viz.* Florida, Maryland, New York etc. operate as subsidiary sovereign bodies deriving their powers not from an act of the congress but from the constitution itself. The Congress, therefore, has no authority to modify or withdraw any of the powers granted to the states by the constitution.[86]

However, a unitary political system secures uniformity of law and administration throughout the length and breadth of a country; does not divide the allegiance of the citizens, is the most flexible, efficiently conducts its foreign affairs and effectively maintains its national defence, is highly economical and saves much of the wasteful and extravagant expenditure because of absence of multiplicity of legislative and administrative authorities as is in a federal political system.

But the critics of a unitary political system point out that there is concentration of authority in it; centralisation of authority destroys the local liberties; discourages popular interests in public affairs and leads to the creation of large centralized bureaucracy, is undemocratic and discourages popular interest and participation in public affairs.

Nevertheless, Great Britain, France, Norway, Sweden, Denmark, New Zealand, and many other unitary democracies have avoided these pitfalls.[87] A unitary political system can be as democratic as a federal. Moreover, a popular interest and participation depend upon many factors entirely apart from the form of government. For example about 80% of the British voters regularly exercise their right to vote, while the percentage of American voters usually lags far behind.[88]

### *3.2.1.2. The Federal form of Political System*

A federal political system, however, is one in which a number of coordinate states unite for certain common purpose.[89] But every kind of association of states cannot be called a federation. According to Dicey, "A federal state is a political contrivance intended to reconcile national unity and power with the maintenance of state rights."[90] Michael Curtis, on the other hand, points out that "A federal state is one in which the functions of government are shared between a central authority and regional authorities, both sets being autonomous in certain areas and deriving their respective powers from the constitution or interpretations

of it, not from each other."[91] The distribution of powers is determined by the Constitution itself, which is written and generally rigid. A federal political system, therefore, signifies a division of governmental powers between the national government and constituent units. Such a division of power is specified in the constitution. Although the constitution can be amended, the amending procedure is invariably more difficult than the enactment of ordinary law.

A federal state, therefore, owes its origin to a constitution, which is in fact, a charter of rights and duties of the federal and state authorities.[92] As the powers to the federal government or to the federating unit governments derived from the constitution, there is the supremacy (known as doctrine of the supremacy) of the constitution.

Dicey mentions the following three consequences flowing from the doctrine of the supremacy of the constitution :[93]

Firstly, the constitution of federal political system must almost necessarily be a written one in order to remove misunderstandings and disagreements about the terms and conditions which have been agreed to among the federating units at the time of forming a federation.

Secondly, the constitution must be a rigid one. It implies that the power of amending the constitution should be beyond the competence of either federal or state legislature. Such rigidity is quite natural as the parties to a federation would like to prevent further encroachment upon their rights.

Thirdly, every legislature in a federation is subordinate to and controlled by the constitution and the validity or unconstitutionality of its laws depends upon whether these follow or violate the authority conferred upon it by the constitution.

Another essential feature of federalism is the distribution of powers between the federal government and the governments of federating units. However, the matters of national importance are generally placed under the control of the national or federal government, while those which are primarily of the local or regional importance remain in the hand of federating units (or states). "National and state government mu have complete freedom from natural control and encroachment in t determination of their powers and the way in which they are exercised is this freedom which is the soul of federalism."[94]

The third essential characteristics of federalism is the creatior an independent Supreme Court with the power to decide dispute wl may arise between the federal government and the state governm The Supreme Court is to see that the rights and duties of the federa regional governments keep to the schedule laid down in the constitu

In short in all matters affecting the constitution, the Supreme Court in federal set up acts as the final arbiter.

Though federal systems were in existence in ancient Greece, yet the United States of America, which came into being by the constitution of 1789, was the first federal state in modern times.[95] Dominion of Canada (another federation) came into being in 1867. Similarly, Republic of Switzerland, the Commonwealth of Australia, Federal Republic of West Germany (other federations) were established by their constitution of 1848, 1900 and 1949 respectively.

In older countries like U.S.A., Canada or Switzerland federalism was created to preserve strong existing diversities while maintaining sufficient unity to ensure that limits were put on the power of the centre. Sometimes, it has been a result of a political bargain between those wishing to extend the area of territorial control and those prepared to surrender part of their independence."[96] In the same manner in newer nations such as India, Nigeria and other the device of federalism has been used to hold together societies in which tribalism is strong and divisive, and nationalist sentiments and allegiance are weak.[97]

These federal political systems may be put in the form of following Table :

**TABLE 4**

| S. No. | Name of continent to which the federal political system fall | Name of the countries |
|---|---|---|
| 1. | Asia | India, Pakistan, Burma, Malaysia, U.S.S.R. and (a part of it). |
| 2. | Africa | Australia, Nigeria, Cameroon, Tanzania, Libya. |
| 3. | America | Canada, U.S.A., Mexico, Venezuela, Brazil and Argentina. |
| 4. | Europe | U.S.S.R. (a part of it), Czechoslovakia, Yugoslavia, Austria, West Germany and Switzerland. |

(Table is framed on the information given by Maheshwari, Sriram in his book Comparative Government and Politics, *op. cit.*, pp. 100-101).

Rodee, Andersan, Christol and Greene further added that "the federal system is particularly well adapted to states embracing wide areas, with sectional diversities due to geography, climate, resources, economic factors and social conditions, as well as to heterogeneity of race, nationality, language or religion."[98]

We may put it in the following tables.

**TABLE 5**

| Groups | Names of Political systems | Number of federating units | Area (sq. miles) | Population |
|---|---|---|---|---|
| 1 | 2 | 3 | 4 | 5 |
| **Group-A** The Federal political systems with wide areas | 1. Union of Soviet Socialist Republic | Fifteen Republics | 8,570,600 | 266599 (Thousands) |
| | 2. Dominion of Canada | Ten provinces and two territories | 3,621,616 | 24 million |
| | 3. United States of America | Fifty states | 3,615,221 | 220 million |
| | 4. Federating Republic of Brazil | Twenty-three states three territories, and a federal district | 3,266,170 | 123 million |
| | 5. Commonwealth of Australia | Six states, two territories | 2,974,581 | 14.7 million |
| | 6. Republic of India | Twenty-five states and six union territories | 1,196,995 | 820 million |
| | 7. Republic of Argentina | Twenty-two provinces, and one national territory | 1,078,266 | 28 million |
| | 8. United Mexican states (MEXICO) | Thirty-one states | 760,373 | 70 million |
| | 9. Libyan Arab Republic | N.A. | 679,358 | 3 million |
| | 10. Pakistan | four provinces | 364,218 | 82 million |
| | 11. United Republic of Tanzania | Union of Tanganyika and the Islands of Zanzibar | 362,688 | 17 million |

| | | | | |
|---|---|---|---|---|
| | 12. Federal Republic of Nigeria | Twenty states | 365,093 | 100 million |
| | 13. Republic of Venzuela | Twenty states and the federal district and two territories | 352,143 | 6 million |
| | 14. Socialist Republic of the Union of Burma | Seven states and seven divisions | 261,610 | 33,310,000 (Thousands) |
| | 15. United Republic of Cameroon | Seven provinces | 178,361 | 8.5 million |
| | 16. Malaysia | Eleven states | 129,594 | 14.5 million |
| **Group-B** The Federal political systems with medium size | 17. Socialist Federal Republic of Yugoslavia | Six republics two autonomous provinces | 99,079 | 22.5 million |
| | 18. Federal Republic of Germany | Ten landers (may be called states) | 95, 914 | 56,174,826 (Thousands) |
| **Group-C** The Federal political systems which are extremely small nations | 19. Czechoslovakia | N.A. | 49,356 | 13,745,577 (Thousands) |
| | 20. Republic of Austria | Nine provinces | 32,369 | 7.5 million |
| | 21. Switzerland | Twenty full and six half cantons | 15,944 | 6.3 million |

(This table is framed on the information given in : 1. World Encyclopaedia on Political Systems Vol. I & II edited by George E. Delury, Longman, Burnt, Mill, Harlow Essex), U.K. 1983. 2. Hammond World Atals and Gazetteer, Hammond and Co. Maple Wood, U.S.A. 3. Sriram Maheshwari's book *Comparative Government and Politics, op. cit.*, pp. 100-101).

**N.A : denotes :— Information not available.**

We then again put these countries in the various groups or clusters depending upon the level of similarity in regard to federalism which may operate:[99]

**TABLE 6**

| Grouping | Level of similarity in regard to federalism | Name of the Countries |
|---|---|---|
| Group-I | Countries which have been successful in their practice of federalism and have reached a state of advanced maturity. | U.S.A., Switzerland, Canada, Australia, West Germany. |
| Group-II | Countries in South America where a federal government has not been able to become a reality. | Federal Govt, in most of Latin America, *i.e.*, Mexico, Venezuela, Brazil and Argentina. |
| Group-III | Communist countries where the though constitution is federal in nature yet an extreme measure of Unitarian and regimentation prevail | U.S.S.R., Czechoslovakia, Yugoslavia, Austria. |
| Group-IV | The decolonised country which has been operating a federal system more or less successfully dispute its strong centrist atributes. | India. |
| Group-V | Newly emerged Asian and African federations, which are still on probation. | Nigeria, Cameroon, Tanzania, Libya, Malaysia, Burma, Pakistan. |

(Table framed from the grouping given by Sriram Maheshwari in his book *Comparative Government and Politics, op. cit.*, p. 101).

Many critics have argued that federalism is absolescent; essentially negative in its effect and is unsuitable for positive action; cannot act rapidly, too reliant on compromises; financially expensive due to the duplication of work and waste of time in compromises and negotiations; difficult to determine responsibility of the different units and the conflict of loyalties may confuse individual rights and obligations; limits the powers of the centre and the states may be as subject to political pressure as the centre, and may resist reform desirable for the welfare of the whole. Moreover, the existence of a number of non-democratic federal systems suggest that even federalism does not always inevitably safeguard political liberty or provide for an opposition to be expressed through the units.[100]

But all the above mentioned points of criticism are not true. In all countries the power of central authorities has been increasing. In federal regimes also the centre now has power to act in areas such as labour, education, crime, taxation, health, housing and recreation where the federating units may not possess resources to take appropriate action. Moreover, by adopting the policy of 'co-operative federalism' and 'creative federalism' certain federal regimes have sought to create conditions in which the states would have greater flexibility and local government would play larger roles within a framework established by the centre.[101]

### 3.2.2. Parliamentary and Presidential Political Systems

On the basis of relationship between the executive and the legislature, the liberal democratic political systems may be classified into parliamentary and presidential types. In other words, liberal democratic political systems have two broad patterns of functioning namely through parliamentary and presidential systems. A comparison of the two throws up certain important distinction between them, emphasises the essential characteristics of each, and, further underlines the limitations of any form of classification.[102] However, the Parliamentary system is traditionally associated with government of Great Britain and the United States of America offers the classic example of the presidential system.

#### *3.2.2.1. Parliamentary Form of Political System*

A political system adopts a particular pattern (parliamentary or presidential) depending upon several factors—both historical and immediate. For instance in Great Britain, parliamentary system from where many democracies have borrowed this system, as a result of historical struggle between the monarchs and the people. In France, under Fifth Republic, however, the parliamentary system was adopted as a result of modification of past inadequacies, when executive was very much strengthened to check political instability created by multi-party system under fourth Republic.[103]

Although the parliamentary form by itself is not an index of the democracy or authoritarian characterizing any given political system, yet all parliamentary systems have in common a close institutional relationship between the executive and legislative branches of government.[104] The executive emerges from, and is responsible to, the legislature, which is popularly elected, and elections are free and competitive. There exist an opposition in the legislature, whose current task is to criticise and oversee the government and whose expectation is to form the government in future.

The chief executive is a Prime Minister (as in Great Britain) or a Premier (as in Italy). He selects the other ministers of government, who constitute the Cabinet. Each cabinet minister is responsible for administering a particular department of government. Moreover, the Cabinet as a whole (referred to as the government) is voted into or out of executive office by a majority of the parliament. In the event of a deadlock, between the government and the legislature, the executive however, enjoys the advantage by being able to dissolve the legislature, thereby calling for new parliamentary elections. There is a constitutional requirement that limits the tenure of the legislature, but elections may be called at any time during this period.[105]

By the consolidation of party system in recent years, the Prime Minister's role has gained importance and the description of him as *primas inter pares* (*i.e.*, first among equals) became inaccurate. The Cabinet is no longer the collegial policy-making body, but, instead, it increasingly has submitted itself to the hegemony of the Prime Minister justifying the label, prime ministerial government for parliamentary government.[106]

As the Prime Minister is less restrained by a parliament in which his party has a cohesive majority, the parliamentary system, in practice has become more presidential then even that of U.S.A. without eroding or supplanting the constitutional basis. However, a cohesive party may sometime dismiss the Prime Minister when be proves to be too embarrassing or inconvenient.[107]

Alan R. Ball, however, sums up the major characteristics of the parliamentary system of government in the following points :[108]

1. There is a nominal head of state whose functions are chiefly formal and ceremonial and whose political influence is limited. This head of state may be president, as in West Germany, India and Italy, or a monarch, as in Japan, Sweden and United Kingdom.
2. The political executive (Prime Minister, Chancellor, etc.) together with the Cabinet, is part of the legislature, selected by the legislature, and can be removed by the legislature, if the legislature withdraws its support.
3. The legislature is elected for varying periods by the electorate, the election date being chosen by the formal head of state on the advice of the Prime Minister or Chancellor."

There are, however, insignificant differences within the parliamentary systems of government. The legislature may consist of one chamber or two. There are variations in the methods of selecting the second chamber and in the power of the executive to dissolve the assembly and call an election. There may be a Supreme Court to interpret the constitution or the legislature is legally supreme (Like in U.K.). Moreover, the number and type of political parties will have important consequences for the operation of these systems.[109]

The advocates of parliamentary system support it because it secures an essential coopertion, coordination and harmony between legislature and executive which lead to administrative efficiency. Moreover, the presence of Cabinet inside the legislature gives to the letter's leadership activities and a direction. The parliamentary system makes executive responsible to legislature which ultimately means its responsibility to the electorate; ensures flexibility and elasticity of the government and affords the executive to initiate the legislations.

Critics have pointed out the following points of criticism :

1. Parliamentary system violates the sacred principle of separation of powers by establishing intimate contact between the executive and the legislature.
2. The control of affairs by men belonging to a single political party in parliamentary system leads to a partisan complexions to administration.
3. The parliamentary system aids to breed ground of nasty party-conflicts. Bryce rightly points out that "it intensifies the spirit of party and keeps it always on the boil. Even if there are no important issues of policy before the nation there are always the offices to be fought for. One party holds them, the other desires them, and the conflict is unending —it is like the incessant battle described as going on the blood vessels between the red corpuscles and the invading microbes."[110]
4. As the parliamentary executive has no fixed term and lives instead at the mercy of the legislature, it can hardly adopt and implement a long term plan for development and embark upon any durable projects.
5. The parliamentary system generally leads to Cabinet dictatorship. In other words the Cabinet members with the backing of a solid majority of the legislature care little for the will of the legislature and the wishes of the electorates. The firm control of the Cabinet over the legislature, thus, enables it to get pass a law of its own choice and obstruct the passage of any measure it does not like. An unrestrained cabinet is opt to be a

despotic. But vigilant public and public awareness of this danger may well arrest such a development."[111]

### *3.2.2.2. Presidential Form of Political System*

"What has been called Presidential government, as contradistinguished from Cabinet or parliamentary government, is that system in which the executive (including both the head of the state and his ministers) is constitutionally independent of the legislature in respect to the duration of his or their tenure and irresponsible to it for his or their political policies."[112]

The term 'Presidential government' was originated in Great Britain before the American Civil War and referred to the governmental system prevalent in former Colony—the United States.[113] Walter Bagehot had used this term in 1867, while referring to the English Constitution, to distinguish Presidential system from the British Parliamentary (or Cabinet) system.[114]

Allan R. Ball has summed up the chief characteristics of the presidential system as under :[115]

1. "The President is both nominal and political head of the State.
2. The President is not elected by the legislature, but directly elected by the total electorate. (There is an electoral college in the U.S.A.; but it is of little political significance).
3. The President is not part of the legislature, and he cannot be removed from office by the legislature except through the legal process of impeachment.
4. The President cannot dissolve the legislature and call general elections. Usually the President and the legislature are elected for fixed terms."

The most glaring and outstanding example of the presidential system is that of United States of America. Most other examples are simply immitations of the American system. These are chiefly found in central and south America.[116]

In the relatively democratic presidential system, the chief executive is chosen by the people for the fixed terms. He selects his Cabinet officers, in most cases with the routine approval of the legislature. They are accountable to him and not to the legislature. Moreover, legislature cannot dismiss the government, except under the unusual circumstances of conviction of the President following his impeachment by the legislature. Impeachment process, however, is not likely to relate directly to partisan or institutional differences over public policy.[117]

In political systems with presidential (or non-parliamentary or fixed executive system) the principle of separation of powers seems to be adopted with some regidity. At least in theory the executive and legislature branches of government are strictly separated in such political systems. Such separation, however, does not altogether rule out executive messages and recommendations to the legislature, the veto and the summoning of special sessions. The legislature too has a share in the conduct of the executive business, such as the making of appointments and treaties and the supervision of administration.[118]

In the United States, the presidency has evolved from the largely passive role in policy making envisaged by fathers of the constitutions to one of highly visibility and activism within the American political system. This reflects the fundamental transformation of the United State of America from a rural and agricultural society to a highly industrialized and urbanised one. The functions of government have, thus, changed accordingly and it has the duty of the President to play a major role not only in coordinating the functions of the government but also in initiating policy changes and securing their legislative enactment. But the institutional separation *i.e.* of legislature and executive branches greatly complicates his task, even when the presidency and congress are controlled by the same political party.[119]

Wherever there is presidential government outside the United States of America, there will also be a fragmented party system, weak political institutions or both. For instance in France after 1958, in Pakistan after 1962 and in Chile before the military coup of Sept. 1973.[120] In some of the new independent states with underdeveloped economies governments were initially organised along the lines of a presidential system until the military intervened and removed the civilian politicians from power.[121] The third world countries where civilians politicians continued to rule within the constitutional parameters of a parliamentary system (as in India) have long trandition of parliamentary government inherited from the imperial powers which ruled them as their colonies for a long time.[122]

Most of the countries in Central America and South America (*i.e.*, in Latin America, such as Mexico, Guatemala, Honduras, El Salvador, Nicaragua, Costa Rica, Panama, Guyana, Surinam, French Guiana, Colombia, Venezuela, Ecuador, Peru, Brazil, Chile, Bolivia, Paraguay, Argentina, Uruguay Haiti, Dominican Republic, Cuba etc.)[123] are Republics as well as have adopted the presidential form of government and their chief inspiration in this respect came from the'Big Brother'the United States of America.[124] The Latin American countries commonly share a number of features such as separation of powers; the strong president elected by a popular vote but for four years term; extreme centralisation of authority, provisions for impeachment of the President[125] etc.

The advocates of presidential system plead that it better safeguards the liberty of the people; gives great sense of stability, administrative efficiency, speedy execution of policies, high effectiveness in times of emergencies and its legislatures are less dominated by party spirit. But the critics of presidential system are of the view that it divides responsibilities between the executive and legislature. The former lives in awarded independence whereas latter pursues its own line of policy. Each, thus, shifts responsibility to others. All this may result into frequent deadlocks, executive irresponsibility and autocracy. Moreover, security to tenure combined with the freedom from responsibility provides enough encouragement to the executive to override legislative and popular wills. The separation and disharmony between the executive and legislature as in U.S.A. also leads to wastefulness and inefficiency. They further argued that the fixity of tenure and the stability of the executive make the presidential system extremely rigid. The executive office goes by calender. Everything happens in accordance with the provisions elaborately prescribed by the constitution. "No danger, no crisis can melt the inflexible constitutional rules."[126]

## 3.3. AUTHORITARIAN AND TOTALITARIAN POLITICAL REGIMES

### 3.3.1. Authoritarian Regimes

Although outright tyrannines are rare in the contemporary world, yet authoritarian political systems are almost everywhere.

Most of the regimes around the world and throughout history deserve to be classified as 'Authoritarian'. Monarchies, Aristocracies, Oligarchies and Pentocracies (*i.e.*, rule by the rich) are all authoritarian because the majority of citizens do not have any direct or institutionalized role in policy making.[127]

The "political systems with limited, not responsible, political pluralism, without elaborate and guiding ideology, but with distinctive mentalities, without extensive nor intensive political mobilization, except at some points in their development, in which a leader or occasionally a small group exercises power within ill-defined limits but actually quite predictables ones"[128] are termed as authoritarian regimes. In authoritarian regimes, therefore, liberty is restricted, there is no legally recognised opposition and parliamentary institutions are absent or meaningless. The system is not tyrannical. The society is however, traditionaly oriented and power is exercised by small groups such as military leaders, bureaucrats or religious figures. But the economic activities can still be pursued with considerable independence. There is a certain degree of cultural freedom, and voluntary internal and external travel is possible.[129] A regime that permits only one party in the political system is an authoritarian regime. In such regimes there is no alternative set of political leaders who can take the place of existing elites for the purpose of implementing new programmes, political communication is strictly according to what the government and its ruling party allows. The alteration of governmental personnel and policies must take place within single party, typically only after the death or purging of the dominant leaders.[130] Authoritarian regimes, thus, indicate the relatively low specificity of political institutions, often penetration the life of the society; preventing even forcibly, the political expression of certain group interests (as religion in Turkey and in Mexico after the revolution, labour in Spain) or shaping them by interventionist policies like those of corporativist regimes.[131] Examples of such regimes are Argentina under Juan Person, Spain under Francisco Franco, and Portugal under Antonia Salazar, Brazilian system established in 1964, most of Latin American political systems, U.S.S.R., China, East Germany,[132] India between 1974 to 1976[133] Pakistan under Zia etc.

Since many authoritarian regimes have been founded by military coups and are headed by military men, a distinction between military and non-military authoritarian regimes can be made. But many of authoritian regimes of today are military anthoritarian regimes. Military regimes, with some-exceptions, undergo a process of civilization if they are stable. Military men can carry out a deep cultural revolution like Ataturk; important social and economic changes like Nasser; displaced traditional regimes or prevent a continuing process of change towards democracy and social revolution after a break with tradition with a counter-revolutionary intent like Franco.[134] The constant dilemma for authoritarian systems is that rebellion or revolution may become the only way to register dissatisfication with the regime.[135]

### 3.3.2. Totalitarian Regimes

Since the 1950s some scholars of politics have argued that the most extreme type of authoritarianism is best described as "Totalitarianism."[136] In addition to the characteristics of authoritarian regimes, totalitarian regimes also imply an official ideology which members of the society must adhere to and which covers all aspects of life in the society; a system of terroristic police control, which supports, and supervises on behalf of the leader, and which is directed against the enemies of the state; and central control and direction of entire economy.[137] According to Brzezinski "Totalitarianism is a new form of government falling into the general classification of dictatorship, a system in which technologically advance instruments of political power are wielded without restraint by centralised leadership of an elite movement for the purpose of affecting a total social revolution, including the conditioning of man on the basis of certain arbitrary ideological assumptions, proclaimed by the leadership in an atmosphere of coerced unanimity of the entire population." Franz Neuman has also provided a similar set of defining characteristics.[138] The most famous and most utilised definition of Totalitarianism has been given by C. Friedrick and Z. Brzezinski in their book 'Totalitarian, Dictatorship and Autocracy'.[139] They are of the view that in Totalitarianism there is an official ideology; a single mass party, usually led by one man: terror is used by governments to enforce obedience, the government has a monopoly of communication and monopoly over weapons and there is central directions of the economy.[140] In other words a totalitarian regime has a totalist ideology, a party reinforced by a secret police and monopoly over mass communications; operational weapons and all organizations including economic ones,[141] *i.e.*, of three major forms of interpersonal confrontation in industrial mass society.[142] We may add certain other characteristics of Totalitarianism such as "the subordination of the arts and science to the interest of the political elite and to the specifications of the ideology and the organization of youth groups, labour unions, cultural associations, the educational system and other intermediary social structures for the purposes of broadening the elite's political and social control and supporting its ideological objectives.[143] We may point out that whereas authoritarian governments are content to control the overt behaviour of the citizens and to eliminate any sign of organised opposition; Totalitarian governments however, attempt to control not only the citizens behaviour but his thoughts as well. The basic concept of Totalitarianism is that the state attempts to absorb all of society, to control lives and minds and to mobilise the population, youth as well as adults in all area of life.[144]

The three regimes regarded as Prime examples of the totalitarian model were Nazi Germany, Fascist Italy and Soviet Union under Stalin if not after his death.[145] But they did not embody all the characteristics of the totalitarian model to the same degree. For example, there was in reality less coherence and unity in decision-making in all the three regimes. However, these three regimes were similar in their ruthlessness and extreme dictatorial behaviour.[146] Ball points out that the use of terror as a political weapon had been far more open in the post-Allende Chilian regimes than in any other types of political system.[147] Moreover, none of them was overthrown by the people living under them in peace time.

In Nazi Germany the membership in one or another of the youth organisations was compulsory, power was concentrated in the hands of an individual or group, the regime eliminates opposition parties, controlled communication and mass media, exercised control over the economy and over highly centralised planning, though irreligious used religion for its purpose and made deliberate use of terror as a controlling factor through the secret police, concentration or labour camps, did not tolerate dissension or democracy even within the one party and refused to allow any standard of morality other than that of the party.[148]

In U.S.S.R. under Stalin the opposition parties were forbidden, the dissident groups even within the communist party were dissolved, much of the cruelty and inhumanity were displayed *e.g.*, the murdering of 20 million people including top political leadership; the extreme use of security police was made.[149]

Italian fascism emphasized the glorious past of the country, the national genious, the need for a unity, the necessity for action, the assertion of state authority and the resurgence of Italy as a world power again.[150] According to Michael Curtis, perhaps the closest current approximation to the totalitarian model is China (particularly under Mao-Tse-Tung). The Chinese government totally controls all political activity through the structures of revolutionary committees, mobilizes labour for common purposes, attempts to install a revolutionary will into the peasantry, indoctrinates people to create a new consciousness; has tried to change human nature by removing all bourgeois behaviour or motives and to the family control and the traditional authority of the father and makes advancement contingent upon ideological conformity.[151]

However, the personalities of the dictators, Hitler in Nazi Germany, Stalin in Soviet Russia, and Mussolini in Fascist Italy and Mao-Tse-Tung in China had an important impact on the operation of their respective political systems.[152]

Some of the scholars are of the view that Totalitarian regimes were supported not simply because of economic benefits or promises but also because they seemed to offer a method of solving the problem of personal alientation and the division between individual and society.[153]

Most of the regimes generally described as totalitarian in contemporary world seem to share one important characteristics *i.e.*, their official ideology is essentially socialist.[154] These are Soviet Union, China, Vietnam, Cuba, North Korea and the States of Eastern Europe. Out of Poland, Albania, Hungary, Yugoslavia, Rumania, Vietnam and East Germany some rest on greater degree of repression than other.[155] There are also profound differences in the underlying economic base of these regimes.[156] For instance there is peasant economy of Vietnam and whereas the industrial structure of East Germany.

But Rodee, Anderson, Christol and Greenee pointed out that "It is doubtful whether Fascist Italy, the Soviet Union under Khrushchev and Brezhnev, Castro's Cuba , Franco's Spain or even Maoist China should be labelled Totalitarian.'"[157] They further argued that the label is obviously misleading with respect to contemporary Poland, Hungary, Yugoslavia, South Africa and the two Vietnams and two Koreas and many other authoritarian countries that are insulted rather than described by the epithet 'Totalitarian.'[158]

However, Juan J-Linz in his article 'Totalitarian and Authoritarian Regimes, points out that a system shall be totalitarian if the following characteristics apply :[159]

" 1. There is a monistic but no monolithic centre of power, and whatever pluralism of institutions or groups exists derives its legitimacy from that centre, is largely mediated by it, and is mostly a political creation rather than an outgrowth of the dynamics of the pre-existing society.
2. There is an exclusive autonomous, and more or less intellectually elaborate ideology with which the ruling group or leader, and the party serving the leaders, identify and which they use as a basis for policies or manipulate to legitimize them. The ideology has some boundaries beyond which lies heterodoxy that does not remain unsanctioned. The ideology goes beyond a particular program or definition of the boundaries of legitimate political action to provide, presumably, some ultimate meaning, sense of historical purpose, and interpretation of social reality.
3. Citizen participation in and active mobilization for political and collective social tasks are encouraged, demanded, rewarded, and channelled through a single party and many monopolistic secondary groups. Passive obedience and apathy, retreat into the role of "paro-chials" and "subjects", characteristics of many authoritarian regimes, are considered undesirable by the rulers."

## REFERENCES


1. Curtis, Michael, *Comparative Government and Politics, op. cit.*, p. 54.
2. Suda, Jyoti Prasad, *History of Political Thought*, Vol. I, *op. cit.*, pp. 99-100.
3. *Ibid.*, p. 99.
4. *Ibid.*
5. *Ibid.*, p. 100.
6. Strong, C.F., *Modern Political Constitutions*, Sidgwick and Joackson Ltd., London, 1963, p. 59.
7. Apter, David E., *Introduction to Political Analysis*, Prentice-Hall of India, Pvt. Ltd., New Delhi, 1978, p. 69.
8. *Ibid.*
9. Curtis, Michael, *Comparative Government and Politics, op. cit.*, p. 54.
10. Strong, C.F., *Modern Political Constitutions, op. cit.*, p. 59.
11. Sibley,Mulford Q., *Political Ideas and Ideologies*, Harper and Row Publishers, New York, 1970, p. 97.
12. Strong, C.F., *Modern Political Constitutions, op. cit.*, pp. 59-60.
13. Sibley, Mulford Q., *Political Ideas and Ideology, op. cit.*, p. 98.
14. Strong, C.F., *Modern Political Constitutions, op. cit.*, p. 60.
15. Sibley, Mulford Q., *Political Ideas and Ideologies, op. cit.* p. 98.
16. Strong, C.F., *Modern Political Constitutions, op. cit.*p. 60.
17. Sibley, Mulford Q., *Political Ideas and Ideologies, op. cit.* p. 98.
18. Strong, C.F., *Modern Political Constitutions, op. cit.* p. 60.
19. Sibley, Mulford Q., *Political Ideas and Ideologies, op. cit.* p. 98.
20. Curtis, Michael, *Comparative Government and Politics, op. cit.*p. 55.
21. Strong, C F., *Modern Political Constitutions, op. cit.* p. 60.
22. Sibley, Mulford Q., *Political Ideas and Ideologies, op. cit.*, p. 98.
23. Curtis, Michael, *Comparative Government and Politics, op. cit.*, p. 55.
24. *Ibid.*, p. 55.
25. Sibley, Mulford Q., *Political Ideas and Ideologies, op. cit.*, p. 121.
26. Suda, J.P., *History of Political Thought*, Vol. I, *op. cit.*, p. 205.
27. *Ibid.*
28. Sibley, Mulford Q., *Political Ideas and Ideologies, op. cit.*, p. 122.
29. *Ibid.*
30. *Ibid.*
31. Suda, J.P., *History of Political Thought*, Vol. I, *op. cit.*, p. 205.
32. Sibley, Mulford Q., *Political Ideas and Ideologies, op. cit.*, p. 123.
33. *Ibid.*
34. *Ibid.*
35. *Ibid.*, p. 123.
36. *Ibid.*, p. 124.
37. Sabine, George H., Thorson, Thomas L., *A History of Political Theory*, Oxford and IBH Publishing Co., New Delhi, 1973, p. 159.

38. *Ibid.*, p. 160.
39. *Ibid.*
40. Suda, Jyoti Prasad, *History of Political Thought*, Vol. I, *op. cit.*, p. 208.
41. Sibley, Mulford Q., *Political Ideas and Ideologies, op. cit.*, p. 125.
42. Suda, Jyoti Prasad, *History of Political Thought*, Vol. I, *op. cit.*, p. 208.
43. Sibley, Mulford Q., *Political Ideas and Ideologies, op. cit.*, p. 126.
44. *Ibid.*
45. *Ibid.*
46. Sabine, George H., Thorson, Thomas L., *A History of Political Theory, op. cit.*, p. 160.
47. Sibley, Mulford Q., *Political Ideas and Ideologies, op. cit.*, p. 295.
48. *Ibid.*, p. 299.
49. *Ibid.*
50. *Ibid.*
51. *Ibid.*
52. *Ibid.*
53. *Ibid.*
54. *Ibid.*
55. *Ibid.*
56. *Ibid.*
57. Suda, Jyoti Prasad, *A History of Political Thought*, Vol. II, p. 73.
58. *Ibid.*
59. *Ibid.*
60. *Ibid.*, p. 74.
61. Maheshwari, Sriram, *Comparative Government and Politics, op. cit.*, p. 75.
62. Suda, Jyoti Prasad, *A History of Political Thought*, Vol. II, *op. cit.*, p. 73.
63. Strong, C.F., *Modern Political Constitutions, op. cit.*, p. 61.
64. Maheshwari, Sriram, *Comparative Government and Politics, op. cit.*, p. 74.
65. *Ibid.*
66. *Ibid.*
67. Curtis, Michael, *Comparative Government and Politics, op. cit.*, p. 56.
68. *Ibid.*
69. Maheshwari Sriram, *Comparative Government and Politics, op. cit.*, p. 74.
70. Curtis, Michael, *Comparative Government and Politics, op. cit.*, p. 56.
71. Maheshwari Sriram, *Comparative Government and Politics, op. cit.*, p. 75.
72. *Ibid.*
73. *Ibid.*
74. *Ibid.*
75. Curtis, Michael, *Comparative Government and Politics, op. cit.*, p. 56.
76. Finer, SE., *Comparative Government*, Allen Lane the Penguin Press, London, 1970, p. 62.

77. For details see :
    (i) Finer S.E., *Comparative Government, op. cit.*, pp. 62-66.
    (ii) Ball, Alan R., *Modern Politics and Government, op. cit.*, pp, 42-43.
    (iii) Strong, C.F., *Modern Political Constitutions, op. cit.*, pp. 62-63.
    (iv) Hans Raj, *Comparative Politics, op. cit.*, pp. 279-281.
    (v) Maheshwari, Sriram, *Comparative Government, op. cit.*, pp. 79-83.
78. *Ibid.*, p. 79.
79. Wheare, K.C., *Modern Constitutions*, Oxford University Press, New York, 1966, p. 19.
80. Rodee, Carlton Clymer, Anderson, Totton James, Christol, Carl Quimby and Greene, Thomas H., *Introduction to Political Science, op. cit.*, p. 40.
81. Curtis, Michael, *Comparative Government and Politics, op. cit.*, p. 45.
82. Ray, Amal and Bhattacharya, Mohit, *Political Theory, op. cit.*, p. 273.
83. Strong, C.F., *Modern Political Constitutions, op. cit.*, p. 80.
84. Ray, Amal, Bhattacharya, Mohit, *Political Theory, op. cit.*, p. 274.
85. Strong, C.F., *Modern Political Constitution, op. cit.*, p. 85.
86. Ray, Amal, Bhattacharya, Mohit, *Political Theory, op. cit.*, p. 275.
87. Rodee, Carlton Clymer, Anderson, Totton James, Christol, Carl Quimby and Greene, Thomas H., *Introduction to Political Science, op.cit.*, p. 41.
88. *Ibid.*
89. Strong, C.F., *Modern Political Constitutions, op. cit.*, p. 64.
90. *Ibid.*
91. Curtis, Michael, *Comparative Government and Politics, op. cit.*, p. 45.
92. Ray, Amal, Bhattacharya, Mohit, *Political Theory, op. cit.*, p. 281.
93. Dicey, A.V., *Law of the Constitution*, Macmillian, London, 1959, p. 157.
94. Ray, Amal, Bhattacharya, Mohit, *Political Theory, op. cit.*, p. 283.
95. Maheshwari, Sriram, *Comparative Government and Politics, op. cit.*, pp. 97-98.
96. Curtis, Michael, *Comparative Government and Politics, op. cit.*, p. 45.
97. *Ibid.*
98. Rodee, Carlton Clymer, Anderson, Totton James, Christol, Carl Quimby, Greene and Thomas H., *Introduction to Political Science, op. cit.*, p. 41.
99. Table framed from the groupings given by Sriram Maheshwari in his book *Comparative Government and Politics, op. cit.*, p. 101.
100. Curtis, Michael, *Comparative Government and Politics, op. cit.*, p. 47.
101. *Ibid.*, p. 48.
102. Ball, Alan R., *Modern Politics and Government, op. cit.*, p. 47.
103. Hans Raj, *Comparative Politics, op. cit.*, p. 289.
104. Rodee, Carlton Clymer, Anderson, Totton James, Christol, Carl Quimby, Greene, Thomas H., *Introduction to Political Science, op. cit.*, p. 37.
105. *Ibid.*, p. 38.

106. Maheshwari, Sriram, *Comparative Government and Politics, op. cit.*, pp. 84-85.
107. *Ibid.*, p. 85.
108. Ball, Alan R., *Modern Politics and Government, op. cit.*, pp. 47-48.
109. *Ibid.*
110. Bryce, *Modern Democracies*, The World Press Pvt. Ltd., Calcutta, 1962, pp. 466-468.
111. Ray, Amal, Bhattacharya Mohit, *Political Theory, op. cit.*, pp. 268-269.
112. *Ibid.*
113. Maheshwari, Sriram, *Comparative Government and Politics, op. cit.*, p. 88.
114. *Ibid.*
115. Ball, Alan R., *Modern Politics and Government, op. cit.*, p. 48.
116. *Ibid.*
117. Rodee, Carlton Clymer, Anderson, Totten James, Christol, Carl Quimby, Greene, Thomas H., *Introduction to Political Science, op. cit.*, p. 39.
118. Ray, Amal, Bhattacharya, Mohit, *Political Theory, op. cit.*, p. 271.
119. Rodee, Carlton Clymer, Anderson, Totton James, Christol, Carl Quimby, Greene, Thomas H., *Introduction to Political Science, op. cit.*, p. 39.
120. *Ibid.*
121. *Ibid.*, p. 40.
122. *Ibid.*
123. *World Encyclopaedia of Political Systems*, Vol. I and Vol. II, *op. cit.*
124. Maheshwari, Sriram, *Comparative Government and Politics, op. cit.*, p. 89.
125. *Ibid.*
126. Ray, Amal, Bhattacharya, Mohit, *Political Theory, op. cit.*, p. 272.
127. Rodee, Carlton Clymer, Anderson, Totton James, Christol, Carl Quimby, Greene, Thomas H., *Introduction to Political Science, op. cit.*, pp. 32-33.
128. Greenstein, Fred, I. Poleby, Nelson W., *Handbook of Political Science* (edited) Vol. 3., Anderson-Wesley Publishers Company, London, 1975, p. 264.
129. Curtis, Michael, *Comparative Government and Politics, op. cit.*, p. 61.
130. Rodee, Carlton Clymer, Anderson, Christol, Carl Quimby, Greene, Thomas H., *Introduction to Political Science, op. cit.*, p. 34.
131. Greenstein, Fred, I Polsby, Nelson W., *Handbook of Political Science*, Vol.3, *op. cit.*, p. 265.
132. *Ibid.*, p. 34.
133. Curtis, Michael, *Comparative Government and Politics, op. cit.*, p. 62.
134. Greenstein, Fred, I. Polsby, Nelson W., *Handbook of Political Science*, Vol. 3, *op. cit.*, p. 275.
135. Curtis, Michael, *Comparative Government and Politics, op. cit.*, p. 62.

136. Rodee, Carlton, Anderson, Totton James, Christol, Carl Quimby, Greene, Thomas H., *Introduction to Political Science, op. cit.*, p. 34.
137. *Ibid.*
138. Greenstein, Fred, I. Polsby, Nelson W., *Handbook of Political Science*, Vol. 3, *op. cit.*, p. 188.
139. Ball, Alan R., *Modern Politics and Government, op. cit.*, p. 44.
140. *Ibid.*
141. Greenstein, Fred, I. Polsby, Nelson W., *Handbook of Political Science*, Vol. 3, *op. cit.*, p. 187.
142. *Ibid.*
143. Rodee, Carlton, Clymer, Anderson, Totton James, Christol, Carl Quimby, Greene, Thomas H., *Introduction to Political Science, op. cit.*, p, 34,
144. Curtis, Michael, *Comparative Government and Politics, op. cit.*, p. 68.
145. *Ibid.*
146. *Ibid.*, p, 69.
147. Ball, Alan R., *Modern Politics and Government, op. cit.*, p. 44.
148. For details please see Michael Curti's book *Comparative Government and Politics, op. cit.*, p. 68.
149. *Ibid,*
150. *Ibid.*, p. 69.
151. Curtis, Michael, *Comparaiive Government and Politics, op. cit.*, p. 71,
152. *Ibid.*
153. *Ibid.*
154. Ball, Alan R., *Modern Politics and Government, op. cit.*, p. 45.
155. *Ibid.*
156. *Ibid.*
157. Rodee, Carlton Clymer, Anderson, Totton James, Christol, Carl Quimby, Greene, Thomas H., *Introduction to Political Science, op. cit.*, p. 35.
158. *Ibid.*
159. Greenstein, Fred, I. Polsby, Nelson W., *Handbook of Political Science*, Vol. 3, *op. cit.*, pp. 191-192.

# 4

# Political Parties and Political System—A Theoretical Perspective

## 4.1. ORIGIN AND GROWTH OF POLITICAL PARTIES

For quite some time, political parties were not regarded as respectable or adorable bodies. A party used to be associated with partibility and thus, viewed as something going against national interests. It was, therefore believed that political parties divide the nation. As political parties were distrusted, evaded, and even deplored, for about 150 years, their place and functions were generally unknown.[1] It was, thus, much later in the history of political parties that a positive image of parties developed and their contributions began to be recognised.[2]

Political parties in western Europe, however, came into limelight with the growth of constitutional and representative government.[3] But the modern democratic party was the result of atleast two important political developments—the limitation of the authority of the absolute monarchy and the extension of the suffrage to virtually all the adult population. In other words, "As long as the king enjoyed monopoly of powers and the mass of citizens could not vote, party activity was not only fruitless but also treasonable."[4] Alfred de Grazia, therefore, rightly observed, "Whereas universal suffrage was delayed the political parties in its most advanced democratic form were late in appearing."[5] The rise of modern political parties, thus, coincident with the mass franchise.[6]

Modern political parties first emerged in U.S.A. simply because of the struggle over the acceptance of the new National Constitution as well as the prevalence of adult franchise there. In other words as United States was the first nation to extend the franchise to very large number of its citizens, it was, therefore, the first nation to have modern political parties.[7] La Palombara and Weiner were of the view that although modern parties with substantial following and stable structures appeared in the United States in 1790's with the Federalists of Hamilton and Adams and the Republicans of Jefferson and Madison, it was not until the era of Andrew Jackson in the 1830's that party organisation developed to include strong centres of local power on substantial mass base.[8]

Great Britain and Europe could, however, adopt universal suffrage nearly two generations late and, thus, witnessed the late emergence of political parties in them.[9] In other words Britain did not have parties on the American scale until the 1860's when its electorate was enlarged sufficiently to justify the organisational effort.[10] But according to La Palombara and Weiner, "In England the modern party really got underway with the organisation of the local registration societies favoured by the Liberals after the Reform of 1832."[11] In France and other places on the continent the transformation of Legislative cliques or political clubs into mass-oriented organisation (*i.e.,* political parties) is associated with the revolutionary year of 1848.[12] In Japan, the first of the Asian countries to transplant major Western political institutions, parties did not emerge until after the Meiji restoration of 1867 and perhaps not even until the World War First.[13]

Political parties in the Third World grew up as national movements to fight for national independence and to drive out the colonial powers.[14] "In the new nations there was no system to support the creation of political parties; no legitimacy of governmental procedures within which the parties could operate and to which they could give their support; there was little, if any, experience with representative government; no sense of citizenship defining even limitatively certain common rights which could in turn given rise to legitimate expectations of participation, finally the Stark and close memory of colonial rule had inclucated a propensity for conflict rather than compromise."[15] The parties in the developing and under-developed political systems, therefore, had to deal with problems not experienced by the parties in the West such as working for national independence, framing of the constitution, creation of governmental institutions, taking fundamental decisions on infrastructural development of the country.[16] Maurice Duverger, a French scholar, however, was of the view "that the modern party system with its well oiled organisations and disciplinary regulations is essentially a 20th century phenomenon."[17]

## 4.2. IMPORTANCE AND DEFINITION OF POLITICAL PARTY

Even though, there exists a few political systems without political parties[18], still political parties are regarded as an integral part of the modern political system, no matter whether democratic or totalitarian. La Palombara and Weiner also pointed out, "The Political party is a creature of modern and modernizing political system, whether one thinks of Anglo-American democracies or Totalitarian system such as USSR, Fascist Italy, Nazi Germany, emergent African States in their earliest years of independent evolution or Latin American republic that have hobhled along for over a century; a mammoth ex-colonial areas such as India groping toward democracy or an equally mammoth communist power such as China seeking to mobilize a population through totalitarian methods, the political party in one form or another is omnipotent."[19] According to Alan R. Ball it is difficult to imagine modern political system without political parties. Liberal democratic institutions certainly imply political parties. The party system is, therefore, the essential mechanism of a democratic form of government. Partyless democracy might have been a feasible proposition in a small Greek city-State but it is nothing less than a utopia in modern democratic state. Political parties therefore, exist under different forms of political regimes and have different intentions and motivations depending upon the political systems under which they operate.

Political parties are a very useful and effective link between masses and the rulers, and of course the elites of the society. That is why Neumann observed, "political parties are the life-line of modern politics."[20] Hence, there is no instance of a 20th century democracy that functions without political parties.[21]

To define a political party is not as easy as it seems. How one defines a political party determines to subject and the method of the study. Society is, however, viewed as a dynamic organism wherein competition takes place for prestige, status, power and security. Moreover, individuals and groups wish to shape the environment and the circumstances that condition their lives. Considering in this context, "a political party is mere one of many groups contesting for power."[22]

A political party may also be described in terms of the purpose for which it was organised, the character of the membership, its structure, or the functions it performs. This is why Edmund Burke defines a party "as a group of men who had agreed upon a principle by which the national interest might be served."[23] In other words a political party is "a body of men, united for the purpose of promoting by their joint endeavours the public interest, upon some principles on which they all agree".[24] In a modern German definition a political party is "a battle fellowship established in the form of a permanent association, to obtain power over the State to realize political aims".[25] Others have defined it "as an organised group of individuals seeking to seize power of government in order to enjoy the benefits to be derived from such control".[26] "A political party has also been characterized as a coalition of group interests representing a segment of the social community".[27] Max Weber has defined a political party "as a voluntary society of propaganda and agitations, seeking to acquire power in order to procure chances for its active adherents to realise objective aims or personal advantages or both".[28] Duverger has defined political parties as "groups organised for the purpose of achieving and exercising power within a political system".[29] He further adds that "The term party has since come to be applied to all organised groups seeking political power, whether by democratic elections or by revolution".[30] Joseph A. Schlesinger defines political parties as "Organisations whose goal was the capture of public office in electoral competition with one or other parties. Subsequently the term party was extended to include political organisations not engaged in electoral competition; minor parties which had no realistic expectations of gaining through appeals to the electroate, revolutionary organisations seeking to abolish competitive elections and the governing groups in totalitarian states".[31]

Jean Blondel defines a political party as "Any group which is both open in its membership and concerned potentially with the whole spectrum of matters which the polity faces".[32]

Friedrich, on the other hand, defines a political party "As a group consisting of Cross-sections of human beings more or less stably organised, with the objective in accordance with the condition, of securing or maintaining for its leaders the control of a government, and of giving to members of the party, through such control ideal and material benefits and advantages".[33] Neumann defines a political party, "the articulate organisation of society's active political agents, those who are concerned with the control of governmental power and who compete for popular support with another group or groups holding divergent view".[34]

While defining a political party La Palombara and Weiner point out, "When we speak of political parties we do not mean a loosely knit group of notables with limited and intermittent relationships to local counterparts. Our definition requires instead :

1. continuity in organisation—that is, an organisation whose expected life-span is not dependent on the lifespan of current leaders;
2. manifest and presumably permanent organization at the local level, with regularised communications and other relationships between local and national units;
3. self concious determination of leaders at both national and local levels to capture and to hold decision-making power alone or in coalition with others, not simply to influence to exercise of power; and
4. a concern on the part of the organisation for seeking followers at the polls in some manner striving for popular support".[35]

While considering political party from behaviour viewpoint professor Samuel J. defines it as a "Social group engaging in patterned activity within the social matrix".[36] He further says "when interpreted as a social organism, the party possesses role playing individuals within an identifiable social unit, perceiving and attempting to achieve specific goals".[37] According to him "a party is also a polity or miniature political system with an authority structure, patterns of power distribution, a representative process, and electoral and decision-making systems".[38]

## 4.3. SOCIAL BASIS OF POLITICAL PARTIES

Political parties may emerge slowly from the major broad grouping pre-existing in a society and become legitimate (*i.e.* accepted). One thus finds parties of a 'tribal', clan or clientele nature, based on the allegiance to a persons or on traditional links within a given area or on both; parties based on ethnic groups, religious groups or on classes. But parties may also be imposed through various means of coercion as well as with the help of leaders who happen to have acquired a large national following (as in war of independence). Such parties are more likely to be concerned with educational or mobilising goals than parties having emerged from social groupings. This is one of the ways in which goals relate to the social bases of the parties.[39]

### 4.3.1. The Notion of the Legitimate Party

Legitimacy refers to the acceptance of a certain structure, under certain conditions, by those who live within that structure. A structure is legitimate if within the boundaries of a sphere of action, its intervention is accepted and followers do not question the right of this structure to act.

When we apply the notion of legitimacy to parties, the two points have to be noted—firstly, parties emerge and have to emerge from pre-existing groups either communal or associational; secondly, the polity itself can be deemed to be a group for the creation of parties. Thus, we may say that parties are not legitimate, they become legitimate when support from the parent group has lasted long enough, to a situation when supports of the party no longer refer to the group. In other words when support ceases to be indirect and becomes direct.[40]

The process of legitimation of parties can be said to be natural when their goals are accepted by the polity or a large section of the polity, as most of the western parties.

But the process of legitimation said to be imposed when party aims at substituting new goals for those which are prevalent in the polity or in very large sections of the polity. This is the situation in Eastern Communist Countries.[41]

### 4.3.2. Modes of Legitimization of Parties by Natural Development

In a given society generally there exist four types of groups— tribes, ethnic groups, religious bodies class-based organisations. Each group is capable to float a party or parties.[42]

#### *4.3.2.1. Tribal or Clientele Parties*

Tribal or clientele groups produce parties when the leaders of these groups come to some understanding or coalition or fight each other in context of a modern political system.

#### *4.3.2.2. Ethnic Parties*

Ethnic groups may also give rise to parties.

#### *4.3.2.3. Religious Parties*

Religious groups are also likely to place parties in orbit. But the creation of such parties depends on its structure or the size of the religious organisation.

#### *4.3.2.4. Class-based Parties*

These are well known in the Western Europe especially in industrialized countries. The structure of industrial groups, the size of these groups and nature of society account for the importance of class-based parties.

The development of parties shall be natural where more than one groups be able to place a legitimate party in orbit.

### 4.3.3. Modes of Legitimation of Parties by Imposed Development

When a government wishes to see a society to follow different goals from those which are currently followed, the question of imposition comes and becomes critical.[43]

The urge for imposition may also arise from a desire to preserve as well as to change a situation. This urge may prevail among small bodies of men or among the leaders of a broad group, In all cases, the strength of the political system as a whole needs to be involved.[44]

Political system, however, cannot lend more legitimacy that it has by itself. If it has little support in the community as a whole, the support which it will transfer will be small. Coercion will have to play a considerable part and supplement the legitimacy transfer which the political system lends to the party.[45] Some internal resources can be called on—on short term the special appeal of individuals and groups may be used alongside coercion, on long term, education may gradually diminish the attractivers of other patterns of relationships and increase that of new goals.[46] Moreover, the leaders, with national following may play a role.[47]

## 4.4. MAIN CHARACTERISTICS OF THE POLITICAL PARTIES

The following are the main characteristics of the political parties :—

1. There must be certain measure of agreement on fundamental principles which can bind the people together as a political unity. They may differ on details but there should be no differences on basic principles.
2. A party is not a loosely-knit organisation of some persons. Men and women holding similar views must be duly organised.
3. The political parties have general policies, simultaneously and in succession. They, therefore, have to face the question of adding and subtracting or combining these policies. A good party should have broad based for policy decision otherwise it will not last long.
4. Parties constitute an upward channel of communication to communicate the interest they represent.
5. The parties determine policies from the top downward. In other words, these intend to impose policy formulation. In short there should be quick and free flow of communication between local and higher levels of the party organisation.

6. A communication process has to exist within the parties and from the parties to the community at large. This raises the question of representation within the party and the creation of mechanisms by which the various levels of the party hierarchy come to meet.
7. The parties are concerned with their own existence and with the staffing of organisation as pre-requisites to their action.
8. There must be clear distinction between principles and the personalities. The life of the party should not depend upon the life of its personalities (*i.e.*, leaders).
9. A political party must endeavour to promote national interests as distinguished from communal interest when a political party directs its activities to promote sectional interests it degenerates into a faction.
10. The party should be prepared to shoulder responsibilities. It should not be satisfied only with criticism of the others policies or influencing programme of the government by its criticism.
11. A political party should seek to carry out its policy by peaceful and democratic means. It is the ballot box Which should decide the fate of a party and its claim to form government.

According to Rodee, Anderson, Christol and Greene, a party, in general, has the following characteristics, "membership, organization and administration, goals and objectives, and resources (to a greater or lesser degree) including funds, talent, electoral strength, charismatic candidates and so forth".[48]

Some parties, however, place a high priority upon the nurturing and propagation of specific ideologies and value systems, specifying the mode distrubtion of power in society. For example the Socialist parties in Western Europe and Communist parties throughout the World.[49]

"The predominant characteristics warranting attention in other parties may be their unique structure, the party hierarchy, administrative agencies, career positions, internal discipline and mode of liaison with other groups."[50]

## 4.5. FUNCTION OF POLITICAL PARTIES

The functions which the political parties perform mostly depend upon the nature of the political system under which they operate. The functions of a political party in a developing political system are, therefore, different from those of developed political systems. Similarly, the functions of a political party in totalitarian regimes cannot be the same as those in democratic systems. Even within the same political system all parties do not perform the same function. Thus, National Parties have broader functions than that of the regional parties. Lord Bryce is of the view that the primary tasks of political parties are to organise the chaotic public will and to bring order out of the chaos of a multitude voters.[51] According to Sigmund Neumann political parties are brokers of ideas, constantly clarifying, systematizing and expounding the party's doctrine, representatives of social interest groups; bridging the distance between the individual and the great community; maximine the voter's education in the competitive scheme of at least a two-party system and sharpen his free choice.[52] Stanley Hening and John Pinder point out that a political party in a democratic country is normally to recruit personnel for government, particularly on the legislative and administrative side; to ensure that members of a government at different levels are bound together by certain common theories and policies, to act as a link between public opinion and the government; to play a role in interest aggregation and interest articulation, in order to bring stability the parties are to cut across contonal, emotional, ethnic and religious boundaries.[53] According to Finer the political parties perform the six functions *i.e.* to bridge distance, wrestle with the apathy of citizens who are least endowned with or convinced of an interest in politics, seek to overcome ignorance, set a priority scale of values for the fulfilment of the will of many diverse small public, to select spokesmen and leaders, to assume responsibility for these services.[54] According to Peter H. Merkl the political parties seek to recruit and select the leadership personnel; governmental offices; to generate the programmes and policies for the government; to coordinate and control the governmental organs; to bring the societal integration, through satisfaction and reconciliation of group demands or the provision of a common belief; to counter-subversion and to create social integration of individuals or mobilisation of support by political socialization.[55] Michael Curtis, however, points out that political parties are the chief mechanism of informing and influencing the electorate; linking together the electoral areas of the nation; and allowing public opinion to be made known through a choice of candidates or policy; server as brokers of ideas; major source for providing leadership; chief force for modernisation, shaping the government; providing the main link among the different social and economic groups, constituting the chief agency for political education and socialization, breaking down traditional behaviour and acting as the binding force in communities divided by groups.[56]

However, following are certain invaluable functions which each political party is supposed to perform in political systems :

### 4.5.1. Uniting Sectional Interests, Bridging the Geographical Differences and Inducing Cohesion

Political parties unite sectional interests, bridge the geographical differences, and induce cohension. For example, the American Democratic Party has provided a bridge to bring together the southern Conservatives and northern Liberals; the French Radical Party gave a parliamentary coherence to a loose group of local based notables, whose only elements in common have consisted of anti-Catholic and anti-Marxist platform; and the German Christian Democratic Party, likewise, had bridged the gulf between Protestants and Catholics in West Germany. In other words the various interests and demands are aggregated through the political parties. Individuals and groups, therefore, constantly make demands upon a political party. For example, an individual may wish to participate in the political process and request the party to make the opportunity available. Similarly, pressure group may demand that social reforms be effected by means of redistribution of the wealth through a new tax system; that the government should grant subsidies for an agricultural crops; that the state should go to war because of some alleged affront; or that party should alter its policy regarding membership of minority groups. Demands may be made directly on the party, internally within the party organization or to the government through the party."[57]

As the diverse interests are accommodated within the party system, and as the governmental process operates mainly through the interaction of parties, the demands of groups are likely to be satisfied. This, therefore, ensures both order and system maintenance. The political parties, therefore, convert the various interests and demands into coherent policies and decisions. Thus, they bring together sectional interests, mobilise diversive culture and linguistic groups and weld them within a common framework. According to Duverger, "Parties lend to crystalize opinions, they give skeletal articulation to a shapeless and Jelly-like mass. Finally, they cause similar opinion to coagulate, they minimise individual differences and smooth down personal idiosyncrasies to mould them into a few great spiritual families —public opinion being, thus extricated from the mass of private opinions, the parties continue to keep it constantly informed, to guide and canalise." Lowell also points out "their function is to make candidates and interests known to the public and draw people together in large masses so that they can speak with a united voice, instead of uttering an unintelligible babel of sound."[59]

### 4.5.2. Identifying and Articulation of Interests

A party is regarded as an institution or a mechanism that stands between the public, particularly the voters in political society, and the government. It helps the people identify and articulate their interests. The party provides, a forum for discussion, a platform of position on issues, leaders to express views and propaganda literature 'pros' and 'con', all representing the interests of some segment of the public.[60] The parties serve as a catalyst through which business, agriculture, labour, civil liberarians, doctors and conservationists represent their concerns to government."

While performing this function a party especially a broad-based party, balance the various interests and reaches a compromise among them.[61]

### 4.5.3. The Political Recruitment

The political parties perform the political recruitment functions. They recruit both leaders and the caders. While the leaders run the government or perform the opposition role, the caders are instrumental for day-to-day contact between the people and the parties.[62] According to James Bryce the chief thing of the American political parties, is the selection of candidates. There is hardly a person who today attains high public office without belonging to or at least without being supported by a political party.[63]

This is a very important in Communist totalitarian regimes where party provides the only avenue to political power. It is also significant in competitive party systems in which the main source of political recruitment is through political parties. In a democratic political system, apart from representatives in the Legislature, the political parties offer their candidates for various other important public functionaries like President, Vice-President, Governor, Judges of Lower Courts etc. where they are to be elected.

### 4.5.4. To Provide a Link between the Government and the People

Political parties seek to educate, instruct and activate the electorate. They use the mass media and local organisation to maintain contact with the relatively political inactive and lead them to the awareness and acceptance of various policies. They seek to mobilise the population. The parties run the electoral process, which is a primary selective mechanism for public service. Moreover, party membership is the most widely used door to power and position in government.

### 4.5.5. To Provide Political Education to the Masses as well as Widen Political Participation

The masses in general are indifferent and apathetic towards the business of government. But if this ignorance of the masses allowed to continue, the popularity of a government would decline and it would meet a tragic end.

The increasing propaganda and activities carried on by the political parties in favour of their candidates and against the candidates and programmes of the opposition therefore, proves highly informative to an average voter. The political parties, thus, arose public spirit and prompt the masses to take active interest in public affairs and keep them vigilant and awaken about governmental activities, programmes and policies. In short, political parties make the people to realise that they are masters on their own destiny and therefore, exercise their judgement freely and openly.

Political parties by presenting, defining and clarifying the issues for the electorates, setting values and goals for the society not only increase the scope of political activities but also widen the possibilities of greater popular participation in the political activities.

### 4.5.6. Policy Formulations

Political parties formulate policies and programmes for adoption and implementation. That is why Ball points out that all political parties have philosophical bases, no matter how blurred and no matter how divorced from the actual political behaviour of the party, they are.

Philosophical base and ideology is important for the workers to justify their commitment to the party. It is equally important for the leadership because that alone distinguish as one party from the others. Such an ideology can be a challenge to the prevailing ideologies or an expression of agreement between the parties on existing political structure and political goals.[64]

In totalitarian societies, where there is a single party, ideological goals for society are more rigid than that of liberal societies. For example the German Nazi party emphasised racial purity and the communist parties proclaim the dictatorship of the prolitariate and economic and social equality. The total aims of the party, therefore, become the total aims for the society. Moreover, the party ideology and goals are taken the form of a secular religion.

### 4.5.7. An Instrument of Political Socialization, Political Modernisation and Socio-Economic Development

In a new independent as well as in the developing states where political habits and traditions are yet to grow up, the political parties help in political socialization of the masses and, thus, become the instruments of political modernisation. The political parties, therefore, strive to maintain and strengthen the structure of democratic norms and values to secure maximal community mobilisation for social and economic development, to shape the government, provide the main link among different social and economic groups, constitute the chief agency for political education and socialization and break down traditional behaviour. They have, therefore, induced both political and socio-economic development in newly emerging democracies.[65]

### 4.5.8. Social Welfare Function

Political parties in recent days perform social welfare functions. They work for the alleviation of the suffering of the people during the days of famine, drought, epidemic, wars etc. Parties also work for the eradication of social evils like illiteracy, superstitions, untouchability, casteism, communalism etc.

### 4.5.9. Political Parties Acts as the Conductors of Government, Critics of Government, Provide Alternative Government and Stability to the Political System

In a parliamentary form of government political party acts as the conductor of government when it returns to power. It acts as critics of government if it is not in a majority in the legislature. In other words the majority party in the house assume the responsibility of conductor of government. Minority parties on the other hands act the role of opposition. In constitutional crisis the minority party may provide government if it is asked to do so. Thus, political parties in parliamentary democracies provide much needed stability to the political systems.

### 4.5.10. To serve as Co-ordinating Factors between the Executive and the Legislature

In presidential form of political system, which is based on the theory of separation of powers, political parties serve as co-ordinating factors between the executive and the legislature. The domination of the legislature by the same party which controls the executive may create a degree of harmony between the Executive and the Legislature which the presidential system itself is incapable of realising otherwise.

## 4.6. CLASSIFICATION OF POLITICAL SYSTEMS

The traditional method of categorizing party systems is to describe them according to the number of parties they contain *i.e.*, the "numbers approach" to party system. For example one party systems, two party systems and multi-party systems. The empiricists are however, critical to this approach of classification. Gabriel A. Almond, on the other hand applied the concept of the aggregative function as a criterion and classified party systems : (i) Authoritarian party system, (ii) Dominant non-authoritarian party system, (iii) Competitive two party system and (iv) Competitive multi-party systems.[66]

Maurice Duverger, by using party strength as a criterion, classified party systems as (i) parties with a majority bent on commanding an absolute majority in a parliament, which he found commonly in two party systems and only exceptionally in multiparty systems; (ii) majority parties without hope of ever obtaining an absolute majority and forced to accommodate to the necessity of operating as part of a coalition of parties; (iii) medium parties incapable of forming a minority government and confined to either following the lead of a major party or keeping the opposition divided; and (iv) minority parties unable to play a political role either with government parties or with parties in opposition.[67]

But Roy C. Macridis employs three criteria for classifying party systems. "The first is sources of party support and here he distinguishes between comprehensive parties, which attempt to solicit votes from the entire electorate, and sectarian parties, which seek adherents from a particular class, region or ideology. The second criterion relates to internal organisation. A classed party restricts membership, and an open party permits virtually anyone to join. The third criterion specifies modes of action as specialized or disffused. The former follows conventional procedure for controlling the government for a limited purpose and for a linked time. The latter is pragmatic in utilizing practically any means to come to power, and it stresses permanent and total control.[68]

## 4.7. STRUCTURE AND ORGANISATION OF POLITICAL PARTIES

### 4.7.1. Party Structure

According to Ball the structures of political parties relates very closely to the functions and the methods political parties employ to realise their aim of capturing or retaining political powers.[69] The parties which wish to widen their electoral support and operate at a parliamentary level will, therefore, need a different structure than that of the party forced underground by restrictive legislation,[70] or from a party conducting guerrila operations from a rural base against urban-centred political Elites. "The parties which demand wider democratic participation such as extension of franchise, may have, in theory, a more democratic structure than the parties which seek to perpetuate the power of existing political Elites."[71]

Maurice Duverger has, however, put forward four-fold structures of the political parties. These are (a) The Caucus; (b) the Branch; (c) the Cell; and (d) the Militia.[72]

The Caucus or committee is characterised by its small membership and always resists to seeking wide mass membership. It always lays stress on the quality of member and becomes very active during election days. Its members consist either local notables elected for their individual qualities and local influence or of delegates of local organisations which have combined to form the party. Its strength does not depend on the number of its members but on their quality.[73]

The term "branch" designates a basic element which is less decentralized than the Caucus. It is only part of the whole and its separate existence is inconceivable. But the parties founded on branches are more centralised than founded on caucuses.[74] Moreover, the branch party is mass party seeking to control the maximum membership. Its political activities are permanent and not merely confined to election periods. The branch structure was invented by the European Socialist parties after the extension of franchise to the working classes. The branch, like the caucus, has a local basis, narrower than that of the caucus, but still geographical. The cell, on the other hand, has an occupational basis. There are factory, workshop, shop, office and adminstration cells.[75] It unites all party members who work at the same place. It is an invention of revolutionary communist party. "The cell is smaller than the branch and is geared to continual political activity."[76]

The 'militia' is a kind of private army whose members are enrolled on military lines. The members are subjected to the same discipline and the same training as soldiers. Like them they wear uniforms and badges, ready to march in step preached by a band and flags, and ready to meet the enemy with weapons in physical combat.[77]

The party structure is, therefore, the militia type of organisation in which the structure takes on the hierarchical character of an army.[78] It is adopted by revolutionary parties. But no political party has ever been exclusively formed on the basis of militia.[79] Every organisational structure will be available in a mixed rather than pure form.[80]

Ball while summing up points out that in any examination of party structure, the following factors should be considered:

1. "The role of the leadership and the method of selecting it.
2. The degree of organisational centralisation.
3. The power of the leadership in relation to the rank and extent of disciplinary powers; participation in decision-making and policy initiation.
4. The control of the party bureaucracy.
5. The relationship of the parliamentary wing to the rest of the party.
6. Basis and extent of membership."[81]

### 4.7.2. Party Organisation

Michael Curtis, Maurice Duverger and others have envisaged the following three chief possible types of party organisation:[82]

#### *4 7.2.1. The clique*

The party as an aristocratic clique with politics, revolving around shifting personal alliances was common in Britain between 1689 and 1832.[83] At the end of 19th century also Liberal Party was still dominated by the aristocratic Whigs who controlled the cabinet.[84] Similar relationship may exist in developing political systems.

In the developed countries, this type of party—the "cadre" party or "party of individual representation"—consist of a group of important figures influential in the local areas of the country. It shall be small, decentralised, lacking in discipline and cohesion both inside and outside the legislature.[85] It will have no real programme or ideology and will be held together by the scent of political office. France, in particularly, has large number of such parties.[86]

#### *4.7.2.2. The mass party*

The increasing extension of the suffrage and the effect of class divisions led to the rise of the modern party—the party of integration. Most of this type of parties are found in developed political systems of 20th century.[87] For example European socialist parties of today with large mass organisation dominated by professional leadership, exercising central control over branches and units organised horizontally throughout the country. These parties have well disciplined inside and outside the parliament.[88] In developing nations mass parties have been created by elite groups or they sought mass support either to achieve certain objectives and the implementation of ideological convictions or to maintain or extend their control. In such parties, however, there is always tension and struggle for influence among the different groups, the mass organisation, the party leadership and local constituent bodies. Party conferences are the place where party programmes debated and framed.[89] But the real powers generally lie in the parliamentary leadership of the party.[90]

#### 4.7.2.3. *The extremist party*

Extremist parties are akin to the extremist ideological groups. They are dedicated to overthrow the system. Moreover, these are based on small cells or millitant groups and subject to strong discipline and the acceptance of the policy of the leadership, which is difficult to displace.[91] Relations between the party organisation and parliamentary groups also differ from that of the clique and mass party. In other words, unlike the clique and the mass party, in extreme ideological parties the party organisation tends to dominate the group and tightly control parliamentary representatives in a variety of ways such as financial dependence, voting discipline and possible expulsion for differences from accepted policy.[92] Party also tries to obtain harmony through a number of ways such as by party caucuses, at which parliamentary and non-parliamentary leaders can meet; by organisation of the executive committee of the party to include parliamentary representatives, by allowing the executive committee to attend meetings of the parliamentary party, or by overlapping of the leadership of the different groups.[93]

Writers like Gaetans Mosca, Robert Michels, and Yilfredo Pareto and others have pointed out that the differences between the different types of party organization and structure are less significant than the essential similarity.[94] Michael Curtis, however, says that in all parties, as in groups, leadership is oligarchic, difficult to control and often securely in command of the organisation even when subject to election. It controls Committee memberships, party newspapers, educational programmes as well as the party programmes.[95]

## 4.8. SYSTEM WITHOUT PARTIES

Although political parties exist in most of the political systems of contemporary world yet they are not universal. There are still certain systems, though small in number, without parties. The growth of military regimes shows that the total disappearance of the systems without parties is not likely to be very near.[96] Moreover there are cases in which no party is allowed to exist by the law of certain nations. According to Jean Blondel there were thirtyone polities in the world without parties at the end of 1960's.[97]

Systems without parties, however, tend to be either dynastic or military. But rarely both.[98] The dynastic regimes are those in which a king or emperor runs the state with the help of a parliament to which members are elected but on a non-party basis. Fourteen out of thirtyone countries are belonging to this category. Majority of them are located in the Middle East, "from Afghanistan to Libya, although Ethiopia, Laos and Nepal are at the periphery of the main area."[99] Many of the countries of this group are small or very small, such as the State of the Persian Gulf. But some of them are of middle size such as Iran or Ethiopia. These political systems can be said to be below or before the level of party development. They never experienced a party system in the past.[100]

Moreover, dynastic regimes are based on the popular allegiance to one or a number of traditional groups such as tribal, ethnic, religious etc. There is either no challenge or if any, it can be easily suppressed.[101] The elections are also on ethnic or clientele basis.[102]

Most of these countries are ideologically conservative. But popular pressure sometimes obliges the monarch to carry out a moderately radical policy. According to Jean Blondel and Valentine Herman a dynastic leader can choose between two broad types of policies. He may either buttress the traditional group structure along with to resist the development of the forces which lead to creation of such new groups or he may champion some of the new developments in order to appear as leaders among the new groups, while retaining his position as leader of older structures[103]

The later type of policy therefore appears to be more satisfactory in the long run as it helps the leader to controls both the traditional structures and the new groups. But the new groups may sometime be so numerous and strong that a system without party may be in danger and the leader may also fear for his own position. That is why regimes of this type have been marked by zigzaging policies *i.e.* between the two types of policies, mentioned above. For example as in Morocco or Ethiopia before 1972.[104]

The other political systems with parties are ruled by the military. There were 16 to 20 regimes of the military type at the end of 1960's. These were located in Africa, South of the Sahara and in South-East Asia.[105] Greece and a few Latin American countries were in the group and showed the wide variety of situations in which military regimes could be found. Such situations ranged from countries previously of the multiparty to very new nations in which party structures have scarcely had a time to develop.[106] Military regimes may emerge in new nations with a low levels of socio-economic development and low legitimacy.[107]

Military regimes need not be necessarily radical but it does oppose the traditional type of rule termed as dynastic regime.[108] Military regimes, however, are more concerning with discipline, national preparedness and strength. Military regimes correspond to a situation in which traditional groups do not have legitimacy. Feelings of identity, in one institutional group *i.e.* the military are strong enough. Military personnel, therefore, want to take power and keep it.[109]

The dynamics of military rule generally leads logically and rapidly to the civilization of the regime or to the threat of further military coup.[110]

## 4.9. ONE PARTY SYSTEM

This type of regime is characterized by the party in power either dominating all other groups, trying to absorb the political opposition, or in the extreme case suppressing all opposition, groups which are regarded as counter-revolutionary or subversive of the regime as forces dividing the national will.[111]

The one party state is founded on the assumption that the sovereign will of the state reposes in the leader and the political elite. This authoritarian principle has found expression first in monarchies and more recently in dictatorships or in totalitarian.[112] It is found in democratic system also. Thus one party system has two sub-categories—-totalitarian and democratic. There exists a single party system of totalitarian or dictatorial model if the party in power allows no other party or group to live or act in opposition to its authority. The single party system is democratic in case the ruling party exercise its authority in a way that it may sometimes take the help of another party, or there are parties that even when put together are not in a position to wrest power from dominant party or there is one party absorbing all other parties. In other words, feeling the need of a monopoly of power to survive, the modern dictatorship abolishes all opposition parties. The official party, thus, takes on the characteristics of an army and is thoroughly integrated with the state.[113] In order to check stiff recurring resistance it is driven to adopt techniques of physical coercion, such as purges and liquidations, and employ it through extensive and vigorous propaganda campaigns. Even a dictator must create machinery through which the masses appears to participate in the political process because some semblance of popular support seems mandatory in these days.[114] The technique devised by Hitler, Mussolini and Stalin has been termed as "dictated plebiscite".[115]

In the late 1960's slightly over a third of the world polities were classified as one party system.[116] In other words there were 49 one party systems out of 138 states existed at that time.[117] At present there are about twentyone party systems in Africa. These are Democratic and popular such as Republic of Alegeria, United Republic of Cameroon; People's Republic of Congo, Ethiopia; Gabonese Republic; Ghana; People's Revolutionary Republic of Guinea, Republic of Guinea-Bissau, Republic of Ivory Coast; Kenya; Republic of Liberia; Republic of Mali; Republic of Niger; Republic of Sierra Leone, Somali Democratic Republic, Democratic Republic of Sudan; United Republic of Tanzania, Republic of Tago; Republic of Tunisia; Republic of Zambia.[118] The emergence of the Soviet one party system, after Russian Revolution, had led to the development of Fascist and Nazi one party system in the inter war-period. This imitation also led to the creation of non-communist one-party states even in post-World War Second period.[119]

According to Jean Blondel "one-party systems can develop in one of the three ways".[120] Firstly, this may be result of legal compulsion, arising from the fact that the constitution of the state mentions one party or allows one party. For example in the USSR or several other communist states. Secondly, one party system may arise because of extra-constitutional repression of opposition. Thirdly, the one-party system may be of a 'natural kind' in which only one party comes to emerge in a polity as a result of the natural structure of the polity.[121] But this situation is more likely to be maintained in relatively small states, such as the Brazilian party system before 1930 and the party system in Northern Nigeria before the military coup of 1966; and in the existence of very small parties reaching perhaps 10% of the votes which cannot affect the position of the dominant party such as in Madagascar and Mexico.[122]

A one party state is proverbially on the side of the authoritarian. It, therefore, proclaims its own brand of philosophy and a peculiar way of life to which the whole society is forced to confirm the legislatures become mere facades, oppositions are suppressed and manifold socio-economic diversities are mechanically reduced to unified pattern. "The monopolisation of legality that empowers a party to be the sole custodian"[123] of the truth spells a grave danger for civilisation itself. According to Finer, Dictatorial parties are not parties, but doctrinal or personal despotism; they do not spread and encourage leadership but monopolise it.[124]

It is argued that in a developing democracies there are many socio-economic and political problems which can be solved by a powerful and strong government. This strength in a democratic system can only be provided when there is a strong one party system.[125]

Totalitarian and militaristic one party organization may appear to be the strongest of all party systems. But it is exceedingly vulnerable. In the first place, no successful formula has yet been devised by which one dictator may transfer his authority to a successor. Nor has it been possible completely to serve the bond of political tradition by substituting new myths and symbols for accepted values through the use of force. Moreover, it is improbable that an atmosphere of fear and suspicion through coercion and terrorism can be maintained indefinitely. Lastly, the ferment of class and group interests in society with its attendant social tensions, cannot be accommodated without substantial alteration in the rigid, stratified structure of a totalitarian state.[126]

## 4.10. SYSTEM OF MORE THAN ONE PARTY

According to Jean Biondel and Valentine Herman, slightly over two-fifths of the political systems of the contemporary world are run on the basis of party systems of more than one party. But variations in ideology, structure and social bases of the parties are as large as the variations in their number and relative strength. In some polities where the norms are liberal democratic, the party system has existed for several decades. The party system there has usually reached in equilibrium. The variations from one election to the next are small and scarcely affect the relative position of the parties. Even long term changes are small and the movements occur on pendulum basis around a mean which can be defined as the 'type' of party system of these countries.[127]

There are four types of such party systems—the *two party system*, in which the electorate divides almost equally between the two major parties, with other parties being very small and almost insignificant. *The two-and-a-half party system; the Multi-party system with a dominant party; and multi-party system proper.*[128]

## 4.11. TWO PARTY SYSTEM

A two party system may be said to exist when there are only two parties sufficiently strong to share the major part of electoral vote and to exercise political control, though other parties may exist but obtain some seats in the representative assembly. The two-party systems also exist when the major parties alternate in the exercise of powers.[129]

There can also be two party system in a polity where there are no ideological differences between the parties. But still the parties function because the tackling of problems confronted them are quite different. In other words they have ideological similarity and issue conflict, for example as Democratic and Republic parties in the USA.[130] According to Michael Curtis, the existence of two party system is because of dualism in human behaviour and in political orientation. Individuals, therefore, are attracted either to passion or to reason; to order or to change; to right or to left, the hierarchy or to equality; to conservatism or liberalism. They thus, fall into two basic personality groups. Individuals developing personalities with liberal or conservative tendencies are then attracted to parties that support or resist change.[131] But this theory of political dualism was challenged by the very moderation forced on the parties in their effort to obtain electoral support, which may lead them to adopt very similar political positions.[132]

According to J.C. Johari, a two party system may be said to have three sub-categories.[133] The first, there is, two party system where alteration of power takes place between two major parties. Secondly, two-plus party system where some other party or parties may seldom have a chance to share power with either of the two major parties. Thirdly, two party system in the midst of many where parties other than the two major ones have chances, now and then, to share power. A two-party system has its two more sub-categories distinct and indistinct. It is district two party system where two major parties have policies and programmes, clearly different from each other and the struggle for power. The Conservative and Labour parties of England are of this category. The case of indistinct bi-party system is found in USA where Democrates and Republicans have no ideological differences. In other words, they have ideological similarity and issue conflict.[134]

In bi-party system it may sometime happens that both the parties may be powerful enough to form government on the basis of their own strength. But at the same time need or assistance of some minor party is needed for either formation or strengthening of the government.[135]

Great Britain and the United States of America are the two classic examples of bi-party system. In 1966 election in G.B., 617 out of 630 successful members of parliament came from the Labour and Conservative parties.[136] Both parties together got 89.8% of the vote. There was also direct fight between 234 candidates of both the parties.[137] In 1974 elections both these parties secured 596 out of 635 seats with 75.1% of the total votes.[138] Under the two party system in the USA the Republicans and the Democrates compete in almost all the congressional districts. No third party has been able to establish an adequate nation-wide base of party strength."[139]

The two parties Democrates and Republicans have become so flexible in the matter of accommodating varied interests in a single programme that they now embrace a vast and heterogeneous membership,[140]

The flexibility in the platforms of the major two parties is derived in part from the fact that the electorate have accepted the basic principles of democracy. An overwhelming majority of citizens, have, therefore, accepted the principles of representative government, civil liberty, separation of church and state, and the economic theory of capitalism as tenets of the American creed.[141]

Two-party system has been as effective in British Parliamentary system as in the American Presidential system. But by contrast with the British situation, the American two-party system has been criticised for lacking national coherence and strong national machinery, discipline and unity; dependence on coalitions of factions for electoral purposes and the lack of clear alternative electoral programmes, more corrupt and boss dominated; and less ideological oriented.[142] It is in this sense unrepresented and, therefore, undemocratic. The structure of the parties is too loosely knit, discipline is lacking. As a result elected officials are unresponsive to party platforms both before and after election. American public is also suspicious of the motivation of politicians. It is not clear whether they wish to serve the body politic or their own materialistic ends.[143]

But all these criticism contain some element of truth. Nevertheless, the merits of the two-party system—stability and continuity, consensus and competitiveness—are impressive. In a pragmatic sense it has prevailed and in certain respect it best reflects the expectations arising from the American socio-economic culture.[144]

Some of other two-party systems are New Zealand, Australia, till 1966, Austria, Uruguay, Colombia since 1957, Luxembourg etc.

While concluding we may point out that the two party system has been praised for producing stability and compromise because each party seeks the widest political support. Moreover, the two-party system is successful only if the political culture is one in which both parties are prepared to accept each other as alternative governments and if they are not committed to fixed ideological positions.[145]

## 4.12. TWO AND A HALF PARTY SYSTEM

The two and a half party system is that in which two major parties are equal in strength and a third, though much smaller, party plays a significant part.[146]

In the Atlantic area, two and a half party systems are imbalanced. The third party is much smaller than the other two. The first party is substantially larger than the second.[147] According to Blondel by the end of 1930's there were about thirteen such systems outside the Atlantic area.[148] In Malaysia, Somalia and Uganda although the party system might resemble with two and a half party system, yet one party dominated the second and the third parties were of little significance. Ceylon and Morcco had a rather balanced system of two major parties.[149] But the role of the independents reduced the overall strength of these two parties.[150] However, Lesotho and Guyana were so well balanced that these might have moved towards a two party situation.[151]

By the end of 1970, the some of the two and half party systems were Ceylon, Malaysia, Barbadoes, Lesotho, Morcco, Guatemala, El Salvador, Somalia, Sudan, Guyana and Uganda.[152]

## 4.13. MULTI-PARTY SYSTEM

Duverger points out that multi-partism is often confused with absence of parties.[153] A country, in which opinion is divided amongst several groups that are unstable fluid, and short-lived is not an example of multi-partism but a prehistoric era of parties[154] such as central European countries between 1919 to 1939, most of the young nations in Africa, the East and the Middle East, many Latin American states and great Western states of the 19th Century.[155] A multi-party system according to Duverger, is that where political parties varies from three parties to infinity.[156] But according to Blondel and Valentine a multi-party system is that where four or five parties are almost equal in strength.[157] Michael Curtis, however, points out that in multi-party system there is multiplicity of political parties. There is no political party which has absolute majority of the electrorate, with itself. In other words, no one party is able to obtain majority control over the legislature in multi-party system. There have been rare exceptions in the past such as the Congress Party in India, the Liberal Democrates in Japan and the Gaullist combination in France[158] Amal Ray and Mohit Bhattacharya point out that France has today about thirteen parties, Western Germany seven, Italy eight and Switzerland about seven or eight major parties. Japan has four major parties.[159]

Sigmund Newmann points out that one reason for multiparty system is the persistence of deep cleavages in a political society caused by differences in nationality and religion.[160] Divisive forces are often inflamed by irreconcible elements within the nation or by external revolutionary movements.[161] Moreover, if political revolution is accompanied by great social transformations, groups in society may differ on both the new goals to be achieved and the means to implement them. Such groups, therefore, seek differing solutions through the creation of new or separate political parties.[162] The powerful elite may also utilize the multi-party system in order to divide and rule political society.[163] Moreover, once the multi-party system is entrenched, it can be perpetuated by mechanical and legal devices such as proportional representation, party machinery and electoral laws.[164] Vested interests of individuals, party organisations and economic and cultural interest groups, thus become firmly established and to a large extent self-perpetuating.[165] As Multi-party system faithfully lives up to the democratic ideals and allows every opinion group to organise itself freely is more elastic than the bi-party system; provides opportunities to groups to unite and separate with every change of the situation; and liberates the opinion groups from a common organisation to formulate their doctrines without compromise; allows the voter to choose among more parties and candidates than that of in bi-party system; it is a characteristic feature of the democratic system of continental Europe[166] as well as exists in most of the countries of the world today.

But multi-party system often leads to formation of coalition in nature and character; the possibility of instability of governments, lack of coherent policy; ambiguity of political responsibility. intensification of the complexity of choice; bewildering the general mass of electorates; complicating the electoral procedure, allowing parties to indulge in unpractical and acrimonious discussions and each party to stress its own interests or those of one section of population.

Multi-party system is, however, of two types stable and unstable :

### 4.13.1. Stable Multi-Party System

It is wrong to say that multi-party system always and everywhere leads to instability of government. A number of multi-party systems have shown stability of the Government. For example Switzerland, the Scandinavian countries, Netherlands, Israel, Germany, Japan recently.

In Switzerland, which has atleast nine parties, three of them share about 73% of the vote and four of them share about 90% of the votes. According to Michael Curtis all Swiss federal governments are coalitions composed of members of the four major parties, while members of the other parties may be included in the coalitions of the cantons into which Switzerland is divided.[167] Social Democrat, Radical Democratic, Conservative-Christian, Social and Farmer's Traders and citizens parties generally struggle for power but no party pushes political system to its disintegration.[168]

The Scandinavian countries although witnessed considerable instability in the pre-war period yet in post-war period the Labour parties, being pivotal to the coalitions formed with 40% of the votes provided stability to the coalition governments. Michael Curtis divides the Scandinavian systems into blocks, pro and anti-socialist.

In Sweden the Social Democrates have been the dominant party since 1932.[169] In Norway, Labour Party won every post-war election until 1961.[170] In Denmark minority government have alternated with coalitions.[171] Finland with seven parties has mainly had non-Socialist coalition governments.[172] In Germany two parties have dominated the political scene but neither is capable of ruling alone. The coalitions have been, therefore, organised around the leading Christian Democratic party until 1969 and around Socialist party since then.[173]

Similarly in the French Fifth Republic the U.N.R. and Gaullists had a stable majority in 1962 in spite of the fact that eight parties were represented in the National Assembly.[174] In Israel the Mapai party was the leading party with 35% of the poll and constituted the core of alliance of parties of the left until 1977.[175] The post-war multi-party Japanese political system has been dominated by the Liberal Democratic party.[176]

### 4.13.2. Unstable Multi-Party System

According to Michael Curtis France and Italy provide the best examples of unstable multi-party systems.[177] France had witnessed 26 governments with an average life of five and one-half months each from the liberation in 1944 until the end of the 4th Republic *i.e.* 1958.[178] The longest government was 16 months Guy Mollet government in 1956-57.[179] There were, however, six Prime Ministers in the fifth Republics *i.e.* from 1958 to 1975.[180]

Similarly, Italy had witnessed 38 governments between 1948 to 1975.[181] Because of the uneven impact of industrial development, political systems in the north tend to follow the lines of ideological commitment and bureaucratic organisation. In the south, the more traditional and agrarian patterns of client-patron relationships prevail. This personalist style of politics, or clientismo, is characteristic of all Italy. It has rendered much of Italian political competition between and within parties a matter of who knows whom and who has done what for whom. Thus, because of the lower level of industrial development in the south and because of the south's traditional patterns of monarchical and feudal type social relationships, the system of clientelismo does appear to be more characteristic of southern Italian politics.[182]

Moreover, "ideological groups in the North are reduced in the south to congeries of local notables who mouth the slogans of their party with little sincerity. Politicians change party label at will and their constituents join them with dispatch".[183]

The internal differences in both the countries have been sufficiently acute to present any single party from obtaining an absolute majority in parliament.[184]

Instability of government is a result also from the fact that few of the political parties have disciplined organisations to control the behaviour of their parliamentary members.[185]

## 4.14. POSITION OF LEFT AND RIGHT PARTIES

In every day political parlance where there are more than one or two political parties, we try to impart some conceptual order to our understanding of political competition.[186] We, thus, frequently describe a particular government, ideology, individual or group as Leftist while others as Rightist (or Centrist also).[187]

According to Rodee, Anderson, Christol and Greene the conceptual dichotomy between ideological left and right probably was derived from earlier days of political organisation when the king, sitting in council, arranged his closest supporters near his right hand. These included his most trusted advisers and those responsible for various administrative tasks of state. Those seated to the king's left were not hostile to his rule, but represented alternative points of view on governmental policy.[188]

After the French Revolution of 1789 was under way, when king and parliament struggled for supremacy, the deputies seated in the National Assembly distributed themselves according to the extremism of their view. The most anti-royalist deputies sat on the far left while the king's strongest supporters sat on the far right. Those groups with more moderate views sat in between.[189] Michael Curtis, however, points out that the ideological left-right terms have being the outcome of the arrangement in a semi-circle hall of representatives according to their self-determined place in the political spectrum in the French council of 500 established in 1798.[190]

Even today not only in French parliament but in other houses of parliament in the world the governing party and its cabinet officers sit to the right of the Speaker. The opposition parties sit to the Speaker's left. Moreover, parties advocating political and social change also run in a spectrum from left to right.[191]

In Britain the left would be those members of the Labour Party who advocate the nationalizatian of the means of production, greater spending on social services and high progressive taxation. The centrist Liberals, on the other hand, call for decentralization, individualism and humane social laws on the right, however, the conservatives plead for a reduced income tax, oppose any further nationalization, dismantle the national health service and public building programmes.[192] In France, the Leftist is a revolutionary critical of the communist party, but seemed to endorse a common platform and political relationship with the socialist party. The right, on the other hand, includes social reformers as well as conservatives. In West Germany the Left are the Social Democrates who do not contemplete further nationalization but have extended the principle of worker determination in industry. In Sweden, the left wants controls of industry through ownership of capital by labour groups and approximate equality of income through high taxes. The right, on the other hand, accepts the social system but calls for incentives for private business and for lower taxes, and citizens bureaucracy.[193]

There are today few important and permanent groups believing in a right-wing ideology. For example Fascist or Nazi parties or like minded bodies like the Iron Guard in Rumania, the Arrow Cross in Hungary and the Endek party in Poland in the pre-war period, which were anti-communist and supported traditional values and authorities.[194] These parties appealed to emotions of race, blood or nation and were prepared to use ruthless methods to attain their ends.[195] In post-world war period the right wing Christian party in Norway draws in strength from the backward areas of the country; the Walloon Popular Movement in Belgium arose largely to protest against closing of marginal coal mines.[196] The Japanese right wing has stressed action and violence, militarism and imperialism.[197] The rightist parties in India like Jan Sangh and other have emphasized racial or cultural superiority, an aggressive nationalism, symbols of greatness, national solidarity, the exclusion of religious or ethnic minorities from membership of the nation and protection of the holy cow.[198]

These are generally traditional and moderate conservative organisations, accept the existing political institutions, economic system; authority structure; inequalities and privileges; advocate order and stability and do not equate change with progress.[199] In the contemporary world they accept the liberal consensus, support policies for full employment, a welfare state, social services, and redistribution of taxes.[200]

Since the Russian revolution of 1917, the major split in left has been between communist parties, having faith to the views and policies of the Soviet Union *i.e.* the revolution and the dictatorship of the Proletariate and Social Democratic group concerned with social reforms rather than revolution. The basis of socialism has been opposition to capitalism, revolution against the inhumanity of the industrial system and bringing about fundamental change in the structure and nature of society.[201]

## 4.15. NATION BUILDING—MEANING, IMPORTANCE AND POLITICAL PARTIES AS AN INSTRUMENT OF NATION BUILDING

Nearly 50% of the states of the world today have attained their independence and sovereignty only since 1945.[202] These new nations have been engaged in a form of social change that makes nation building and material development simultaneous political problems.

Professor S.C. Dubey, in his article problems of Nation Building,[203] however points out that during the last three decades the less developed countries of the world have been engaged in the twin tasks—Nation Building and Development. The accent in their effort was on development. The leaders of these developing nations wrongly assumed that the acceleration of the developmental process would automatically take care of divisive forces and would contribute towards the emergence of a durable and cohesive national bond.

But the faltering progress of development and many setbacks encountered by ambitious plans of economic growth and technological transformation brought home to these countries that nation-building and development are complementary processes. They, in fact, support and sustain each other. Overemphasis on either one to the neglect of the other proves counter productive.

Prof. S.C. Dubey further points out that faint murmurs of discontent in time, manifest themselves as powerful currents of dissent and protest, undemocratic localised troubles. Therefore, often flared up and assumed the dimensions of major upheavals. It, thus, led to the shift of focus from developmental objectives to crisis management which often made economic progress first casualty. The strategies of nationbuilding, therefore have to lay equal emphasis on strengthening the forces that go into the making of a viable and durable nation, as well as on plans of economic development.[204]

Many of the newly independent nations are old societies. But these have become click. Moreover, these were also not well integrated and most of them loosely structured. The fragile social bonds were recognised and encouraged pluralism. The different constituent units of the plural society enjoyed varying degree of autonomy and avenues for self-assertion. The national bonds, uniting different segments are often feeble and tenuous".[205] Almost in every case the complex interplay between centripetal and centrifugal forces have shown up their vulnerability. "Building a nation, out of a highly fragmented and historically divided society without resort to authoritarianism, evolving an impressive infrastructure for economic growth and building institutions that can endure major vicissitudes" are the most difficult tasks.[206]

The leadership of these countries by inciting the spirit of nationalism among the masses had engineered rebellion against foreign regime. The foreign rulers had completely destroyed administrative and economic structure, before granting them independence. The attainment of the independence had put the same leaders into the saddle of power. They, therefore, suddenly came face to face with the practical problems of overhauling the administration, strengthening the economy and building the nation.[207]

Professor Dubey further points out that the particularistics interest, which were temporarily submerged but not dead in the strong current of nationalist aspiration aiming at dislodging foreign domination were strong enough and re-emerged and articulated themselves with a ferocious tenacity in the newly independent nations after independence. The same happened in India also. The national leaders first tended to ignore them and underplay their strength. But when the leaders realised their significance, they eagerly tapped them for mobilising support. In this process, these divisive forces acquired a new political legitimacy. The task of building of a nation, thus, has become more difficult in the developing world.[208]

### 4.15.1. Definition of the Term Nation-Building

Before we define the term 'National Building' we should know the meaning of the term 'Nation' and 'Nation-Growth'.

#### *4.15.1.1. Definition of the Term Nation*

According to Karl Deutsch "A Nation is any sizeable population or group of persons which can be called :

(i) independent—in the sense that it is not ruled from outside;

(ii) cohesive—by virture of its markedly more effective habits of easy and varied social communication and cooperation;

(iii) politically organised—in the sense that it provides a constituency for a government which exercises effective rule with it;

(iv) autonomous—in the sense that it accords to this government such acclaim, consent, compliance, and support as to make its rule effective;

(v) internally legitimate—in the sense that its habits of compliance with and support for the government or towards mutual political cooperation and members in nation, are connected with broader beliefs about the universe and their own nature, personalities, and culture so that their support for the nation, even in times of adversity is likely and thus ensures its endurance".

#### *4.15.1.2. Definition of the Term Nation Growth*

The concept of nation-growth is an organismic one, used in order to refer to the historical process through which the present nation-system envolved in the west.

#### *4.15.1.3. Definition of the Term Nation Building*

Yogesh Atal points out that "to my mind nation-building is a distinctive concept related to the development of a polity that is characterized by stability and people's firm commitment to it.[209] He further points out that nation-building is a process directed towards the creation of an integrated whole. It is synonym of modernisation or another name of national integration. Yogesh Atal further addes that "building a nation is social engineering. It is a process of creation of apertures and formation of insulators at appropriate levels".[210] Rajni Kothari is also of the view that nation-building is a social process.

Nation-building, therefore, refers to the social process by which national consciousness appears in certain groups. These social processes proceed through institutionalised social structures to attain political antonomy for the society. According to Reinhard Bendex "The central fact of nation building is the ordinary exercise of a nation-wide public authority. It means that innumerable problems such as the quest for national culture, the unity in linguistic feelings, reconciliation of differences in ethnic, religious and regional feelings, elimination of corruption, freedom from narrow loyalties, formation of laws etc. have got to be tackled and resolved so that there is homogeneity in the people as a whole. Thus, the feeling of oneness despite minor differences has got to be obtained".[211] According to Rajni Kothari "Nationbuilding is not an exercise in fragmentation but rather a necessary step in the evolution of world society based on the principles of freedom, justice and participation."[212]

Nation-building is, however, different from nationalism. Nationalism proceeds nation-building activity. It is the sentiment of belongingness that creates the desires among the people to assert their identity and exert their influence. But when the sentiments give rise to a constructive activity it becomes the process of nation-building.

Nation-Building exercise is unique for each country, because no two countries are identical in their social structure or history or ideological commitment.

Goegraphic contiguity, one language, one religion, economic development, modernisation, common culture, education system, the media of mass communication etc. are some of the important agencies or the factors which help in building a nation.

## 4.16. POLITICAL PARTIES AS AN INSTRUMENT OF NATION BUILDING

The role of political parties in the blending of ethnic, sub-cultural, sub-racial and other groups into a nation is ambiguous.

On one hand, it has been admitted that the excessive multiplicity of small political parties, many of them dominated by power hunger leaders are not conducive to' the unification of the nation. The inter-party and intraparty conflicts are responsible for a long period of political instability, insecurity, disruption and division of population into religious, regional, caste, ethnic, racial and communal groups in most of the developing countries. Moreover, the ideological and political disagreements on the national level are reflected on the regional and village levels. In other words regional, religious and caste-based and class based parties particularly mostly responsible for the exploiting petty interests and sentiments and stimulate disintegrative and disruptive factors and forces. The political parties are, thus not only responsible for social disruption but also the main obstacles in the way of building a nation in most of the developing countries.

But at the same time, political parties have made significant contribution towards the welding of the new nations in some of the countries including developing countries also.

In their pursuit of national and democratic principles, the parties have organised themselves ignoring ethnic, sub-cultural, sub-racial and local, regional and religious boundaries.

Although the numerical dominance of a specific ethnic group can be observed in the membership of certain parties yet hardly there is a national party which has restricted itself to the ethnic criterion in recruitment of its members or even its leaders.

Over and above the traditional, local and ethnic loyalties, there develop a new sense of national belonging suffusing the structure and membership of the political parties and declared goals of their activities.

In this way the ethnic, religious, regional, sub-cultural and sub-racial and local groups, steeped in their age-old traditions, have lost their grip on the individuals and their ability to impede the formation of a new-nation. Political parties are, therefore, one of the few social structures, potentially capable of involving large number of the people in political action. The parties by involving the people in political activities, ensure both communication and participation. The parties stimulate and remiforce existing political attitudes and belief or inculcate new one. Thus, they try to inculcate new political culture and infuse the sense of oneness in their supporters.

The prime objective of nation-building on the political levels is to foster an inherent awareness among the people that each one of them is an equal citizen of the state. Equally crucial to this process of national socialization is to create a willingness on the part of the people to submit themselves to the authority of the state and its various institutions. The national political parties perform these functions.

However, every general election provides an opportunity to different contending parties to articulate their ideas in the form of an ideology and make it known to the people through manifesto. Manifestos are nothing but a varnish of logic, an academic, philosophical exercise. Anxious to obtain the mandate from the people, the parties or ruling parties ask for a vote for its programme. The parties share some of the views in common. That is to say that on certain issues parties share common views. This common thinking or identical thinking brings about the identical thinking in the masses and ultimately develops the common consensus. Moreover, all the national level parties plead for secularism and democracy. It will naturally help in the growth of integration and nationbuilding.

William N. Chambers in his article 'Parties and Nation Building in America', however, mentions that the following functions[213] are being performed by the American political parties in the process of Nation-building there :

1. "Establishing and maintaining a national authority, or the operating political system itself.
2. Expressing and aggregating interests .... and if possible, containing conflict within a spectrum which will prevent immobilism or disruption.

3. Meeting the crisis of participation and meeting related problems of coordinating political action in a politics of popular participation.
4. Recruiting and training at all levels new leaders who are capable of managing the problems or loads at hand.
5. Effecting a "Pay-off", in Lipsets terms or meeting the "crisis of distribution" in order to maintain the political system by convincing at least substantial segments of the population that it is an instrument through which they may accomplish their objectives.
6. Arriving at a position with reference to possible opposition to governing elites within the polity".

## REFERENCES

1. Puri, S., *Modern Political Analysis, op. cit.*, p. 92.
2. Maheshwari, Sriram, *Comparative Government and Politics, op. cit.*, p. 129.
3. Rodee, Carlton Ciymer, Aderson, Totton James, Christol, Carl Quimby, Greene, Thomas H , *Introduction to Political Science, op. cit.*, p. 316.
4. *Ibid.*
5. Grazia, Alfred de, *Political Behaviour*, Vol. I, The Free Press New York, 1962, p. 2.
6. Greenstein, Fred I, Polsby Nelson W., *Hand Book of Political Science, op. cit.*, Vol. 4, p. 231.
7. *Ibid.*
8. La Palombara, Joseph and Weiner, Myron, *Political Parties and Political Development* (Edited), Princeton, New Jersey Princeton University Press, 1966, p. 6.
9. Maheshwari, Sriram, *Comparative Government and Politics, op. cit.*, p. 130.
10. Greenstein, Fred I, Nelson Polsby W., *Hand Book of Political Science, op. cit.*, Vol. 4, p. 231.
11. La Palombara, Joseph and Weiner, Myron, *Political Parties and Political Development, op. cit.*, p. 6.
12. *Ibid.*
13. *Ibid.*
14. Maheshwari, Sriram, *Comparative Government and Politics, op. cit.*, p. 132.
15. Macridis, Roy C., *Political Parties : Contemporary Trends and Ideas* (Edited), Harper Torch Books, New York, 1967, p. 16.
16. Maheshwari, Sriram, *Comparative Government and Politics, op. cit.*, p. 132.
17. Duverger, Maurice, *Political Parties*, Methuen & Co. Ltd., London, 1954.
18. Blondel, Jean, *Comparative Government, op. cit.*, p. 141.
   "The thirtyone polities were without parties at the end of the 1960's".

19. La Palombara, Joseph and Weiner, Myron, *Political Parties and Political Development, op. cit.*, p. 3.
20. Neumann, Sigmund, *Modern Political Parties* (Edited), *op. cit.*, p. 1.
21. Greenstein, Fred 1, Polsby, Nelson W., *Hand Book of Political Science*, Vol. 4, *op. cit.*, p. 231.
22. Rodee, Carlton Clymer, Anderson, Totton James, Christol, Carl Quimby, Greene, Thomas H., *Introduction to Political Science, op. cit.*, p. 317.
23. Ray, Amal; Battacharya, Mohit, *Political Theory, op. cit.*, p. 434.
24. Finer, Herman, *The Theory and Practice of Modern Government*, Methuen & Co. Ltd., London 1965, p. 240.
25. *Ibid.*
26. Rodee, Carlton Clymer, Anderson, Totton James, Christol, Carl Quimby, Greene, Thomas H., *Introduction to Political Science, op. cit.*, p. 317.
27. *Ibid.*
28. Maheshwari, Sriram, *Comparative Politics and Government, op. cit.*, p. 130.
29. Encyclopaedia Britannica Vol. 14, p. 677.
30. *Ibid.*
31. International Encyclopaedia of the Social Sciences, Vol. 11, p. 429.
32. Blondel, Jean, *Comparative Government op. cit.*, p. 99.
33. Ray, Amal; Battacharya, Mohit, *Political Theory, op. cit.*, p. 435.
34. Neumann, Sigmund, *Towards a Comparative Study of Political Parties*, New York, 1963, p. 351.
35. La Palombara, Joseph and Weiner, Myron, Political Parties and Political Development, op. cit., 1966, p. 6.
36. Rodee, Carlton Clymer; Anderson, Totton James; Christol, Carl Quimby ; Greene, Thomas H., *Introduction to Political Science, op. cit.*, p. 318.
37. *Ibid.*
38. *Ibid.*
39. Blondel, Jean and Herman, Valentine, *Workbook for Comparative Politics*, Weidenfeld & Nicolson, London, 1972, pp. 43-44.
40. Blondel, Jean, *Comparative Government, op. cit.* p. 99.
41. *Ibid.*
42. *Ibid.*, p. 100.
43. *Ibid.*
44. *Ibid.*
45. *Ibid.*
46. *Ibid.*
47. *Ibid.*
48. Rodee, Carlton Clymer; Anderson, Totton James; Christol, Carl Quimby; Greene, Thomas H., *Introduction to Political Science, op. cit.*, p. 318.

49. *Ibid.*
50. *Ibid.*, p. 319.
51. Newmann, Sigmund, *Modern Political Parties, op. cit.*, p. 396.
52. *Ibid.*, pp. 396-97.
53. Hening, Stanley and Pinder, Jon, *European Political Parties (Edited)*, George Allen & Unwin Ltd., Ruskin House Museum Street, London, 1969, pp. 15-18.
54. Puri, S., *Modern Political Analysis, op. cit.*, pp. 99-100.
55. Merkl, Peter H., *Modern Comparative Politics*, Hinsdale, Drydon Press, London, 1977, p. 99.
56. Curtis, Michael, *Comparative Government and Politics, op. cit.*, pp. 154-56.
57. Rodee, Carlton Clymer, Anderson, Totton James, Christol, Carl Quimby, Greene, Thomas H., *Introduction to Political Science, op. cit.*, p. 319.
58. Maheshwari, Sriram, Comparative Government and Politics *op. cit.*, p. 132.
59. Amal, Ray ; Battacharya, Mohit, *Political Theory, op. cit.*, p. 442.
60. *Ibid.*
61. Maheshwari, Sriram, *Comparative Government and Politics, op. cit.*, p. 132.
62. Ray, Amal, Bhattaraya, Mohit, *Political Theory, op. cit.*, p. 442.
63. Maheshwari, Sriram, *Comparative Government and Politics, op. cit.*, p. 133.
64. Hansraj, *Comparative Politics, op. cit.*, p. 161.
65. Ray, Amal, Bhattacharya, Mohit, *Political Theory, op. cit.*, p. 444.
66. Almond, Gabriel and Goleman, James S., *Politics of Developing Areas, op. cit.*, p. 40.
67. Rodee, Carlton Clymer, Anderson, Totton James, Christol, Carl Quimby, Greene, Thomas H., *Introduction to Political Science, op. cit.*, p. 322.
68. *Ibid.*
69. Bal, Alan R., *Modern Politics and Government, op. cit.*, p. 81.
70. *Ibid.*
71. *Ibid.*
72. Duverger, Maurice, *Political Parties, op. cit.*, p. 17.
73. *Ibid.*, p. 18.
74. *Ibid.*, pp. 23-27.
75. *Ibid.*, p. 27.
76. Ball, Alan R., *Modern Politics and Government, op. cit.*, p. 82.
77. Duverger, Maurice, *Political Parties, op. cit.*, p. 36.
78. Ball, Alan R., *Modern Politics and Government, op. cit.*, p. 83.
79. Duverger, Maurice, *Political Parties, op. cit.*, p. 37.
80. *Ibid.*
81. Ball, Alan R., *Modern Politics and Government, op. cit.*, p. 84.
82. Curtis, Michael, *Comparative Government and Politics, op. cit.*, p. 167.

83. *Ibid.*
84. *Ibid.*
85. *Ibid.*
86. *Ibid.*, p. 168.
87. *Ibid.*
88. *Ibid.*
89. *Ibid.*, p. 169.
90. *Ibid.*
91. *Ibid*; p. 172.
92. *Ibid.*
93. *Ibid.*
94. *Ibid.*
95. *Ibid.*
96. Blondel, Jean and Herman, Valentine., *Workbook for Comparative Government, op. cit.*, p. 57.
97. Blondel, Jean., *Comparative Government, op. cit.*, p. 141.
98. Blondel, Jean and Herman. Valentine, *Workbook for Comparative Government, op. cit.*, p. 58.
99. Blondel, Jean, *Comparative Government, op. cit.*, p. 142.
100. *Ibid.*
101. Blondel, Jean and Herman, Valentine, *Workbook for Comparative Politics, op. cit.*, p. 58.
102. Blondel, Jean, *Comparative Government, op. cit.*, p. 142.
103. Blondel, Jean and Herman, Valentine, *Workbook for Comparative Government, op. cit.*, p. 59.
104. *Ibid.*
105. Blondel, Jean, *Comparative Government, op. cit.*, p. 142.
106. *Ibid.*
107. Blondel, Jean and Herman, Valentine, *Workbook for Comparative Politics, op. cit.*, p. 144.
108. *Ibid.*, p. 58.
109. *Ibid.*
110. *Ibid.*, p. 144.
111. Curtis Michael, *Comparative Government and Politics, op. cit.*, p. 165.
112. Rodee, Carlton Clymer, Anderson, Totton James, Christol, Carl Quimby, Greene, Thomas H., *Introduction to Political Science, op. cit.*, p. 327.
113. *Ibid.*
114. *Ibid.*
115. *Ibid.*
116. Brondel, Jean, *Comparative Government, op. cit.*, p. 143.
117. *Ibid.*, p. 144.

118. World Encyclopaedia of *Political Systems*, Vol. I & Vol. II, Edited by George E. Delury, Longman, 1983.
119. *Ibid.*
120. *Ibid.*
121. *Ibid.*, p. 45.
122. *Ibid.*, p.145.
123. Ray, Amal, Bhattacharya, Mohit, *Political Theory, op. cit.*, p. 452.
124. Finer, Herman, *The Theory and Practice of Modern Government, op. cit.*, p. 362.
125. Hansraj, *Comparative Politics, op. cit.*, p. 170.
126. Rodee, Carlton Clymer, Anderson, Totton James, Christol, Carl Quimby, *Introduction to Political Science*, p. 327.
127. Blondel, Jean, Herman Valentine, *Workbook for Comparative Government, op. cit.*, p. 65.
128. *Ibid.*
129. Curits, Michael, *Comparative Government and Politics, op. cit.*, p. 175.
130. Hansraj, *Comparative Politics, op. cit.*, p. 171.
131. Johari, J.C., *Comparative Politics, op. cit.*, p. 428.
132. Curtis, Michael, *Comparative Government and Politics, op. cit.*, p. 176.
133. *Ibid.*
134. Johari, J.C., *Comparative Politics, op. cit.*, p. 428.
135. Hansraj, *Comparative Politics, op. cit.*, p. 171.
136. Curtis, Michael, *Comparative Government and Politics, op. cit.*, p. 176.
137. *Ibid.*
138. *Ibid.*
139. Rodee, Carlton Clymer, Anderson, Totton James, Christon, Carl Quimby, Greene, Thomas H., *Introduction to Political Science, op. cit.*, p. 323.
140. *Ibid.*
141. *Ibid.*
142. Curtis, Michael, *Comparative Government and Politics, op. cit.*, p. 179
143. Rodee, Carlton Clymer; Anderson, Totton James; Christol, Carl Quimby; Greene, Thomas H., *Introduction to Political Science, op. cit.*, p. 323.
144. *Ibid.*
145. Curtis, Michael, *Comparative Government & Politics, op. cit.*, p. 180.
146. Blondel, Jean and Valentine Herman, *Workbook for Comparative Government, op. cit.*, p. 65.
147. Blondel, Jean, *Comparative Government, op. cit.*, p. 167.
148. *Ibid.*
149. *Ibid.*
150. *Ibid.*
151. *Ibid.*

152. Blondel, Jean & Valentine Herman, *Workbook for Comparative Politics, op. cit.*, p. 70.
153. Duverger, Maurice, *Political Parties, op. cit.*, p. 228.
154. *Ibid.*
155. *Ibid.*
156. *Ibid.*
157. Blondel, Jean & Herman, Valentine, *Workbook of Comparative Government, op. cit.*, p. 65.
158. Curtis, Michael, *Comparative Government and Politics, op. cit.*, p. 180.
159. Ray, Amal, Bhattacharya, Mohit, *Political Theory, op. cit.*, p. 452.
160. Neumann, Sigmund, *Toward a Comparative Study of Political Parties, op. cit.*, pp. 395.
161. Rodee, Carlton Clymer, Anderson, Totton James, Christol, Carl Quimby, Greene, Thomas H., *Introduction to Political Science, op. cit.*, p. 325.
162. *Ibid.*
163. *Ibid.*
164. *Ibid.*
165. *Ibid.*
166. *Ibid.*, pp. 452-53.
167. Curtis, Michael, *Comparative Government and Politics, op. cit.*, p. 181.
168. Hansraj, *Comparative Politics, op. cit.*, p. 172.
169. Curtis, Michael, *Comparative Government and Politics, op. cit.*, p. 182.
170. *Ibid.*
171. *Ibid.*
111. *Ibid.*
173. *Ibid.*
174. *Ibid.*
175. *Ibid.*, pp. 182-83.
176. *Ibid.*, p. 184.
177. *Ibid.*, p. 185.
178. *Ibid.*
179. *Ibid.*
180. *Ibid.*
181. *Ibid.*
182. Rodee, Carlton Clymer, Anderson, Totton James, Christol, Carl Quimby, Greene, Thomas H., *Introduction to Political Science, op. cit.*, p. 224.
183. *Ibid.*
184. Curtis, Michael, *Comparative Government and Politics, op, cit.*, p. 185.
185. *Ibid.*
186. Rodee, Carlton Clymer, Anderson, Totton James, Christol, Carl Quimby, Greene, Thomas H. *Introduction to Political Science, op cit.*, p. 91.

187. *Ibid.*
188. *Ibid.*
189. *Ibid.*
190. Curtis, Michael, *Comparative Government and Politics, op. cit.*, p. 158.
191. *Ibid.*
192. *Ibid.*, p. 159.
193. *Ibid.*
194. *Ibid.*
195. *Ibid.*
196. *Ibid.*
197. *Ibid.*
198. *Ibid.*
199. *Ibid.*, p. 160.
200. *Ibid.*
201. *Ibid.*, p. 161.
202. Pulparampit, John K., *Models of Nation Building*, A Critical Appraisal Amarko Book Agency, B-12, Amar Colony, New Delhi, p. 17.
"The most prominent among such new states are: India, Indonesia, Malaya, Singapore, Philippines, Vietnam, Laos, Cambodia, Burma, Ceylon, UAR, Libya, Tunisia, Cyprus, Morocco, Algeria, Sudan, Nigeria, Tanganyika, Uganda, Mali, Guinea, Bangla Desh etc."
203. The Times of India of 30th June, 1980, p. 5.
204. *Ibid.*
205. *Ibid.*
206. Kothari, Rajni, *State and Nation Building* (Ed.), Allied Publishers Pvt. Ltd., New Delhi, 1976, p. 193.
207. The Times of India of 30th June, 1980, p. 5.
208. *Ibid.*
209. Atal, Yogesh, *Building A Nation*, Abhinave Publications, New Delhi, 1981, p.
210. *Ibid.*
211. Bendix, Reinhard, *Nation-Building and Citizenship: Studies of Our Changing Social Order*, Wily Eastern Ltd., New Delhi, 1969.
212. Kothari, Rajni, *State and Nation Building* (Edited), Allied Publishers Pvt. Ltd., New Delhi, 1976, p. viii.
213. La Palombara, Joseph and Weiner, Myron, *Political Parties and Political Development* (Ed.), op. cit., pp. 89-90.

# 5

# Political Culture

Traditionally, the study of comparative government has focussed on structural analysis in terms of basic Constitutions and institutions of government such as Legislature, Judiciary, Bureaucracy etc.[1] But the politics of the newly emerging nations chiefly in Africa and Asia could not be studied by referring to the structures of their governments alone. As the parliamentary institutions and the political parties there function on unconstitutional lines, these therefore cannot fit in with well known models existing in the contemporary Western democracies. In order to study, understand and explain the basic character of political changes and the political development particularly in the third world, the behaviouralists sought to lay greater stress on the study of the informal processes of politics and less on the State political institutions.[2] They rightly pointed out that comparative politics could be meaningfully discussed only in the terms of individual and group orientation *i.e.*, finding out the ways in which the people develop, sustain and alter their political institutions.

The study of the traditions of a society, the underlying spirit of public institutions, the collective attitude of the people, the role of the leadership has become an important fact of the intellectual inquiry particularly of the contemporary developing nations. The Behaviouralists lay greater stress on the study of inter group behaviour as well as informal process of politics *i.e.*, on the non-governmental and social groups, political processes and politically oriental behaviour of individual and groups.

Thus, the study of political culture like 'political socialisation' followed in the wake of the wider intellectual concern for the indepth analysis of the Comparative Politics.[3] Moreover it has not only constituted an examination of the sociological aspect of the subject of political development but has also come to stand as a very important touchstone for a morphological study of the political systems. It has also influenced the system theorists to assert that one political system is distinguished from another not only in terms of its structure but also in respect of the Political Culture in which it lays embedded.[4] That is why the parliamentary system of government which developed and worked well in Western democracies failed to have a similar success in most of the underdeveloped and developing political systems of the contemporary world—particularly of Asia and Africa.

## 5.1. POLITICAL CULTURE—CONCEPT

The concept 'Political Culture' is somewhat new in the discipline of Political Science.[5] One version is that it was in 1960's that this concept became a part of modern political analysis. Gahril A. Almond and Sidney Verba have pointed out that the concept of Political Culture, like other concepts in the field of Political Science, was originated between two world wars.[6] It was first introduced by Gabriel A. Almond in one of his paper titled "Comparative Political System," published in 1956.[7] It was first introduced by Gabriel A. Almond in 1956 in his early attempt to offer a classification for comparing Political Systems.[8] Political Culture, however, has been popularised by some of the leading Amercian writers like Samuel Bear, Admulams and Gabriel A. Almond. It, thus, has become an important tool for making comparative study of Political Systems.

'Political Culture' is, however, closely lined with 'Political System' and in fact the formal regulates the latter. Moreover, political Culture is not static but changes with changing times. This concept has, therefore, offered a new method of having knowledge of comparative politics. One political system may be different from other in respect of Political Culture. It is Political Culture which explains why in some Political Systems democracies or parliamentary democracy failed and replaced by military dictatorship and in others it was replaced by civilian totalitarianism. It is not only the legal framework that matters but there is something more which affect this development. For example the Constitutions and Political systems of two nations may be the same still their politics may differ. This may not only due to the facts that different issues involved but also the general attitude, beliefs and behaviour of the people in their respective nations. In other words there are differences of their Political Cultures.

Each society, however, imparts its own characteristic set of norms and values to its people, and the people in turn have distinct sets of idea about how the Political System is supposed to work, about what the Govt, may do them, and about their own claims on the system and their obligation to it. This set of beliefs, symbols, and values about the Political System forms the Political Culture of a nation. In the simplest words, Political Culture is the Psychology of the nation in regard to Politics.[9]

The term Political Culture has therefore been defined by Sidney Verba as the system of empirical beliefs, expressive symbols and values which define the situation in which political action takes place.[10] By empirical beliefs he means the ways people perceive and interpret the nature of a political relationship. By expressive symbols, he means the ways people feel towards political institutions and leaders; patterns of political loyalty, identification, and commitment in the political system. By values he means the standards used to set the general goals of the Political System; standards used to evaluate political demands, processes and products. A political culture can, thus, be characterized by relative, empirically determinable levels of consensus in the sharing among people of these beliefs, symbols and values.[11] In other words political culture is defined in terms of political orientations and attitudes held by individual, in relation to their Political system.[12] According to Dennis Kavanagh "A Political Culture is composed of the attitude, beliefs, emotions and values of society."[13] Alan R. Ball points out that these attitudes may not be consciously held, but may be implicit in an individual or group relationship with the political system. In a collaborative effort with Powell, Almond, however, elaborated further his conception of Political Culture, trying it both to the Political System and political development, and defined Political Culture as[14] 'The pattern of individual attitudes and orientations towards politics among the members of a Political System.[15] They further added that it is the subjective realm which underlies and gives meaning to Political Action.[16] It is "the set of attitudes, beliefs and sentiments that give order and meaning to a political process and that provides the underlying assumptions and rules that govern behaviour in the Political System."[17] In certain political community, it sands for the pattern of individual attitudes and orientation toward politics of that community among the measures of the polity.[18] Lucian W. Pye viewed 'Political Culture' as providing "an ordered subjective realm of politics, which is found on two levels. For the individual the political culture produces controlling guidelines for effective political behaviour, and for the collectivity it gives a systematic structure of values and rational considerations which insures coherence in the performance of institutions and organisations."[19] Political culture, therefore, is the product both of collective histories and of individual life histories of the political system. It, thus, evolves from conscious learning about politics.[20]

Many interpretations of Political Culture, however, diverge to some extent from the Almond-Pye-Verba formulation. Samul Beer, for example, described 'political Culture' as a pattern of ideas and traditions about authority; Beer conceived it at the national level and Roy Macridis points out that it is made up of shared goals and commonly accepted rules of individual and group interactions.[21]

## 5.2. CULTURE AND POLITICAL CULTURE

The concept of 'Culture' is fundamental to anthropology and sociology. For an anthropologist the concept of culture provides a total picture of the life, action and beliefs of a community.

### 5.2.1. Culture

E.B. Taylor had introduced the concept of 'culture' to anthropology in 1871 and defined it as "that complex whole which includes knowledge, belief, art, morals, law, custom, and any other capabilities and habits acquired by man as a member of society."[22] Frans Boar — an anthropoligist while giving a descriptive definition to the concept 'culture', which was similar to that of Taylor, pointed out that ' 'Culture embraces all the manifestations of social habits of a community, the reactions of the individual as affected by the habits of the group in which he lives, and the products of human activities as determined by these habits."[23] Ralph Linton had stressed historical feature of culture, such as social inheritance or social tradition.[24] But O. Klineberg emphasizing a normative connotation pointed out that "Culture is that whole way of life which is determined by the social environment."[25] C.S. Ford, on the other hand, presented culture in terms of its psychological implications, as a means of satisfying needs and solving problems and said that ' 'Culture consists of learned problem-solutions."[26] The widely accepted definition has been given by Clyde Kluckhohn "Culture consists of patterns, explicit and implicit, of and for behaviour acquired and transmitted by symbols, constituting the distinctive achievement of human groups, including their embodiments in artifacts; the essential core of culture consists of traditional (*i.e.*, historically derived and selected) ideas and especially their attached values; culture system may, on the one hand, be considered as product of action, on the other as conditioning influences upon further action."[27]

Talcott Parsons being a sociologist has defined culture as "patterned or ordered systems or symbols which are objects of the orientation of action, internalized components of the personalities of individual actors and institutionalized pattern of social systems."[28] According to Graham Wallas "Culture is an accumulation of thought, values and objects, social heritage acquired by us from preceding generations through learning."[29] It is different from biological heritage which is passed on to us automatically through genes.

Culture, on the whole, is a social concept and very much concerned with group behaviour. Since it is communicated from one generation to the other, it has a link with the past. It is always idealised and can exist after meeting social needs as well as ever increasing demands. It also manifests men's mind to a varying degree and constantly undergoes certain changes. Moreover, every new element which gets introduced in it gets integrated in it. In fact internal adaptation of culture is absolutely necessary due to environmental developments which is taking place all the time.

### 5.2.2. Political Culture

There has been a substantial effort to view culture in a political context in Political Science in general and in comparative politics in particular. For a political scientist "the shared values of a community or group are embodied in its political culture, "which in the reflection of its attitudes towards politics and which conditions the manner in which functions are exercised and the nature of the persons who perform those functions."[30] According to Dogan and Rose the concept of "political culture is a conventional shorthand way of referring to the values briefs, emotions, that give meaning to political life."[31] Ross points out that "the political culture of a nation consists of the characteristic attitudes of its population towards basic features of the political system . . ."[32] Walter A. Rosenbaum defines it as "The collective orientation of people towards the basic elements in their political system."[33] S.P. Verma points out that 'Political culture includes not only the attitudes to politics, political values, ideologies, national character and culture ethos but also the style, manner and substantive form of politics."[34]

## 5.3. POLITICAL CULTURE AND ITS COMPONENTS—INCLUDING ORIENTATION

As political culture is the pattern of individual attitudes and orientations towards politics among the members of a political system,[35] it is the subjective realm which underlies and gives meaning to political actions.[36] Such individual orientations involve several components which are as under:

### 5.3.1. Cognitive Orientation

Cognitive orientation refers to peoples' knowledge, accurate or otherwise, of political objects and beliefs. In other words congnitive orientation involve knowledge about political objects and familiarity with the way the political system actually works. Thus, an individual may have relatively high degree of accurate knowledge about how his political system works, who are leading figures and what are the current problems faced by the country. In developing countries majority of people are more or less ignorant as to how political system is run and about the role of the Prime Minister, President and the Courts. Majority of them have limited contact with the political system also.

### 5.3.2. Affective Orientation

Affective orientation refers to emotional feelings of the people towards their political system. In other words it stands for subjective feelings of attachment to or alienation from the political system. It also refers to the standard of criteria with the help of which the people judge their political system. Affective orientation, therefore, includes the feelings of attachment, involvement, rejection and the like, about political objects. This emotional feelings are very important because they affect the activities of the people as well as of the government.

### 5.3.3. Evaluative Orientation

Evaluative orientation refers to judgements and opinions about political objects, which usually involve applying value standards to political objects and events.

These three orientations are closely interrelated and would be found in the psyche of a single individual in different combinations.[37]

Almond and Powell have rightly observed that the orientation patterns "constitute the latent political tendencies, the propensities for political behaviour,"[38] which are of crucial importance in explaining and predicting political action in a particular political system.

## 5.4. TYPES OF POLITICAL CULTURE

According to Alan R. Ball "political culture can be classified according to whether members of society take an active role in the political process and expect benefits from governmental activity, or whether there is a passive relationship in which individuals know very little about governmental activity, and do not expect to share in the decision — making process."[39] Almond and Verba, in order to characterise political culture in terms of distribution of general attitudes toward the political system and toward the input and the output processes, have classified political culture into the following three types:[40]

(i) Parochial political culture,
(ii) Subject political culture, and
(iii) Participant political culture.

### 5.4.1. Parochial Political Culture

People who exhibit little or no awareness of the political system fall in this category. In other words it includes people who have no inclination to participate in input process and not aware of the output process. They are, thus, not interested to play any role. According to Michael Curtis "a parochial orientation is that when the individual is not aware of nor has opinions about the system as a whole but only of the local community."[41]

Such type of people are found in every society. Their number is, however, more in traditional societies and rare in western developed societies. There is, therefore, no specialisation and no special political roles in the society which has parochial political culture. In such a society the headman or chieftain alone assesses political, economic and religious role as in African chiefdoms.

Thus, from parochial culture we mean a system in which there is low cognition of political objects. The people by and large have no awareness of national political system. The society is, therefore, by and large traditional and backward.[42]

### 5.4.2. Subject Political Culture

People, who have high frequency of orientation towards a differentiated political system and toward the out-put aspects of the system but their orientation towards input objects and toward self as an active participant is zero, are included in this category.

In other words, this category includes all those individuals who are oriented to the political system or aware of various governmental roles such as collection of taxes, law making etc., and of the government-good or bad, legitimate or illegitimate.

But they were not oriented to take part in output structure as they do not have any clear knowledge of the way in which they can influence the political system. They have, therefore, no inclination to play any role. According to Michael Curtis a subject orientation is that when the individual is aware of the system but is essentially passive and accepts decisions.[43]

Such type of culture is generally found in monarchical system of government.

### 5.4.3. Participant Political Culture

Participant political culture is one in which the members of the society tend to be explicitly oriented to the system as a whole *i.e.,* to both the political and administrative structures and processes. In other words members of the society of this category are oriented to both the input and output aspects of the political system. It may further said that individuals of this category may be favourably or unfavourably oriented to the various classes of political objects. They also tend to be oriented towards an 'activist' role of the self in the polity. However, their feelings and evaluations of such a role may vary from acceptance to rejection, people of this category are always engaged in the articulation demands on the political system and are also participating or involved in the making of public decisions. According to Michael Curtis, participant orientation is that when the individual is an active member of the polity.[44]

This type of culture exists in a highly developed societies where people take active part in the political activities by considering themselves as the active members of the polity and are well conscious of their rights and duties.

But all the above mentioned three types of political culture are inter-dependent and one cannot replace the other. Usually all the three get mixed and combined with each other.[45] It has also pointed out that the political cultures in different communities can be classified according to the combination of these three types of political cultures.

Almond and Verba point out that the threefold classification of political culture such as parochial, subject and participant is only the beginning of the classification of political cultures. But each one of these major classes may has its sub classes also.[46]

### 5.4.4. Political Sub-Culture

In addition to the above mentioned three types of political culture, some of the writers talk of a few other types of political culture. One of them is political sub-culture.

They are of the view that entire population of a political system may not have the same culture. Some sections of the society may have developed participant political culture while others may not. It may be caused due to differences in education, ethnic membership, geographical location, religious faith, economic and social programmes.

It may also happen as a result of the inadaptability of the political structure with the political culture. In other words, some time structure remains static while orientation of part of population changes rapidly. Some time new structures are introduced by the elites but the certain sections of the people may not cope with them. Thus, different sections of population may have different political orientations.

When a particular set of political orientation is distinguishable from the other in the same political system, we speak of political Sub-Culture. In developing nations, for example, Political Sub-Culture is due to the differences of language, religion, class, caste etc.

### 5.4.5. Mass Culture

In every society a distinction may be drawn between the culture of the rulers or power holders and the masses. In other words those who deal with power and have responsibilities for taking decisions of the government, develop outlook on politics different from those of people who simply remain observer or perform marginal activities. The formal group of people exhibit Elite Political-Culture whereas latter group of people reflects Mass Political Culture.

While analysing the Indian Political Culture, even Myron Weiner points out this distinction in Indian society.

### 5.4.6. Elite Culture

As already pointed out that the Political Culture reflected in the ruler or power holder or decision maker is Elite Culture. So far as India is concerned, it is reflected in national planners, leaders and senior bureaucrates. It is widespread in the army also and among the English speaking intelligentsia.

### 5.4.7. The Civic Culture

In order to study the cross-national differences in Political Cultures, found in five different nations, Almond and Verba interviewed some five thousand people in five different nations,[47]—USA, Britain, West Germany, Italy and Mexico-in 1959 and I960,[48] They identify the people's orientations towards the political life basically falling into three categories—allegiance, apathy and alienation. Allegiance refers to a positive attitude, apathy indifference and alienation is negative. In other words the authors tested the following important three variables:

(a) What impact the people felt government had on their lives;

(b) What obligations they felt they had towards government; and

(c) What they expected from government.

What emerged was a picture of five different political cultures. The United States was found to have a largely "participant" political culture. The American citizens, on the whole, were actively and emotionally involved in political events and issues and had a high degree of respect for civic participation. An average American thought that it was natural that he should help to determine government policy. Many of them were of the view that all problems could be solved if the politicians would only follow the instructions of the electorate.

The Britishers also felt strong sense of personal involvement in government, but were more likely than American to defer to the judgement of those with superior knowledge and experience. But in Italy, where the people have lived under a long series of unstable and short-lived governments since World War Second, political attitudes of the people were characterized by a high degree of alienation, little national pride, and little sense of obligation to participate in government decision making processes. The Mexican Political Culture was a combination of alienation and aspiration. The tradition of discipline had a powerful influence on the German Civic Culture. The German people were highly informed and confident of the fairness of government. That was why they had not yet developed a sense of participation in its processes. They tended to regard themselves as subjects rather than involved participants in a democracy and still bowed to authority with little hesitation. Social discipline was still prized above individual independence.

On the basis of the information Almond and Verba put forward their "concept of civic culture." It is an allegiant participant culture. In other words civic culture is a participant Political Culture in which the Political Culture and Political Structure are congruent.[49] American society is, therefore, usually quoted as an example of Civic Culture because the Americans are very much involved in politics and also have a high Civic Competence. No doubt in American Society too, there is racialism which resulted in political in equality, yet on the whole it is liberal and considerable importance is attached to liberal values. In this type of culture, the rulers cannot act on their own will as the people are quiet conscious about their rights and duties.

Almond and Verba have, therefore, shown that National Cultures vary considerably in their (people's) view toward government and politics and that governments in turn vary according to their cultural environments. They further added that no stable Political Structure can be grafted onto a national culture which is completely alien to it, the political system is, therefore, a part of a nation's political culture and as such it reflects the total experience of that society. Moreover, political Cultures change over times and in response to events, some of them created by government.

"In a highly regarded civic culture respect for authority is combined with individual independence and the acceptance of the legitimacy of the political system with the belief that an individual can and should influence the system."[50]

Almond and Verba have identified the following four different types of Political cultures in broader terms[51]:

1. *The Anglo-American*, with values of freedom, welfare, and security, homogeneity in ends and means, and differentiation of political roles.
2. *Continental European*, where strong sub-cultures exist and Political roles are often embodied in the sub-cultures.
3. *The Pre-industrial*, which exhibits tension because of cultural mix and political instability because of an imperialist past imposed on a traditional political culture.
4. *The totalitarian*, in which there is a monopoly of political power by one party, strong coercion, and no voluntary associations.

### 5.4.8. Mixed Political Culture

Purely one type of Political Culture is unlikely to be found in modern society. Rather we find a mixture at different orientations within a society. In other words Political Culture will represent a blend of different elements found in the above mentioned types of Political Cultures. Even Almond and Verba have pointed out that the mixture of types would have a profound influence upon the ability of a nation to support a democratic system — and most importantly their interests.

## 5.5. FACTORS RESPONSIBLE FOR THE DEVELOPMENT OF POLITICAL CULTURE

The Political Culture is, however, is a product of several inter-related factors — historical, geographical and socio-economic. In other words Political Culture is fashioned by historical, geographical and socio-economic factors. Even Lucian W. Pye points out that political culture is shaped by the general historical experiences of the country and also by the private and personal experiences of the individuals.

### 5.5.1. History or Historical Factors

Historical facts and truths do have their impacts on the general attitude, beliefs, values and behaviours of the people of a Country. For example Political continuity of Great Britain is due to the fact that the old values of its people have been allowed to emerge with modern attitudes without any disturbance. Unlike France, there has been no revolution in Britain. That is why the English people are more conservative and the French more radicals.

The historical fact that the English people continued their association with India, has made India to learn the values of Parliamentary democracy. Whereas people of Algeria and Vietnam have learnt from their French masters the lesson of revolutionary struggle.

### 5.5 2. Geography or Geographical Factors

Geographical factors also help to fashion Political Culture of the people of a nation. For example Britain being an island, has been protected since time past from foreign invasion. In other words it Political Culture has not been disturbed by the foreigners. That is why British people have as well as harmonious Political Culture.

Whereas Indian geographical situation is such that foreign invasions and annexations were followed one after the others. As a result there was massive influx of foreign races who stayed and settled here permanently. That was why there developed the values of secularism or secular political culture.

### 5.5.3. Socio-Economic Factors

The socio-economic structure of a society is another determinant of its Political Culture. For example a predominantly urban industrialised society is a complex society. With emergence of a rapid communication, higher educational standard, group consciousness and participating in decision making process. All these may provoke a change in political values and believes with subsequent strains on political system. In this way there may be continuous development in Political Culture. But rural society with predominently peasant population tends to be more conservative in attitudes, beliefs and values, and it may not geared to the changes.

### 5.5.4. Other Determinants of Political Culture

Some of the writers have mentioned that ethnic differences,[52] holding of the traditions, degree of trust on the political leaders, spirit of tolerance, degree of love for their liberty, loyalty to the masses and social harmony may be some other determinants of the Political Culture of a nation.

## 5.6. CONTRIBUTION OF THE CONCEPT AND ITS DIMENSIONS OF POLITICAL CULTURE

The concept Political Culture and its dimensions have made most significant contributions to the study of Comparative Politics. According to Lucian W. Pye, the theory of Political Culture developed to bridge the growing gap between the level of micro analysis based on psychological interpretation of the individual's political behaviour and the level of macro-analysis based on the variables common to Political Sociology.[53] In other words it provides a useful link between micro and macro-politics, powerful means of explaining and predicting political behaviour in specific country situations, helps in regulating not only input demands but also influence conversion of system outputs into new or modified inputs, comparing different political systems, studying the degree of congruance which exist between culture and structure, laying down norms which can ensure coherence in proper operation of institutions and organisations, and to understand as to why different societies move in different directions during the course of their political development. Moreover, it is with the help of the study of Political Culture that focus has been shifted from the study of the individual to that of the society.[54]

## REFERENCES

1. Ray, Amal, Bhattacharya, Mohit, *Political Theory, op.cit.*, p. 230.
2. Johari, J.C., *Comparative Politics, op.cit.*, p. 20.
3. Ray, Amal, Bhattacharya, Mohit, *Political Theory, op.cit.*, p. 231.
4. Johari, J.C., *Comparative Politics*, Sterling Publishers Pvt. Ltd., New Delhi, 1930, p. 154.
5. Dr. Hans Raj, *Comparative Politics, op.cit.*, p. 86.
6. Almond, Gabriel A., Verba, Sidney, *Civic Culture*, Princeton, New Jersey, USA, 1972, p. VII.
7. *The Journal of Political System*, Vol. 18, 1956.
8. Chilcote, Ronald H., *Theory of Comparative Politics, op.cit.*, p. 223.
9. Cord, Robert L., Medeires, James A., Jones, Walter S., Roskim, Michael G., *Political Science : An Introduction*, Prentice-Hall Inc., New Jersey, 1985, p. 128.
10. Pye, Lucian W., and Verba, Sidney, *Political Culture And Political Development, Princeton University Press*, USA, 1965, p. 513.
11. Sprengel, Denald P., *Comparative State Politics*, Charles E. Merriol Publishing Company, Columbus OHIO, pp. 13-14.
12. Chilcote, Ronald H., *Theory of Comparative Politics, op.cit.*, p. 224.
13. Kavanagh, Dennis : *Political Culture*, London, 1972, pp. 9-19.
14. Ball, Alan R., *Modern Politics And Govt.*, The Macmillan Press Ltd., London, 1979, p. 52.
15. Almond, A. Gabriel & Powell, G., Bingham, *Comparative Politics: A Developmental Approach*, Oxford & IBH Publishing Company, New Delhi, 1978, p. 50.
16. *Ibid.*
17. Pye Lucian W., *Aspects of Political Development*, Boston, Little Brown, 1966, p. 104.
18. Ray, Amal and Bhattacharya, Mohit., *Political Theory, op.cit.*, p. 231.
19. Chilcote, Ronald H., *Theory of Comparative Politics, op.cit.*, p. 225.

20. *Ibid.*
21. *Ibid.*
22. *Ibid.*, pp. 218-19.
23. *Ibid.*
24. *Ibid.*
25. *Ibid.*
26. *Ibid.*
27. *Ibid.*, p. 219
28. *Ibid.*, pp. 220-221.
29. Hans Raj, *Comparative Politics, op.cit.*, pp. 86-87.
30. Curtis, Michael., *Comparative Government And Politics, op.cit.*, p. 26.
31. Dogem, Mattei and Rose, Richard, *European Politics*, Little Brown and Company, Boston, 1971.
32. Rose, R., *Electoral Behaviour : A Comparative Handbook*, New York, 1974.
33. Rosenbaum, Walter A., *Political Culture.*
34. Verma S.P., *Modern Political Theory.*
35. Almond A, Gabriel and Powell, G. Bingham Jr., *Comparative Politics : A Developmental Approach*, Oxford & IBH Publishing Co; New Delhi, 1978, p. 50.
36. *Ibid.*
37. Ray, Amal and Bhattacharya, Mohit, *Political Theory, op.cit.*, p. 232.
38. Almond, A. Gabriel and Powell, G. Bingham Jr, *Comparative Politics : A Developmental Approach, op.cit.*, p. 50.
39. Ball, Alan, R., *Modern Politics And Government, op.cit.*, p, 53.
40. Almond Gabriel And Verba Sidney, *The Civic Culture, op.cit.*, pp. 116-17.
41. Curtis, Michael, *Comparative Government And Politics, op.cit.*, p. 27.
42. Hans Raj, *Comparative Politics, op.cit.*, p. 88.
43. Curtis, Michael, *Comparative Government And Politics, op.cit.*, p. 27.
44. *Ibid.*
45. *Ibid.*, p. 89.
46. Almond, Gabriel A. and Verba, Sidney, *The Civic Culture, op.cit.*, p. 21.
47. Ashraf, Ali and Sharma, L.N., *Political Sociology : A New Grammar of Politics*, Universities Press Pvt. Ltd., Madras, 1983, p. 136.
48. Cord, Robert L., Medeirous, James A, *Political Science :* Michael G. Jones, Watters and Robins, *An Introduction*, Prentice-Hall. Inc, Englewood Clifs, New Jersey 1985, pp. 17-18.
49. Ashraf, Ali, Sharma, L.N., *Political Sociology: A New Grammar of Politics, op.cit.*, p. 136.
50. Curtis, Michael : *Comparative Government and Politics, op.cit.*, p. 27.
51. *Ibid.*
52. Ball, Alan R., *Modern Politics And Government, op.cit.*, p. 55.
53. Ray, Amal, Bhattacharya, Mohit, *Political Theory, op.cit.*, p. 234.
54. Hans Raj, *Comparative Politics, op.cit.*, p. 91.

# 6

# Political Socialization

Like 'Political Culture', the term 'Political Socialization' is also one of the key concepts in contemporary Political Analysis. It is primarily a Psychological concept which deals with orientation of individuals towards political objects.[1] As it is a process by which political cultures are maintained and changed,[2] it plays a vital role in the study of comparative politics. It is an important means of inter-generational and inter-continental transmission of culture.[3] It is the way a society transmits its political culture from generation to generation and from one continent to another. This process helps societies to achieve cohesion through a shared understanding of values, norms and symbols.[4]

It also helps in the process of establishment and development of attitudes and beliefs about political system.[5] It may encourage loyalty to the nation, the fostering of particular values, and may increase either support for or alienation from the system. It is also particularly important in the degree of participation in political life that is expected of groups and individuals.[6] Almond and Powell point out that the study of Political Socialization seems to be one of the most promising approaches to understand political stability and development.[7] Moreover, changes in the patterns of political culture also come about through political socialization.[8] Thus, process by which individuals in political system learn their political orientations and dispositions is called Political Socialization.[9]

It is a process, however, not confined to the impressionable years of childhood but one that continues throughout life.[10]

The need for the study of the subject political socialization specially felt by the newly emerging countries to instil among their citizens the support for the political community, the regime and the occupants of political roles.

## 6.1. POLITICAL SOCIALIZATION — CONCEPT

Political Socialization is the induction into Political Culture and the developmental process through which we learn the accepted attitudes and values of our political culture and sub-cultures.[11] According to Michael Curtis Political Socialization means the transmitting of political values and norms of the society.[12] Ball regards it as the establishment and development of attitudes to and beliefs about the political system.[13] J.C. Johari is of the view that Political Socialization seeks to inculcate values, norms and orientations in the mind of the individuals so that they trust in their political system and thereby keep themselves like well functioning citizens and also leave their indelible imprints on the mind of their successors.[14] That is why Rush and Althoff describe it as the process by which an individual becomes acquainted with the political system and which determines his perceptions of politics and his reactions to political phenomena.[15] Easton and Dennis define it as those developing processes through which persons acquire political orientation and pattern of behaviour.[16] According to Robert Levine Political Socialization is the means by which individuals acquire motives habits and values, relevant to participation in a political system.[17] According to Peter H. Merkl, Political Socialization refers to acquisition of political attitudes and behaviour patterns by members of a political system of sub-system."[18]

Fred I. Greenstein defines it as 'all political learning, formal and informal, deliberate and unplanned at every stage of the life cycle including not only explicitly political learning but also nominally non-political learning that affects political behaviour, such as, learning of politically relevant social attitude and the acquisition of politically relevant personality characteristics."[19]

The end product of political socialization is, therefore, a set of attitudes congnitions, value standards and feeling—towards the political system, its various roles, and role incumbents. It also includes knowledge of values and feelings affecting the inputs of demands and claims and the authoritative output.[20]

Political Socialization is, however, different from socialization. Socialization, being sociological concept, is that process by which individuals learn to conform to the norms of the group and social beings establish wider and profounders relationship with one another.[21] Whereas political socialization deals with economic and political structures of the society.[22] It, therefore, includes all those processes by which people acquire political orientation and pattern of behaviour.[23] Roberts Sigel also points out that political socialization is the gradual learning of norms, attitudes and behaviours acceptable to on-going political system.[24] While explaining the concept Waloby points out that political socialization is a process by which people acquire political values not simply during active political participation but even before engaging themselves in political activities.[25]

Political Socialization, therefore, includes all formal, informal, deliberate, unplanned learning at every stage of life. Political Socialization which means learning of political attitudes and social preferences is crucial to stable government.[26]

## 5.6. TYPES OF POLITICAL SOCIALIZATION

According to Almond and Powell, Political Socialization is of following two types :[27]

6.2.1. Manifest

6.2.2. Latent

It is manifest when it involves the explicit communication of information, values or feelings toward political objects.[28] In other words Political Socialization is manifest when certain values or feelings towards political system are put into the minds of others directly, clearly and manifestly. It includes the process of formal instruction given in schools or colleges about the political objects.

Lesson in the advantages of democracy, rights of the citizens, respect for authority, love of political system, the civics courses in American Public school, compulsory courses of Marxism — Leninism in the earstwhile Soviet Union at school level simplify manifest political socialization.

But the usual methods of manifest socialization, being formal education given in educational institutions, lectures and use of mass media is either for political stability or for political changes or maintain status quo.

Political Socialization is latent when attitude to non-political things becomes as attitude towards political things. In other words latent Political Socialization is the tramission of non-political attitudes which affect attitudes toward analogous roles and objects in political system.[29] For example the attitude of submission to the authority of the father in a family makes us to submit to the authority in one political system. It is deep rooted and usually it works unnoticed and more or less automatically.[30] Latent political socialization, therefore, involves many of the most fundamental characteristics of the general culture, which may, in turn, have great effect on the political sphere.[31]

In addition to these two main types of Political Socialization, there are following other types of it:[32]

6.2.3. Particularistic;

6.2.4. Universalistic;

6.2.5. Affective;

6.2.6. Instrumental;

6.2.7. Specific; And

6.2.8. Diffuse.

Particularistic Socialization is that process in which individual is taught only one and not more than one role. He does not learn anything about other roles, *i.e.*, socialising an individual into particularistic values only.

In universalistic socialization cosmopolitan outlook is developed. One, therefore, learns several roles.

In affective socialization there is stress on emotional values and loyalties, *viz.* pride in one's political system, loyalty to the one's country, respect for ruler etc.

In instrumental socialization the emphasis is on pragmatic bargaining and calculating strategies *i.e.*, the brief that a political system should be supported not for all times, but as long as one drives benefits from it.

In specific socialization, specific attitude and values are imparted by specific political structures.

There is diffused socialization where there is learning about vague things such as religion, politics, economy, society etc. It is found in such societies in which there is no differentiation between state and society.

## 6.3. THE AGENTS OF POLITICAL SOCIALIZATION

Almond and Powell has identified a number of agents of political socialization.[33] It is through these agencies that the influence process works and reaches out to the individual mind. These are the socialization structure in a society which regularly performs the function of socialization. These are :

6.3.1. The Family

6.3.2. The School

6.3.3. Peer Groups

6.3.4. Work or Employment Situation

6.3.5. Mass Media

6.3.6. Direct Contacts with Political System

6.3.7. Religion

6.3.8. Caste

6.3.9. Politics

The family unit is the first socialization structure encountered by the individual. It has been described as the child's first window on the world outside, that is to say it is child's first contact with authority. This primary organization has an authority structure and a decision making process. The influences—both latent and manifest—to which the child is exposed at the early state have a decisive impact on his orientation toward authority and obedience in other spheres including the political.[34] The collective decisions taken by the family are authoritative for the child as they are backed with political sanction. Moreover, an early experience with participation in decision making can increase the child's sense of political competence, provide him with skills for interaction, and thus enhance the probability of his active participation in the political system when he becomes an adult.[35] Children tend to identify with the parents and to adopt their outlook toward the political system. Studies of the intergenerational continuity of party identification in the USA show how children may be disposed to consider themselves republican or democrats according to their parents' loyalties.[36]

## The School

It is the second most powerful agent of Political Socialization. Manifest transmission of political knowledge and opinion take place at the school level. Different competitions, debates, discussions and other decision-making modes in the school expert influence in later life on the individuals' performance in other roles.

The five-nation study found without exception that educated persons were more aware of the impact of government on their lives, paid more attention to politics, had more information about political processes and manifested a higher degree of political competence.[37] Almond and Powell further pointout that schools can also pay an important role in shaping attitudes about the unwritten rules of the political game, as the traditional British Public Schools inculcate the values of public duty, informal political relations and political rectitude. They can bring an awareness of other values and circumstances, providing a basis for new political aspirations.[38]

## Peer Groups

Peer groups which are also termed as reference groups, work outside educational institutions. They play an important role in shaping values and orientations. They play most vital role in an industrial society where family ties are loosened or where family training seems incongruous with the youth's social environment. In such a atmosphere and situations the formal and informal peer groups have considerable impact on individual views of politics. Moreover, the ways in which peer groups contacts affect these orientations has a bearing on future political behaviour.[39]

### Work or Employment Situation

Experience in employment may also shape political orientations. The job and the formal and informal organisation built around it *viz.*, the union, the social club etc., may act as channels for the explicit communication of political information and beliefs.[40] In other words political orientations are shaped through participation in unions, collective bargaining, demonstrations, strikes and other forms of decision making. Similarly informal groups of employees exert influence on their member's attitude toward political objects and events.[41]

The striking labourer not only learns that he can shape the authoritative decisions being made about his future, but he gains knowledge of specific action skills, such as demonstrating and picketing which may be used in political participation.[42]

In short it is in employment that one learns to dominate, to be subordinate, the art of organising unions, strikes, bargaining for better wages. All these qualities have always gone a long way in political socialization.[43]

### Mass Media

Radio, television, newspaper, and other forms of mass media also provide information about political happenings. That is why manipulation of media is often resorted to in different countries to influence, and change the political orientation of citizens. A controlled system of mass media, can, therefore, be a powerful force, in shaping political beliefs, and also can provide bases of support as important to a totalitarian state as its Police forces.

### Direct Contacts with Political System

Individual orientation to politics is very often conditioned by the direct contacts with the political system. His direct relationship with political parties, pressure groups; influential political leaders would naturally determine his attitude towards politics. Almond and Powell rightly point out that no matter how positive the view of the political system which has been inculcated by family and school, when a citizen is ignored by his party, cheated by his police, starved in the bread line, and finally conscripted into the army, his views of the political realm are likely to alter.[44] Similarly direct formal and informal relationship with specific elites in the political system are inevitably a powerful force in shaping orientations of individuals to the system.[45]

## OTHER AGENTS OF POLITICAL SOCIALIZATION

### Religion

Some of the writers are of the view that religion is also an agent of political socialization. The Roman Catholic Church, for instance, has been influential in imparting certain political attitudes to its followers especially to women.

### Caste

The role of caste as an agent of socialization is also regarded as potent particularly in the third world nations. Voters are seen to vote on caste lines and the candidates also reflect caste allegiance in their political behaviour. The ideology underlying the system of reservation for scheduled castes and tribes is that their members are so socialized as to be sympathetic to the cause of these disadvantaged communities.

### Politics

Politics itself is a powerful agent of political socialization. The ways in which the politics of a country is conducted is a deep learning experience for the citizens. Citizens are exposed to the method of selection of candidates in elections, mode of election campaign, behaviour of political activists, nature of electoral competition gives the most significant political experiences to the individuals. That is why Peter H. Merkl rightly observed "One of the most immediate and effective agents of the political socialization of children and adults is the spectacle of politics itself. As the group and sports help to socialise, so the game of politics, especially its competition, may get adolescents and adults involved."[46]

## 6.4. CONCLUSION

Political Socialization is, thus, a relatively new area of study, but it performs functions which are vital to the political system no less than to the individuals. This is when even a totalitarian regime is keen to monopolise the socialisation process so that people develop positive attitudes towards it however, deplorable it may be from the larger humanistic standpoint.

But the study of political socialization, like political culture, has special and vital significance for the third world countries where the political culture is in flux and change and is yet to take a definite shape. The great issues of politics in the emerging nations such as political stability, political development and change can be much more meaningfully studied and discussed with the help of the concepts like political culture and political socialization.

## REFERENCES


1. Hans Raj, *Comparative Politics, op.cit.*, p. 92.
2. Almond, Gabriel A. Powell, G. Bingham Jr., *Comparative Politics: A Developmental Approach, op.cit.*, p. 64.
3. Ashraf, Ali, Sharma, L.N., *Political Sociology. A New Grammar of Politics, op.cit.*, p. 172.
4. *Ibid.*
5. Almond Gabriel A. Powell, G. Bingham, Jr., *Comparative Politics: A Developmental Approach, op.cit.*, p. 65.
6. Ball, Alan R., *Modern Politics and Government, op.cit.*, p. 63.
7. Almond, Gabriel A., Powell, G. Bingham Jr., *Comparative Politics: A Developmental Approach, op.cit.*, p. 64.
8. *Ibid.*, p. 64.
9. Maheshwari, S.R., *Comparative Govt., and Politics, op.cit.*, p. 53.
10. Ball, Alan, R., *Modern Politics And Government, op.cit.*, p. 63.
11. Cord, Robert L., Medelros, James A., Jones, Walter S., Roskin, Michael G., *Political Science : An Introduction, op.cit.*, p. 20.
12. Curtis, Michael; *Comparative Government And Politics : op.cit.*, p. 7.
13. Ball, Alan, R., *Modern Politics And Government, op.cit.*, p. 63.
14. Johari, J.C., *Comparative Politics, op.cit.*, p. 140.
15. Ashraf, Ali, Sharma, L.N., *Political Sociology—A New Grammar of Politics, op.cit.*, p. 172.
16. *Ibid.*
17. Geetz, Clifford, *Old Societies and New States*, Amerind Publishing Co., 1971, New Delhi, p. 280.
18. Almond, Gabriel A., and Coleman, James S., *The Politics of the Developing Areas*, Princeton University, Princeton, 1970, p. 27.
19. Fred I., Greenstein, '*Political Socialization*' in International Encyclopaedia of the Social Sciences, Vol. 14, p. 551.
20. Hyman, Herbert, *Political Socialization*, The Free Press, New York,: 1959, p. 25.
21. Hans Raj, *Comparative Politics, op.cit.*, p. 92.
22. *Ibid.*
23. *Ibid.*

24. *Ibid.*, p. 93.
25. *Ibid.*
26. Cord, Robert, Medeiros, James A, *Political Science*, James Walter S., Roskin, Michael G., *op.cit.*, p. 20.
27. Almond, Gabriel A, Powell, G. Bingham Jr., *Comparative Politics: A Developmental Approach, op.cit.*, p. 65.
28. *Ibid.*, pp. 65-66.
29. *Ibid.*, p. 66.
30. Hans Raj, *Comparative Politics, op.cit.*, p. 95.
31. Almond, Gabriel A, Powell, G. Bingham Jr., *Comparative Politics: A Developmental Approach, op.cit.*, p. 66.
32. Hans Raj, *Comparative Politics, op.cit.*, p. 95.
33. Almond, Gabriel A, Powell, G. Bingham Jr., *Comparative Politics: A Developmental Approach*, pp. 66-67.
34. Ray, Amal, Bhattacharya, Mohit, *Political Theory, op.cit.*, p. 235.
35. Almond, Gabriel A, Powell, G. Bingham Jr., *Comparative Politics: A Developmental Approach, op.cit.*, p. 66.
36. *Ibid.*, pp. 66-67.
37. *Ibid.*, p. 67.
38. *Ibid.*, p. 67.
39. *Ibid.*, p. 69.
40. *Ibid.*
41. Ray, Amal, Bhattacharya, Mohit, *Political Theory, op.cit.*, p. 235.
42. Almond, Gabriel A, Powell, G. Bingham Jr., *Comparative Politics: A Developmental Approach, op.cit.*, p. 69.
43. Hans Raj, *Comparative Politics, op.cit.*, p. 97.
44. Almond, Gabriel A, Powell, G. Bingham Jr., *Comparative Politics: A Developmental Approach, op.cit.*, p. 69.
45. *Ibid.*
46. Maheshwari, S.R., *Comparative Politics, op.cit.*, p. 60.

# 7

# Political Development

The massive political changes on international scene in the late 1950s and early 1960s were dramatic. By 1960s a host of new nations chiefly in Africa and Asia had burst onto the world's stage, not only significantly expanded the universe of Political Science in general and of Comparative Politics in particular but also had provided fresh and exciting new developments.[1] These developments had led to the vigorous pursuit of cross-polity studies[2] and also gave legitimacy to the idea that through foreign assistance programmes, the USA could bring the benefits of its system, institutions and accomplishment to the less-favoured nations.[3]

It is equally true that the developing Countries which acquired independence from Western imperialism in Post World War Second era remained technologically backward and Politically dependent and, therefore, economically exploited and indigent. The urge for development, social reforms and economic growth was a part of their struggle for freedom. Their aspiration for independence, national dignity, and development found a practical basis for the academic concern with modernisation and Political Development.[4]

The rise of newly emerging nations on the international chess board, however, opened the new dimensions in the discipline of Political Science. No doubt the Sociologists, Anthropologists, Economists and Historians also tried to study these new societies. But when these societies began to take the shape of new states, the attention of Political Scientists was drawn towards them.

The term 'Political Development', therefore, entered the lexicon of Political Science in the 1950s[5] when the newly emerging nations began formulating development plans for the socio-economic well-being of their people.

However, the western Political Science discipline was at that time deeply under the influence of system theory which believed that Political System, being a sub-system of social system, receives the challenges as well as its sustenance from the social system in the form of inputs and yield outputs, which again fed into the political system as the reaction of outputs. The feedback process strengthened or weakened challenges as well as sustenance processes. It was also admitted that though non-western political processes were different from that of the west yet they could be successfully studied by System-Approach in their Socio-Economic cultural background.

Moreover, the Committee of Comparative politics of the Social Sciences Research Council of USA pioneered sustained and systematic interest in the study of Political Development. Some members had suggested that it may be useful to conceptualise and analyse the processes of Political Development in the new emerging nations[6] Gabriel A Almond, who became the Chairman of the Committee and who had soon emerged as leading theoretician of Political Development, stressed that development should not be treated just as a phenomenon to be analysed in a scientific sense but also as a moral, ethical and political 'Good' among the developing nations.[7] Under the auspicies of this Committee the following Social Sciences Research Council Series containing the indepth analysis of Political Development of the developing nations were published between 1963 and 1966 by the Princeton University Press New Jersey:[8]

1. Gabriel A Almond & James S. Coleman : *Politics of Developing Areas.*
2. Lucian W. Pye. : *Communication and Political Development*, 1963.
3. La Palombara J (ed.) : *Bureaucracy and Political Development*, 1963.
4. Robert Eward and Dankwart A. Ruston : *Political Modernisation in Japan and Turkey*, 1964.
5. James S. Coleman (ed.) : *Education and Political Development*, 1965.
6. Lucian W Pye and Sidney Verba (ed.) : *Political Culture and Political Development* 1965.
7. La Palombara and Myron Weiner (ed.) : Political Parties and Political *Development*, 1966.

Two more books were published in 1971 and 1975.

These are :[9]

| | | |
|---|---|---|
| 8. Leonard Buider, James. S. Coleman, Joseph Lapalombra, Lucian W. Pye, Sindeny Verba and Myron Weiner (ed.) | : | *Crisis and Sequences in Political Development*, 1971. |
| 9. Charles Tilly (ed.) | : | *The Foundation of the National States in Western Europe*, 1971. |

In the meantime a huge amount of statistical and quantitative data on the social, demographic, Economic, Political etc. characteristics and about attitude, values and behaviour pattern of the people of the new nations were being brought out by the Survey Research Developed in U.S.A. at different centres *viz.*,

(*i*) The Yale Political Data Programme;

(*ii*) The Inter-University Consortium for Political Research at Michigan;

(*iii*) The International Data Library and Research Service at Berkeley and UCLA Stanford Michigan state, Pennsylvania, Yale and other Universities;

(*iv*) The Council of Social Science Data Archieves in New York; and

(*v*) The Centre for International Studies at the M.I.T.

With the help of these statistical data revolution it was, thus possible to analyse and even measure the level of Political Development.

## 7.1. POLITICAL DEVELOPMENT — CONCEPT

The world wide interest in the plight of the newly emerging nations, which were actually old societies, had produced a babel of terms during 1950s and early 1960s. Some of these expressed the aspirations of the statesmen, and policy makers, others were the pompous pretensions of calculating politicians and still others were merely the euphemisms of people who thought that they might be talking about delicate matters.[10] In other words there is no agreed framework of Political Development. One comes across a variety of connotations of the term. According to Rostow, the norms of Political behaviour and the institutional appratus evolved by the industrial societies constitute the bases of political development for the non-industrial societies. Industrial societies are, therefore, the pattern-setters of political development for other societies.[11] A few other scholars seek to devise indices of social and economic change, and link these to the process of Political Development. Edward Shills equates Political Development with nation-state-building.[12]

In spite of the fact that several attempts had been made by them to give a proper and suitable definition to this concept, yet there is still considerable ambiguity and imprecision in the use of the term Political Development.[13]

### 7.1.1. Lucian W. Pye Views

Lucian W. Pye was, however, among the first batch of scholars who has made an indepth analysis of the concept Political Development. Though he was then in the evolutionary stage, yet his contribution to this subject was original and extensive.[14] He has compiled a list of all the conflicting and overlapping connotations, notions and ideas commonly used in popular as well as professional interpretation of what was involved in Political Development. But at the same time he pointed out that there were other possible interpretations of the term also.

It shall be helpful to elaborate the confusing connotations of this Concept given by Pye not only to accept or reject any particular but rather to illuminate a situation of semantic confusion which impeded the development of theory.[15] These are:

#### *7.1.1.1. Political Development as the Political Prerequisite of Economic Development*

This definition links Political Development solely with Economic Development.

Economists like Baram, Ellis, Buchaman and others are of the view that Political and Social condition can play a quite decisive role in impending or facilitating the Economic growth as well as Political Development. Pye found following weaknesses[16] in this Concept of Political Development :

(i) It has a negative character that is it is easier to know the ways in which performance of Political System may impend or prevent Economic growth and development than about how it can facilitate Economic growth and Development.

(ii) Such a concept of Political Development does not focus on a common set of theoretical considerations. For some it would mean no more than whether or not government is following intelligent, and Economically rational policies. For others it involves far more fundamental considerations about the basic organisation of Polity.

Problems of Political Development would, thus, vary according to the economic problems faced by each Country.

(iii) Moreover the prospects for rapid Economic development have become exceedingly dim in most of the poor countries.

(iv) In most of the underdeveloped countries people are concerned with far more than just material advancement. They are anxious about Political Development quite independent of its effects on the rate of Economic growth.

Thus, to link Political Development solely to economic events would be to ignore much that is of dramatic importance in the developing Countries.

In other words this definition is too narrow because the criterion of Political Development would be Economic capacity which means that the problem of Political Development would vary according to the particular Economic problems in question. But there is a need for independent criteria for Political Development.

#### *7.1.1.2. Political Development as the Politics typical of Industrial Societies*

This view identifies the process of Political Development with the pace of industrialisation. In other words the industrial societies whether democratic or not — set certain standards of Political Development. And they represent appropriate goals of development for all other Political systems.

This definition is nothing but the extension of the first. Pye rejects it on the ground that it ignores the role of other factors. For example reckless actions — that threaten the hold of vested interests; an appreciation of the values of orderly legal and administrative procedures; an acknowledgement that the politics is rightfully a mechanism for solving problems and not an end in itself; a stress on welfare programme and acceptance of some form of mass participation.[17]

In other words this connotation is based on an assumption and is not warranted by the differences in the Political Culture of industrial societies.

#### *7.1.1.3. Political Development as Political Modernisation*

It means that Political Development is synonymous with Political modernisation.

Some social theorists like Coleman, Deutsch and Lipset are of the view that Political Development means a study of developed or Western or industrialised Countries and their ways. In other words the advanced industralised nations are the fashion makers and pace settlers in most phases of social, economic and political life.

Pye says that such a view has its own shortcomings. It fails to distinguish between 'Western' and 'modern' concepts. It ignores the fact that the backward or developing Countries may have their own historical traditions and that they may not like to give up for the sake of merely emulating everything that is western of modern.[18]

### *7.1.1.4. Political Development as the Operation of Nation State*

Some writers point out that Political Development consists of the organisation of Political life and the performance of Political functions in accordance with the standards expected of a modern nation State. In other words Political Development is identified with nationalism.

Pye rejects this view. He is of the view that nationalism is only a necessary condition but far from being a sufficient condition to ensure Political Development. Political Development may, however, be identified with Nation-building and not merely with nation State.[19]

### *7.1.1.5. Political Development as Administrative and Legal Development*

Writers like Max Weber, Talcott Parson Stress that Political Development is intricately linked with legal and administrative orders of the Community. The establishment of effective bureaucracy is, therefore, an essential for the process of Political Development.

But Administrative Development is associated with spreading of rationality, the strengthening of secularism, legal concepts and the elevation of Technical and specialised knowledge in the direction of human affairs.

Pye is of the view that if administration is over stressed it can create imbalances in the Polity which may impend the Political Development. Moreover, this view also overlooks the problem of citizenship training and popular participation which are the essential features of Political development.[20]

Nation building comprised institutions building as well as citizenship development and both of them are essential for Political Development.

### *7.1.1.6. Political Development as Mass Mobilisation and Participation*

Some writers like Clifford, Greetz, Rupert Emerson, Bert F. Hoselitz and Eisenstandt emphasised the role of politically awakened citizens and the behaviour of people in the direction of an expanding popular participation. Extention of franchise is also taken as a mark of diffusion of the decision making process through mass participation.

Pye, has, however, taken into his consideration the disastrous effects of the politics of mass manipulation and points out that such a view of

Political Development is accompanied with danger of emotionalism or corrupting demagoguery which can weaken or sap the strength of a society.[21]

In other words this connotation is also narrow and can be misleading in itself.

#### *7.1.1.7. Political Development as the Building of Democracy*

Joseph La Palombara and J. Ronald Pennoch hold that the case of Political Development is closely connected with the building of Democracy and inculcating values of a democratic order in the mind of the people. In other words Political Development is synonymous with the establishment of democratic institutions and practices. Many people, therefore, believe that the only form of Political Development worthy of the name is the building of democracy.

Pye, however, disagrees with this view and points out that such a concept will exclude the cases of those countries where democracy is non existence. Moreover, democracy is a value laden concept while development is value free. To use the building of democracy as the key to Political Development seems as an effort to push upon others American or Western values.

Political Development is, therefore, different from democracy. The very attempt to introduce democracy can sometime be a positive liability to Development.[22]

#### *7.1.1.8. Political Development as Stability and Orderly Change*

Deutsch and Riggs are of the view that stability is legitimately linked with the concept of Political Development. They have pointed out that any form of economic or social advancement generally depend upon an environment in which uncertainty to be reduced to minimum.

Pye differs from this view as it does not answer how much order is necessary or desirable and for what purpose change should be directed. Moreover stability and change are that which occur in the mind of the middle class and at least in the societies which are better off than most of the currently underdeveloped ones. They preach to maintain status quo and thus are anti-revolutionary. Stability also leads to stagnation. But political Development calls for a somewhat more positive action.[23]

#### *7.1.1.9. Political Development as Mobilisation and Power*

James S. Coleman, Gabriel A Almond and Talcott Parsons are of the view that the Political Development can be evaluated in terms of the level or degree of absolute power which the system is able to mobilise. This view emphasises that states differ in proportion to their inherent resources base. As a result the measure of development is the degree to which they are able to maximise and realise the full potential of their given resources.

Pye criticises this view on the plea that such an explanation is applicable to the case of a democratic political system and ignores the case of development in others where the mobilisation of power is deliberately kept limited.[24]

### *7.1.1.10. Political Development as One Aspect of a Multi Dimensional Process of Social Change*

Some writers like Donald L.M. Blachmer and Daniel Learner argued that it is unnecessary and inappropriate to try to isolate completely political development from other forms of development. They further add that for sustained Political Development to take place it can only be within the contex of multi-dimensional process of social change in which no segment or dimension of the society can long lag behind.

Pye appreciates this view on the plea that here all forms of development are related. Development is much the same as modernisation, and it takes place within a historical context in which influences from outside the society impinge on the process of social change.[25]

### *7.1.1.11. Political Development As Sense of National Respect in International Sphere*

Some writers point out that development means a sense of national respect and dignity in international sphere or refers to post-nationalism era when nation state will no longer be regarded as the basic unit of political life.

Pye says nothing about this view. He neither accepts it nor rejects it.[26]

After reviewing the different connotations of Political Development Pye seeks to isolate the characteristics of Political Development which seem to be most widely held and most fundamental in the general thinking about the problems of development. He then therefore gives his own explanation of the Political Development which bears the following three characteristics.[27]

(a) Equality; *i.e.*, an attitude toward equality;

(b) Capacity; *i.e.*, capacity of political system; and

(c) Differentiation, *i.e.*, specialisation of structures, resulting in increasing functional specificity of the various political rolls within the system.

The first broadly shared characteristic is an attitude towards equality involving not only mass participation and popular involvement in political activities but also laws should be of a universalistic nature; applicable to all and more or less impersonal in their operation; all people to submit to the same dictates of law and the recruitment to political office should reflect achievement standards of performance and not the ascriptive considerations of a traditional social system. In short this characteristic implies the attitude of the people towards equality — equality among national citizens, legal order and role allocation.[28]

'Capacity' refers to the capacity of a Political System by which it can give outputs and extent to which it can affect the rest of the society and economy. It also associates with governmental performance and the conditions that directly or indirectly influence such performance. It also includes the extent to which it is capable of execution of public policy, rationality in administration, secular orientation towards policy and government's action to be guided more by deliberations and justification that seek to relate ends and means in a systematic manner.[29]

The third characteristic of Political Development is differentiation and specialisation of structure resulting in increased functional specificity of various political rolls within the system. The offices and agencies tend to have their distinct and limited functions. There should be an equivalent of a division of labour within the realm of government. But differentiation does not mean fragmentation and the isolation of the different parts of the Political system but specialisation be based on an ultimate sense of integration.[30]

Pye also makes two more points.[31] Firstly, all the three characteristics as elements of Political Development may and may not fit together and there may not be tension between the demands for equality, the requirements for capacity and the process of greater differentiation. In other words a pressure for greater equality can challenge the capacity of the system. On the other hand differentiation can reduce equality by stressing the importance of quality and specialised knowledge. Secondly, that development is not unilinear nor it is governed by sharp and distinct stages, but rather by a range of problems that may arise separately or concurrently. The structural functionalism approach popularised by Gabriel A. Almond and others also treated the Political Development as a dependent variable. By late 1960s 'Political Development' was striving for release from such a dependence.

A study of Political Development in the wider perspective of Comparative Politics show that characterstic of equality is concerned with political culture. The problems of capacity are related to the performance of the authoritative structures of government and the questions of differenciation touch mainly on the performance of the non-authoritative structure.[32] This suggests that in the ultimate analysis the problems of Political Development revolve around the relationship between the Political Culture, the authoritative structures and general Political process. These are not closely linked with each other and it is difficult to link the three to achieve coherent results.

Lucian Pye further points out that the sign of Political Development can be traced at following three different levels :

(i) with respect to population as a whole,

(ii) with respect to the level of governmental and general systematic performance; and

(iii) with respect to the organisation of the polity.

So far as first the citizens should behave no longer like a subject passively receiving orders from the higher authorities and carry them out but as active participants and contributor in shaping and sharing Political decisions. In other words the greater involvement of the masses in developing Political system. This will lead to greater sensitivity on the part of the people to the principles of equality and wider acceptance by them of universalistic laws.

Secondly with the Political Development there should develop a greater capacity in Political System to manage public affairs, control controversy or cope with popular demands.

Thirdly, a developing Political system implied greater structure differentiation, functional specificity and integration of the participating institutions.

He, therefore, advises to search for the characteristic of equality, capacity and differentiation in developing Political systems and determine the degree of their advancement.

These characteristics were subsequently described by James S. Coleman as "Developmental Syndrome".

Early writers like Lucian W. Pye were more concerned with identifying characteristics which distinguish the developing societies of the third world from the developed societies of the West. But they did not mention the stages through which societies moved toward political development or of the forces which induced and accelerated the process of Development.

Some members of the Committee on Comparative Politics of the Social Science Research Council of USA, have suggested that it may be useful to conceptualize the processes of political development as involving essentially six crisis, all of which must be successfully dealt with for a society to become a modern nation state.[33] In other words the subject of Political Development is riven with certain crisis. Lucian W. Pye has mentioned these as under :[34]

1. The Identity Crisis.
2. The Legitimacy crisis.
3. The Penetration crisis.
4. The Participation crisis.
5. Integration crisis, and
6. The distribution crisis.

The first and the most-fundamental crisis is that of achieving a common sense of identity. The people in a new state must come to recognise their national territory as being their true homeland. They must feel as individuals that their own personal identities are in part defined by their identification with their territorially delimited country. In most of the new states traditional forms of identity ranging from tribe or caste to ethnic and linguistic groups compete with the sense of larger national identity. The identity crisis also involves the resolution of the problem of traditional heritage and modern practices. As long as people feel pulled between these two identities they cannot have the firm sense of identity necessary for building a stable, modern nation state.[35]

The legitimacy crisis being closely related to the identity crisis, is the problem of achieving agreement about the legitimate nature of authority and the proper responsibilities of government. In many new states this crisis led to the emergence of Constitutional problem such as what should be the relationship between central and local authorities? What are the proper limits of the bureaucracy, or of the army in the nation's Political life? Or how much of the Colonial structure of government should be preserved in an independent state.[36]

The penetration crisis is the result of the critical problems of administration in the new state. It involves the problems of government in reaching down into the society and effecting basic policies. But to carry out significant developmental policies a government must be able to reach down to the village level and touch the daily lives of the people. The problem arises when an attempt of the government in this direction, leads to the inculcation of demands explosion that it feels hardly capable of solving.[37]

The participation crisis occurs when there is uncertainty over the appropriate rate of expansion (Popular participation) and when the influx of new participants creates serious strains on the existing institutions. The new segments of participants bring into the Political system new interests. The new issues begin to arise and the continuity of the old polity is broken. Hence the need of re-establishing the entire structure of Political relation is felt. The question, therefore, arises as to whether freedom should be allowed for various parties and groups to operate to influence the decision making process or what restrictions be imposed in order to prevent them from becoming anomic organisations and whether participation facilities should be granted for a genuine democratic purpose or just for the sake of demonstrational politics.[38]

Integration crisis covers the problems of relating politics to governmental performance. It also prepresents the effective and compatible solution of both the penetration and the participation crisis. It, therefore, deals with the extent to which the entire polity is organised as a system of interacting relationship, first among the offices and agencies seeking to make demands upon the system, and finally in the relationship between officials and articulating citizens.[39]

The distribution crisis refers to the question about how governmental powers are to be used to influence the distribution of goods, services and values throughout the society. In some cases governments seek to meet the problem by directly intervening in the distribution of wealth whereas in others the approach is to strengthen the opportunities and potentialities of the disadventaged groups.[40]

Lucian W. Pye, thus tries to show that the nature of the above mentioned crisis eventually determines the sequence of political development in different countries.

### 7.1.2. Fred W. Rigg's Concept of Developmental Trap

Fred W. Riggs in his essay 'Contemporary Political Analysis' has given his doctrine of his 'Development Trap'. While discussing it he points out that many scholars believe that the three dimensions of equality, capacity and differentiation given by Pye may not necessarily fit easily together. In fact there have been great differences between the demands for equality, the requirements for capacity and the process of greater differentiation.

The demand for greater equality may challenge the capacity of the system, Similarly greater differentiation shall affect equality. Riggs, therefore, points out that a balance must be secured between equality, capacity and differentiation. If balance is not secured, there will occur a developmental Trap. He further adds that when a Political system gets caught in a developmental Trap, it will fall into the condition of Political decay or break down.

He does not agree with Samuel P. Huntington's that institutionalisation could serve as a safe guard against this trap. On the other hand he held that institutionalisation itself could serve as a developmental trap. Greek, Chinese, Indian models of Political system, where there were too much of institution building, have broken down.

### 7.1.3. Samuel P. Huntington's Views

Samuel P. Huntington's paper on "Political Development And Political Decay" published in World Politics XVII Oct. 1965 has been further landmark in the field of Political Development. He regarded Political Development process independent of although affected by modernisation. He defined Political Development as "the institutionalisation of Political organisation and Procedures." He further adds that Political Development can occur only if Political Procedures and organisations are given the shape of institutions. According to him, the Political Development of a Society can be measured only by the degree of institutionalisation. He then defines the term institutionalisation as the process by which organisation and procedures acquire value and stability. The level of institutionalisation of any Political system can be defined by the adaptability, flexibility and coherence of its organisation and procedures. In other words the level of institutionalisation of any particular organisation or procedures can be measured by its adaptability, complexity, autonomy and coherence. Complexity here means differentiations, adaptability means flexibility and capacity of institutions is to cope with the changing circumstances.

He argues that what is going on in the Third world today is not Political Development but Political Decay. It is because of the fact that the speed of modernisation in these countries is so fast that the process of institutionalising of values lags far behind. That is the modernisation brings about social and economic mobilisation. Social mobilization and Political participation are rapidly increasing in Asia, Africa and Latin America. These processes are in turn directly responsible for the deterioration of Political institutions in these nations.[41] Because the institutions for the operation of their relationship are not established. He further argues that mobilisation refers to change of residence of occupation, of social setting, of face association, of institutions role and way of acting, of experiences and expectations and personal memories, habits and needs. Thus, there occurs a direct conflict between mobilisation and institutionalisation. For example with the spread of education, revenues for employment should also be created. But it is not being done. Similarly if universal adult franchise is introduced, there should also be creation of institutions for giving new elites a chance to participate in decision making process. Whereas there may be a few positions and roles which are already dominated by traditional elites. New positions are not created with the result that aspirations of the new enfranchised people are not fulfilled. In many developing states even the decline of Party organisations is reflected with the emergence of charismatic leaders who personalised power and weaken institutions which might limit that power. In Turkey, Pakistan and Burma, the Republican People's Party, Muslim League and AFPFL respectively deteriorated and military intervention eventually ensured. In party organisations and bureaucracies, marked increases in corruptions often accompanied significant declines in effectiveness of government services. Particularistic groups — Tribal, ethnic, religions — frequently reassessed themselves and further undermined the authority and coherence of Political institutions.[42]

The Political system, therefore, loses its legitimacy. The newly mobilised, educated and enfranchised people when lose their trust in the impartiability of the institutions and justice of the system, they try to regulate the system in their own way. All this led to the emergence of mass politics. Moreover, a Political System whose level of institutionalisation is low, cannot survive in the face of growing urge for the political participation. This also results in Political instability the alround frustration of the people ultimately paves the way to military coup. *Coups d'etat* and military interventions in politics are one index of low level of political institutionalisation. They occur where Political institutions lack autonomy and coherence. Huntington pointed out that eleven of twelve modernising states outside Latin America which became independent before World War II experienced *Coups d'etat* or attempted Coups after World War II. Of twenty states which got independence between World War II and 1959, fourteen had Coups or Coup attempts by 1963. Of twenty-four states which became independent between 1960 and 1963, seven experienced coups or attempted coups before the end of 1963.[43]

In short the developing nations which do not allow institutions to grow proportionately with the pace of modernisation are not going for Political development but for Political decay.

He further argues that even the increase of literacy rate and education do bring more Political instability. For example Burma, Cylone, Republic of Korea etc., are highly literate but no one of them is a model of Political stability.

Although literacy stimulates democracy yet with 75% literacy rate, Cuba was the first Country in Latin America to establish Communist government. Same was the case in Kerala state of India. Institutional decay has, therefore, become a common phenomenon of the modernising or developing Countries.[44]

In some developing nations like Pakistan and the Sudan, institutional evolution has been unbalanced. The Civil and military bureaucracies are more highly developed than the political parties and the military has strong incentives to move into the institutional vacuum on the input side of the political system and to attempt to perform interest aggregations functions. This pattern is also common in Latin America.[45]

In short Huntington is of the view that the third world countries are heading towards Political Decay.

### 7.1.4. Eisenstadt's Concept of Political Break Down

Eisenstadt in his essay on 'Breakdown of Modernisation' differs from Huntington. He is of the view that the developing Countries alongwith the start of process of modernisation also set up Western type of institutions and refined procedures of work. This has been done with the belief that these institutions would help in the process of modernisation. Modernisation according to him involves "major cluster of old social, economic and psychological commitments are eroaded and broken and people would be come available for new patterns of socialisation and behaviour." Thus, in this process old loyalties, old groups, old values, old ways of living and thinking change to new ones.

But most of the developing societies are incapable of providing institutional framework that could absorb these changes. It, therefore, leads to political breakdown.

By breakdown he means that the institutions copied from the West failed to cope with the changing environment. As a result there arose stagnant situation, which invited revolution or military coup. But the political breakdown does not necessarily mean a stop of the process of economic or social development. These processes actually continued or are made to continue to consolidate the position of the military regime.

### 7.1.5. David E. Apter's Views

Political Development has several stages[46] and needs and problem of each stage are unique. The nature and degree of Political control naturally vary. Following Apter's view we can broadly distinguish between two stages of developmental process. These are Pre-industrial and Post-industrial stages. In a developing society, where a broad-based industrial infrastructure does not exists the political problem of controlling and integrating the process becomes increasingly crucial. The passage to industrialisation, therefore, needs an extraordinarily organised Political system with in-built capacity of maintaining a high-degree control and cohesion. Apter, therefore, suggests the adoption of high control system for a successful transition to industrialisation.[47]

Once the industrial phase of development is completed, the perspective is bound to change. In the industrialised societies there is need of increasing generation and use of new knowledge. Moreover the need in post-industrial societies is for wider devolution of authority, great decentralisation of high-control systems, reducing direct government control, a noncoersive, and high information situation and a government playing a mediating and coordinating role.[48]

### 7.1.6. J.P. Nettl's Views

J.P. Nettl is of the view that Political Development has four implications such as set of definitional priorities, a set of values, interconnection between developed and developing countries, recognition of an implicit rank order of development.

Set of definitional priorities constituted development as a process and in the concept of political development. There is hesitant and discordant division of political theories into social, economic and Political Priorities and the see saw battle between historical analogy and abstract models of utilitarian or rational emphasis. So far as set of values he says that in political development so many value loaded terms had been used that utter confusion being created. But Political Development should be made as value free. He pointed out that whole concept and all terms used in Political Development referred to the Western type of development. But the weaknesses in the Western systems have also been felt. This has some time created hatred in the minds of the people of developing countries against that of American. He is also of the view that there should also be interconnection between developed and developing Countries. The Concept of Political Development should be such that it should suit both the developed and developing nations. The recognition of an implicit rank order of Political Development means that in Political Development due stress should be laid on capabilities of Political system.

### 7.1.7. Leonard Binder's Crises and Sequences In Political Development

Leonard Binder in his book 'Crises and Sequences in Political Development' has referred to 'Political Development' as "Changes" in the type and style of politics. He also regards the three concepts of equality, capacity and differentiation as a shorthand description of the syndrom of modernity.[49] He gives the following five characteristics[50] of Political Development :

1. Change of identity-from the religious to the ethnic and from the parochial to the social;
2. Change in legitimacy from transcendental to immanent sources;
3. Change in Political participation from elite to mass and from family to group.
4. Change of distribution-from status and privilege to achievement.
5. Change in the degree of administrative and legal penetration into social structure and out of the remote regions of Country.

The difficulty is that even the recent writers have not succeeded in freeing themselves from the earlier conceptual framework. The Political realities of the developing societies still continue to elude the western scholarships. As a result the Concept of Political Development continued to be vague, faint, foggy and fuzzy.[51]

But one should not forget that development is a total concept and Political development is to be viewed as but a part of the more encompassing process such as economic development, social development etc.[52] Thus, economic development, social development and political development are closely interrelated, characterised by constant buying and selling" between them. As everywhere in developing society the system comes face to face with the politics of scarcity, it happens to embody and reflect the deeper economic pressures Political Development, there emerges as a dependent variable in the social system.[53]

### 7.1.8. Alfred Diament's Views

He defines 'Political development' as a process by which a political system acquires an increasing capacity to sustain successfully and continuously, new types of goals and demands and the creation of new types of organisation.[54] The definition emphasis that Political Development is a process and whatever characteristics may appear to be acceptable must refer to the viability of a political system in effectively responding to the tentions, challenges and demands of its own framework as well as the environment.[55]

### 7.1.9. Illchman and Uphoff's View

Illchman and Uphoffs view in their book "The Political Economy of Change" pointed out that the new approach of Political economy has premited a number of definitions of the term 'Political Development." It may be defined as :[56]

(a) Increasing level of political solvency;
(b) increasing capacity to meet and induce changing and expanding demands;

(c) Increasing capacity of both generating and processing demands of

(d) increasing capacity to cover an increase in the number of Political enterpreneurs.

They maintain that political development is a function of Political and administrative infrastructure. Political infrastructure consists of Political parties, elections, ideologies and development plans and is used in the mobilisation of support and resources for acquiring and maintaining authority. Its primary functions are, therefore, to provide inputs for policy allocations. Whereas administrative infrastructure is necessary for the exercise of authority. It is responsible for the implementation of policy allocations that is for handling regime's outputs.[57]

### 7.1.10. Marxist View on Political Development

There is, however, an altogether different view point that can be inferred from Marxist social thought. From this perspective Political Development is an integral part of stages of social development.[58] Keeping in mind historical facts, Marx held that successive socio-economic formations emerged at different stages. Each formation is quantitatively different from its preceding one. Political Development ultimately would mean replacement of the exploitative state structure by a participative and equalitarian social formation of the highest order.[59]

## 7.2. INDICATORS OF POLITICAL DEVELOPMENT

Various attempts have been made to evolve indicators, of varying reliability of Political Development. But each such exercise has its own limitations and each of its index is, therefore, subject of criticism. World Handbook of Political and Social Indicator has mentioned eighteen indicators of Political development. However, the tentative indicators[60] are as under :

1. National integration;
2. Voter turnout;
3. Popular participation in governmental decision-making process.
4. Autonomous interest groups;
5. Mass, media circulation, particularly in regional languages;
6. Political and administrative decentralisation;
7. Autonomy of local governmental institutions;
8. Expansion and autonomy of non-bureaucratic sector of society.
9. Duration of legislative sessions.

10. Number and effectiveness of Watchdog organisations overseeing the government and the bureaucracy.
11. Autonomy of quasi-governmental sector *i.e.*, Public undertaking, institutions.
12. Stable Party system characterised by inner democratic functioning.
13. Political Competitiveness.
14. Consensual politics.
15. Tolerance for dissent and protest.
16. Broadening social base of the Political elite.
17. Openness in public administration.
18. Provision for redressal of citizen's grievances.
19. Constituency service by legislators.
20. Education.
21. Urbanisation.
22. Freedom of the Press.
23. Anomic movements within certain limits.
24. Honest, non-partisan election machinery.
25. Independence of judiciary.
26. Apolitical character of the army.

## 7.3. NEGATIVE INDICATORS OF POLITICAL DEVELOPMENT

S.R. Maheshwari has also mentioned some negative indicators of Political Development.[61] These are :

1. Coups.
2. Riots
3. Number of Political Prisoners in Jails.
4. Political assassinations
5. Manipulated defection of legislators.

## 7.4. CONCLUSION

Although a host of political scientists have studied and written about the Political Development, yet there is no Universally accepted theory of Political Development or any pre-determined law of development. No society in the world can claim to be its model to which others may move. The theorists, however, helped in drawing attention of the world to the problem of political Development of the third world nations. Moreover, the scope of empirical political investigations has also considerably widened and made more broad based. Thus, the study of political

Development has helped considerably in orientation of several new theories in the field of Political investigations.

## REFERENCES


1. Wiarda, Howard J.: Directions in Comparative Politics; West View Press — Boulder, London, 1985, p. 15.
2. Ray, Amal Bhattacharya, Mohit : Political Theory; The World Press Pvt. Ltd., Calcutta, 1983, p. 223.
3. Wiarda, Howard J. : Directions in Comparative Politics; op.cit., p. 15.
4. Ashraf, Ali, Sharma L.N : Political Sociology; University Press Pvt. Ltd., New Delhi 1983 p. 120.
5. Maheshwari, S.R.: Comparative Government and Politics; Lakshmi Narain Aggarwal, Agra 1985, p. 186.
6. Kebschull, Harvey G. : (Ed) Politics in Transitional Societies; Appleton — Century — Crofts Educational Division Meredith Corporation, New York 1968, p. 285.
7. Bhushan, Vidya : Comparative Politics; Atlantic Publishers and Distributors, Darya Ganj, New Delhi 1988, p. 10.
8. Wiarda, Howard J. : *Directions in Comparative Politics; op.cit.*, p. 22.
9. *Ibid.*
10. Pye, Lucian W. : *Aspects of Political Development*; Amerioid Publishing Co. Pvt. Ltd., New Delhi 1966, p. 32.
11. Ray, Amal, Bhatacharya, Mohit : *Political Theory; op.cit.*, p. 226.
12. *Ibid.*
13. Pye, Lucian W : *Aspects of Political Development; op.cit.*, p. 32.
14. Masheshwari, S.R : *Comparative Politics; op.cit.*, p. 187.
15. Pye, Lician W : *Aspects of Political Development; op.cit.*, p. 33.
16. *Ibid.*, pp. 33-34.
17. *Ibid.*, pp. 34-35.
18. *Ibid.*, pp. 36-37.
19. *Ibid.*, pp. 37-38.
20. *Ibid.*, pp. 38-39.
21. *Ibid.*, pp. 40 -
22. *Ibid.*, p. 41.
23. *Ibid.*, p. 42.
24. *Ibid.*, pp. 43-44.
25. *Ibid.*, p. 44.
26. *Ibid.*, p. 45.
27. Pye, Lucian W. and Verba, Sideny : *Political Culture and Political Development, op.cit.*, p.
28. Pye, Lucian W : *Aspects of Political Development; op.cit.*, pp. 45-46.
29. *Ibid.*, pp. 46-47.

30. *Ibid.*, p. 47.
31. Johari, J.C. : *Comparative Politics;* Sterling Publishers Pvt. Ltd., New Delhi 1980, p. 102.
32. *Ibid.*
33. Kebschull, Harvey G. : *Politics in Transitional Societies*; Appleton — Century — Crofts Meredith Corporation, New York 1988, p. 285.
34. *Ibid.*, p. 285.
35. *Ibid.*, pp. 285-86.
36. *Ibid.*, p. 286.
37. *Ibid.*, pp. 286-87.
38. *Ibid.*, p. 287.
39. *Ibid.*
40. *Ibid.*
41. Kebschull, Harvey G. : *Politics in Transitional Societies; op.cit.*, p. 290.
42. *Ibid.*
43. *Ibid.*, p. 292.
44. *Ibid.*, p. 295.
45. *Ibid.*
46. Apter, David E. : *Introduction to Political Analysis*; Prentice Hall of India, New Delhi, 1978, p. 469.
47. Ray, Amal, Bhattacharya, Mohit : *Political Theory, op.cit.*, p. 228.
48. *Ibid.*
49. Binder, Leonard: *Crises and Sequences in Political Development*, Princeton University Press, Princeton 1971, p. 66.
50. *Ibid.*
51. Maheshwari, S. R. : *Comparative Government and Politics, op. cit.*, p. 189.
52. *Ibid.*
53. *Ibid.*
54. Ashray Ali, Sharma, L. N. : *Political Sociology, op. cit.*, p. 129.
55. *Ibid.*
56. Illchman, W., Uphoff, N.: *The Political Economy of Change*, University of California, Berkely 1969, p. 8.
57. Ashray Ali, Sharma, L. N. : *Political Sociology, op. cit.*, p. 131.
58. Ray, Amal, Bhattacharya, Mohit : *Political Theory, op. cit.*, p. 229.
59. *Ibid.*
60. The whole list of tentative indicators have been adopted from S. R. Maheshwari book on, *Comparative Government and Politics, op. cit.*, pp. 191-192.
61. *Ibid.*

# 8

# Political Elites

If we carefully study the working of any political system — whether primitive or modern, democratic or totalitarian — we find that every society is ruled by a microscopic minority. That is by those who possess the qualities necessary to rule or to exercise full social and political powers. The political philosophers, from time to time, have also recommended rule by a special class to fit into, the ideal political system they prescribed. Plato's ideal state was entrusted to a small group of philosophers brought up and educated *i.e.,* philosopher kings.[1] In other words Plato's ideal state was entrusted to a small group of the ruling elite—the philosopher kings. While talking of dictatorship of the proletariat, Comrade Lenin — a socialist philosopher meant actually the rule by the Communist Party elite.[2] The increasing complexity of the business of government in classical democracy has destroyed the myth that democracy is based on the will of the majority or on the will of the people.[3] Actually, it is not people but the few who rule with the consent of the majority.[4] Ball rightly points out that there is agreement that all forms of governments are mere disguise to cover minority control.[5] Even the majority cannot control this ruling minority. Thus, in every society a minority makes the major decisions.[6] The origins of the Elitist theory are in Plato's thoughts and writings but its elaboration is in the thought of two leading Italian political sociologists, Vilfred Pareto and Gaetam Mosca.[7] Eliote Theory, therefore, refers to a body of thought which seeks to explain the nature and role of groups in which decision making power is concentrated. Robert Michaels; James Burnham; Milovan Djilas; C. Wright Mills; Harold D. Lasswell etc. have also sought to prove that there may exist in any society a minority of population which takes the major decisions in the society.

The Elite theorists believe in the theory of inequality of mankind. In other words they believe that whereas all men are equal in the eyes of God, they are not equal in the eyes of men. The Elites, therefore, are the chosen element of the people, who come to top position either by their ability or economic status, control of economic and natural resources and even physical strength.

## 8.1. POLITICAL ELITE—CONCEPT

In seventeenth century the word 'Elite' was referred to 'commodities of particular excellence'.[8] Later on it referred to superior social groups like erack military units or the higher ranks of the nobility.[9] But this term did not enter the vocabulary of political science in Europe until the 19th century.[10] In other words this term did not become widely used in social and political writing until late in the nineteenth century in Europe[11]. In the beginning of 20th century, this term was therefore seldom used by social and political writers. The use of this term in United Kingdom and in U.S.A. however began only in the thirties.[12] Some of the theorists traced out this concept to the philosophers like Plato[13] and Aristotle. Plato talked of the rule of a philosopher king—a person who was gifted with reason and capacity to rule. Whereas Aristotle held that some persons were fit to rule while others fit to be ruled.

Elite at present consists of those persons who sit at the top of society over others by virtue of their superior qualities. It is a name given to a group emerged in every walk of life, to a position of leadership and influence at every social level. In other words Elite consists of those successful persons who rise to top in every occupation and stratum of society. For example, there are Elite of business (*i.e.,* Business Elites); Elite of mechanics (*i.e.,* Mechanics Elites); Elite of lawyers (*i.e.,* Lawyer Elites); Elite of Thieves (*i.e.,* Thief Elites); Elite of politics (*i.e.,* Political Elites); Elite of Economics[14] (*i.e.,* Economic Elites) etc.

The elites are, therefore always in minority yet they take all major decisions and ensure that these are implemented. They command social respect, prestige, status, position and authority and control all the sources of distribution.[15] Moreover each one from among the elite tries to pose that he represents the feelings of the group to which he belongs.[16] The concept of Elite is, therefore, used to describe certain fundamental features of organised social life. The basic factor is that a minority within a social collectivity—society, state, party, occupation, business, etc.—exercises a preponderant influence.[17] The political Elites are, therefore, those who come to prominence in the political field by virtue of their superior qualities.

## 8.2. THEORIES OF THE POLITICAL ELITES

The theories of the elites have been a dominant theme in the history of Western thought since the turn of the last century[18] in general and in the united states in the years following the world war second[19] in particular. They have attracted the attention of the political scientists and the sociologists all over the world, especially those who are interested in the studies of distribution of power, influence and decision-making authority in the society.

No single universally accepted elite theory has emerged as yet. These are therefore elite theories. Some studies mention that there is a single power elite drawn from economic class which provides leadership to other elements in the political community.[20] Other reject this view and favour a pluralist model where power is diffused among many interest groups competing for it. Many other theories based on a fusion of the elitist and pluralist theories.[21]

Classical texts on the elite though believe that in each society there is a single cohesive Elite group which dominate the affairs of the society and not controlled by any other group or groups. This group comprised politicians plus civil servants plus economists. In other words classical writers believed in the monistic view of Elitism *i.e.*, a single Elite group.

Contemporary writers of Elite theory, on the other hand, believe that there exist many elite groups in a society and leadership emerges because of competition among them. That is there exists a competition among members of Elite groups. In simple words they believe in the pluralistic version of Elite theory.

But the common points in both of the views is that there exists a minority of people who influence decisions and control powers. It has, however, been argued that these theories are not only relevant but vital for understanding of power structure and power processes in any country of whatever variety it might be.

The core of the elitism is that in any society there is and must be a minority of the population which makes the major decisions in the society and rule over the majority. This minority, called political class or governing elite includes the wider circle of those who influence governmental decisions as well as those who formally decide politics. This minority gains its dominant position by means beyond ordinary elections. Its influence may be due to its embodying certain social or religious values hereditary or certain personal qualities.[22]

### 8.2.1. Vilfred Pareto's Theory of Elite or Views About Political Elite[23]

Pareto proceeded with the basic assumption that individuals invariably differ from one another in their basic abilities. In other words there are biological differences which resulted in inequalities of men and thus makes inequality inevitable in the society. Some individual are, therefore, superior in their attributes while others possess inferior abilities. The former class of superior ability constitutes the Elite. They are known for their qualities of head and heart; capacity to initiate, execute and plan; and dominate all sections of society — social, economic and political in one way or the other.[24]

For Pareto, elite is a value free term. It includes all those who score highest on scales measuring any social value or commodity such as power, riches, knowledge etc. But by the term elite he means the strongest, the most energetic, and most capable — for all good as well evil. Though he was mostly dealing with economic and political Elites, yet he was ready to extend the use of the term to religion (the most holy); to art (the most artistic), and to ethics (the most virtuous). In other words Elite means all those who constitute the higher stratum in society.[25]

He points out that the higher stratum of the society comprised of two classes — Governing Elite and Non-governing Elite. Governing Elites are comprising of individuals who directly or indirectly play a considerable part in government. Whereas Non-governing Elites are comprised of the rest *i.e.* masses.

Pareto is convinced that the study of historical change very largely revolves round the study of Elites. He further points out that the events and decisions among the elites have more consequences for the history of a society than events and decisions among its great masses. But he was not concerned with non-governing Elites, who might have influence on the government.

In the opening chapter of his monograph "The Rise And Fall Of The Elites", Pareto mentions several laws or propositions. Out of them first two are most important. Firstly, he points out that the great part of human actions have their origin not in logical reasoning but in sentiments. Secondly, man although impelled to act by non-logical motives yet he ties his action logically to certain principles. That he invents a posteriori in order to justify his actions.[26]

He addes that psychologically all human actions are the combination of 'Residus' and "Derivations". Pareto locates six residues, which means the major motivation of action. These are :[27]

1. *Combination i.e.,* the tendency to invent and embark on adventures. In other words the quality of cunningness like that of fox.
2. *Persistence of preservation i.e.,* the tendency to consolidate and make secure. In other words to have strength, the quality to fight, force like lion.
3. *Expressiveness i.e.,* tendency to make feelings manifest through symbolisation.
4. *Sociability* tendency to affiliate with others.
5. *Integration* tendency to maintain a good self-image; and
6. *Sex* tendency to see social events in erotic terms.

He is of the view that the first two residues are dominant in an Elite. Both of them are shown in the following table.

| Dominant Residue | Economic Elite | Political Elite |
|---|---|---|
| Combination | Speculator (S) | Fox |
| Preservation | Rentier (R) | Lion |

The main point of the discussion is that by means of the two residues *i.e.,* combination — the quality of cunningness of fox and preservation — the lion's like persistence or use of force, Elite keeps himself in power.

But in order to rationalise or justify his actions (or use of force) he takes recourse to derivations or myths which help him to dupe the masses.[28]

Derivations according to him, are the ways by which actions are made to assume the appearance of logical actions. They are expressed mostly through speeches. Pareto, has, however, classified derivations in the following four categories[29]:

1. Assertion,
2. Appeals to authority,
3. Appeals to sentiments or principles, and
4. Verbal proofs.

### Mixed Residues

Some time first residue *i.e.,* cunningness cannot manage the crisis and let the class rule break down. Similarly, some time second residue *i.e.,* mere use of force cannot help the ruling class to rule longer. The ruling class, therefore, make use of mixture of the two residues *i.e.,* the quality of combination and quality of preservation to keep itself in power. Pareto, however, does not mention about the proportion of mixture.

## Circulation of Elites

While pointing out that "History is a graveyard of aristocracies" he has propounded his well known concept, "The Circulation of Elites". 'Circulation of elites' may refer to a process in which individuals circulate between the elite and the non-elite strata. It may also refer to a process in which one elite is replaced by another elite. Pareto, therefore, not only distinguished between elites and non-elites but also suggested the idea of a circulation of Elites in which one elite replaces another as aristocracies decay or regenerate. There might also be mobility from a non-elite stratum to an elite stratum or governing class of people who rule directly or indirectly.[30] This simply means that new men of money or power replace the old ones. In other words consolidators replace innovators. In the same manner innovators sometimes replace consolidators. There is, therefore, constant change from conservatism to radicalism and so on. He has put this idea in a phrase of Marx's dictum of history "The history of man is the history of the continuous replacement of elites — as one ascends, another declines.[31]" Pareto accounts for this process. He has listed among the causes of this historical change, war and differential fertility.[32] War tends to kill a higher proportion of elites than of the general populations. Elites families also tend to die out, since they have fewer children than the masses. But the most serious cause of circulation of elites occurs when the elites are consisted of innovators only or consolidators only. In such situation elites are unable to meet effectively normal exigencies of life. In other words Elites must sometimes embark on innovating actions and sometime on consolidating actions. When they fail to do so, they are replaced by new elites.

An imbalance between innovation and consolidation can be avoided by an open recruitment into the elite. It is particularly important that elites predominantly comprised consolidators admit intelligent innovators in its stratum. Failure to pursue this policy leads to difficulties and even to revolution. According to Pareto "Revolution come about through accumulation in the higher strata of society—either because of a slowing down in class circulation, or from other causes of decadent elements no longer possessing the residues suitable for keeping them in power, and shrinking from the use of force; while meantime in the lower strata of society elements of superior quality are coming to the force, possessing residues suitable for exercising the function of government and willing enough to use force".[33]

The circulation of elites is almost always aided and accompanied by rising religions — humanitarian sentiments. In such a climate, the existing elite becomes softer, milder, more humane and less apt to defend its own power.[34] If the innovators already dominate at such a stage; it spells doom for the elites. The rising elite is also subject to speech habits justifying its drive to power (derivations) and these are also moulded by the same rising religions — humanitarian sentiments.[35] But after victory, the elite becomes more rigid and more exclusive.[36] Thus the wheel takes full turn. The new elite is then established and the process can start all over again.[37]

Pareto presents another dimension of the 'Circulation of Elite'. He regards elites as representing a definite social interests. The circulation of elites, therefore, occurs with the decline of established interests and the emergence of new ones in the society.[38] He observes, "In the beginning military, religious and commercial aristocracies and plutocracies must have constituted parts of the governing elite and sometimes have made up the whole of it". He then mentions the rise of new elites such as industrial workers producing a trade union elites.[39]

All elites are, therefore, prone to decay and downfall. Originally forceful and decisive Elites become ineffective in course of time as a result of their easy living and addiction to power. A new elite group then arises and replaces the old one.

### 8.2.2. Gaetano Mosca's Theory of Elite

Gaetano Mosca, another Italian scholar, further developed the theory of Elite in his book "The Ruling Class".[40] He fervently believed that regardless of their outer form, all governments were essentially ruled by a minority. Mosca uses the term elite in a restricted sense and by it he means the ruling class. While explaining his fundamental idea, Mosca emphasised "Among the constant facts and tendencies that are to be found in all political organisms, one is so obvious that it is apparent to most casual eye. In all societies — from societies that are very meagrely developed and have barely attained the dawnings of civilization, down to the most advanced and powerful societies — two classes of people appear — a class that rules and a class that is ruled. The first class, always the less numerous, performs all political functions, monopolizes power and enjoys the advantages that power brings, whereas the second, the more numerous class, is directed and controlled by the first, in a manner that is now more or less legal, now more or less arbitrary and violent".[41] He further adds that the second class supplies the first, in appearance at least with material means of subsistence and with the instrumentalities that are essential to the vitality of the political organism".[42] He further points out that in all countries the management of public affairs is in the hands of a minority of influential persons.[43]

He, therefore, refers to two political facts. Firstly, in every political organisation, there is one individual who is chief among the leaders of the ruling class under special circumstances two or three may discharge the functions of supreme control. He or they may not hold power according to law.[44] Secondly, in every political organism, pressures arising from the discontent of the masses who are governed, from the persons by which they are swayed, exert a certain amount of influence on the policies of the ruling, the political class.[45]

Mosca explains the rule of the minority over the majority by the fact that the former is organised, obeys single impulse and thus its domination over the unorganised minority is inevitable.[46] It is difficult for the majority to organise. The larger the political community, the more difficult will it be for the majority to organise itself for reaction against the minority. The ruling minorities, on the other hand, are distinguished from the masses by the qualities they possess. Either they have certain material, intellectual or even more superiority of they are the heirs of individuals who possessed such qualities. They are, therefore, most influential in the society in which they live.[47]

In the primitive societies, military valour and in advanced societies wealth opened access to the political class. Wealth produces power just as political power has been producing wealth. To be rich is to become powerful.[48] Other agencies for exerting social influence are personal publicity, good education, specialized training, high rank in church, public administration and army. All these are always readier of access to the rich than to the poor.

Mosca further points out that all political classes tend to become hereditary in fact if not in law. Political forces seem to possess a quality — the force of inertia (a physics term). They have a tendency to stabilise themselves. This is why certain families develop the quality for manning important offices and continue to be dominating for a long time. Even in democratic elections successful candidates show certain hereditary characteristics. Mosca points out that is why we frequently see in English, French and Italian parliaments, the sons, grandsons, brothers, nephews and son-in-laws of members and deputies of ex-members and ex-deputies.[49] Mosca says that a hereditary caste, after gaining a dominating defacto status turns into a dejuri power holder.[50]

Like Pareto, Mosca also says that governing class justifies its actual exercise of power by resting it on some universal moral principles.[51]

**Circulation of Elites**

Mosca also talks of circulation of Elites. He says "The whole history of civilized mankind comes down to a conflict between the tendency of dominant elements to monopolize political power and transmit possession of it by inheritance, and the tendency toward a dislocation of old forces and an emergence of new forces, and this conflict produces an unending ferment of endosmosis and exosmosis between the upper classes and certain portions of the lower".[52]

While analysing why and when this situation arises, Mosca points out," It will happens as soon as there is a shift in the balance of political forces, when a need is felt that capacities different from the old should assert themselves in the management of the state; when the old capacities lose some of their importance or changes in their distribution occur, then the manner in which the ruling class is constituted changes."[53] Moreover, if a new source of wealth develops in a society, if the practical importance of the knowledge grows, if an old religion declines or a new current of ideas spread, then the ruling class faces serious chances of dislocation. Commerce with foreign people, forced emigration, discoveries and war are also the causes which create new poverty and new wealth, disseminate new knowledge, and bring in new moral, intellectual and religious currents.[54]

The political class also undergoes changes in its membership, ordinarily by the recruitment of new individual members from the lower strata of the society, some times by the incorporation of new social groups and occasionally by the complete replacement of the established elite by a 'counter Elite' as exists in revolution.[55]

Mosca, however, takes a moodest view of the use of force and prefers change through persuation. He, therefore, advises the governing Elites to bring about gradual alteration in the political system in order to make it conform to changes in the public opinion.

He was also in favour of multiplicity of social forces. He also introduced the concept of sub-Elites comprising civil servants, manager of industries, scientists and scholars and treats it as vital element in society.[56]

### 8.2.3. Robert Michael's Theory of Elite

Robert Michaels — an Italian sociologist and disciple of Mosca — reveals another dimension of the Elite phenomenon in his work "Political Parties — A Sociological Study of Modern Democracy".[57]

He made a deep study of the European Socialist political parties and trade union, especially German Socialist Party and found them oligarchic in their power dynamics.[58] He argues that democracy is unconceivable without organisation. In a complex society people can, effectively voice demands only by joining together and forming organisations. But organisations are antithetical to democracy. Rank and file cannot take decision because issues are complex and they demand specialized knowledge which they do not possess. Decisions are, therefore, left to the Executive Committee and people are left with no say except to fall in line with the decision of small groups. Organisations, therefore, invariably produce oligarchy.

This is what he calls the 'iron law of oligarchy'. In other words he purposes a law governing all social organisations and calls it as "The iron law of oligarchy."[59]

Michaels begins with the observations that 'Democracy is inconceivable without organisations.'[60] He adds that not only organisational ability grants power, but even the very structure of any organised society gives rise to an elite.

He tried to test his hypothesis by examining the organisations, which would be expected to offer an outstanding counter example to this law. He analysed the structure of decision making in the socialist parties of Europe, and in particular, the German socialist party in the year before the war. He found that these parties though committed to democracy and socialism, yet allowed power and privilege to a small group of leaders who controlled the party organisation.[61]

He further insists that mass members cannot control the large scale organisations of the modern age. The leadership is, therefore, technically indispensible. He adds that at the outset leaders arise spontaneously and their functions are accessory and gratuitous. Soon after they become professional leaders and in this second stage of development they are stable and irremovable.

According to him the following two set of factors are responsible for the phenomenon of concentration of power in the hands of mling minority :

(i) Organisation; and

(ii) Psychological.

So far as organisational cause is concerned, he points out that a political party campaigning to gain power needs to organise its vote, canvass supporters, supply information for speakers, raise contributions, attend to party's financial structure and its legal standing. It needs to establish a coordinated policy line for the sake of consistency and solidarity. All these activities require expertise which the mass of men may not have the aptitude to develop and for which they lack the leisure.

The leadership, therefore, controls the party funds and the channels of communication. It selects parliamentary candidates and dispenses other kinds of patronage. Its activities are news, publicized even by the opposition press. The leadership works to gain the support of non-party members or those who are on the margin of the party to ensure electoral success. To gain their allegiance, the party moderates its dogma and provide continuity of leadership to give the assurance of stability.[62]

All the above mentioned factors strengthened the hands of two groups — (party bureaucrates, more interested in power than in principles) and the party's parliamentary representatives, (who owe their electoral success to their electoral appeal).

While referring to psychological cause, he mentions that the majority is apathetic towards public matter. Interests and influence in the party are presented by pyramid — Voluntary party officials, a large stratum of those attending party meetings, a large stratum enrolled members and finally — a large number of non-members who merely vote for the party.[63]

Majority is, therefore, too glad to have others to take on political responsibilities even the revolutionary agitation has to be undertaken by a small minority on their behalf. Such apathy, submissiveness and difference, hence, provides ideal conditions for the few with the interest and organisational ability to lead.[64]

Michaels, therefore, insists that the rule of oligarchy is in the same sense applicable to the all organisations including the organisation of the state. He, however, disposes of democracies favourably as they allow competition between several oligarchical structures.[65]

### 8.2.4. James Burnham's Theory of Elite

Under the impact of Pareto and Mosca a large number of studies have been made by the scholars. The hypotheses with regard to Elites were tested, modified and corrected by them with reference to different contexts. James Burnham is one of those belonged to first category. He propounded his views about elite theory in his book "The Managerial Revolution" published in London in 1941.

He agrees with Marx that control of production gives rise to political powers, social prestige as well as wealth and also that capitalism is in decline.[66] But his explanation for the cause of decline of capitalism as well as his preception of the future set up are different.[67]

According to him capitalists were originally both managers and owners of their own enterprises. When these grew into a large and complex organisations, these were left to the professional managers. After sometimes the capitalists did not even finance. Rather they were being fed upon the profits without contributing to production. Thus, in the end the capitalist ruling class was displaced by the technically indispensible managerial elite.[68]

Making similar projections about trends in government and in public administration he predicts that government will increasingly be a matter of executive action rather than legislation. And, thus, it will be run by bureaucrates,[69] whether civil servants in Britain, the state planner in the erstwhile U.S.S.R. or the heads of executives bureaus in the U.S.A.

### 8.2.5. Milovan Djilas' Theory of Elite

Milovan Djilas' Yugoslav critic of totalitarian communism — developed his opinion about elite in his book "The New Class".[70] He describes how after the Bolshevik Revolution in Russia, a new class previously unknown to history has been formed.

This new class consisted of the leaders of the Communist Party, who controlled the party organisation and enjoyed complete power and special privileges and economic preference because of administrative monopoly they hold.[71]

The communist party leaders made up the Elite and used the party as an instrument of their own power and privilege. This class grew stronger, while the party grew weaker.[72] This was the inescapable fate of every communist party in power. The new class arose from the proletariat and worked as the champion of that class. This class obtained its power, privileges, ideology and its customs from one specific form of ownership *i.e.,* collective ownership which this class administered and distributed in the name of nation and society.[73] Its chief weapons were industrialisation and development of production.

All changes initiated by the communist chiefs were dictated primarily by the interests and aspirations of the new class which like every social group lived, reacted and defended itself and advanced with the aim of increasing its power.

Having achieved industrialisation, the new class could do nothing more than strengthened its brute force, political as well as administrative hegemony.[74]

He, however, bitterly predicted that "when the new class leaves the historical scene — and that must happen — there will be less sorrow over its passing than there was for any other class before it".[75]

### 8.2.6. C. Wright Mills' Theory of Elite

C. Wright Mills — an American Sociologist offers a less ambitious theory of elite, based on distribution of power in the democratically governed U.S.A. He developed his concept of Elite in his book "The Power Elites" published in London in 1959. The period of his study was 1950s.[76]

He does not believe in the psychological basis of elite rule but explains it in absolutely institutional terms. He also does not agree that the members of elite necessarily possess superior traits. Rather he stressed that the structure of the institutions in a society is such that those occupying position in the institutional hierarchy are of key significance and those who are holding positions command in them hold the levers of power in the society.[77] In other words he believes that power in a society is attached to institutions and defines the power elite "as those who occupy the command posts".[78]

According to him the corporation, the military and the federal government are three such institutions in U.S.A. and the occupants of top positions in these three institutions constitute three Elites. He, thus, distinguishes three major Elites in the U.S.A. — the corporation heads; the political leaders and the military chiefs.[79]

He also rejects the view point that Elites in a functioning democracy are neither close-unit nor united. He rather stresses, that they are, in fact, a cohesive group. He supports this view by establishing the similarity of social origins, the close personal and family relationship and the frequency of inter-change of personnel between the three spheres.[80]

He describes the American society as a mass society in which the power elite decides all important issues and keep the masses quiet by flattery, deception and entertainment. He also refers to the corruption of the power elite. For which he accounts for by the absence of any organised public to which they are responsible for their decision. He also refers to the dominance of the wealthy and the political influence of military chiefs.[81]

In short, Mills argues that the American society is dominated by this power elite which is of unprecedented power. Power elite makes momentous decisions without any reference to the people. It is not accountable to any one and the people are subjected to 'instruments of psychic management and manipulation'. The power Elite skillfully controls the mass media and manipulates it to make man in the mass think and act what it likes.[82]

### 8.2.7. Harold D. Lasswell's Theory of Elites

H.D. Lasswell too points out that a society can be divided into two categories of persons namely the masses and the political Elites. For him the study of politics is the study of "Influence and influential" and the influentials are those who get the most of what there is to get".[83]

What people want to get is described by him as 'Values' and he lists the basic values as deference, income and safety. Those who get the most, of these values are called Elites. The rest are the masses.[84]

He further points out that Elites differ as they command different values. That is Elite of deference is not necessarily an Elite of safety. He also analyses the methods by which the Elites are protected or superseded.[85]

He argues that the fate of the Elite is profoundly affected by the ways in which it manipulated the environment. This is to say by the use of violence, goods, symbols and practices.[86]

As the time passed he felt that political Elitism was not based on ability, but on power. Those who wielded power, irrespective of ability were really elite.[87]

He stresses that an elite defends and asserts itself in the name of the symbols of the common destiny. Such symbols are the ideology of the established order and the utopia of counter elites. By the use of sanctioned words and gestures the Elite elicits blood, work, taxes and applause from the masses.[88] He finds the various forms of violence to be a major means of elite attack and defence.

According to him the society can be divided into three categories namely most powerful, less powerful and least powerful. In the first category falls political bosses in the elite group; in second those fall who are in the middle of political group whereas in the third category comes the masses who are the least powerful and have no voice in political policies and decision making process.[89]

He stresses that an Elite is subject to domestic attack when it falls to bring in prosperity. The security of elite is, therefore, bound up with shifts in goods and prices. Lasswell, however, felt that insecurities of the contemporary world, sharpened by the vicissitudes of a rapidly expanding and rapidly contracting economy, foster the conditions of perpetual crisis which favour the seizure of power by the agitator, and the retention of power by the man of ruthless violence.[90]

Thus, in any society there is and must be a minority of the population which takes the major decision and rule over the majority. This minority is comprised political elites. They not only influence governmental decisions but also formally decide policies. The elites gain their dominant position by means beyond election. Their influence is due to their embodying certain social or religious values or heredity or certain personal qualities. James Meisel calls these qualities are three Cs (*i.e.,* $C^3$) — group consciousness, coherance and conspiracy, which help them to maintain their power. The power itself is cumulative by its nature. It also gives access to more and more power as it becomes a means to obtain other social goods such as economic influence, social status, wealth, educational advantages for children and so on. All these too are in themselves powers and, therefore, help to maintain the elite's domination in subsequent generations also. The elitists have also described variously the qualities and social opportunities a group is needed to possess in order to gain an elite position. The Elitist doctrine also believes that this dominant minority cannot be controlled by the majority whatever democratic mechanism it may use. The elitist writers also believe that there is circulation between different categories of the governing elite inself as well as between elite and the rest of the population. The Elite is, therefore, not a permanent group that rules rather its membership changes over a period of time.

## 8.3. RECAPITULATION OF ELITE THEORIES

Many scholars have contributed to the development of the Elite Theory and a wide range of views have been expressed. By recalling the above discussion we may say that at the hands of Vilfredo Pareto and Gaetano Mosca — the two Italian sociologists — Elite theory has become critique of democracy and even defendant of despotism. Both describe the phenomenon of circulation of Elites *i.e.,* circulation between different categories of the governing elites itself and between elite and the rest of the population also. Thus, it is not a permanent group that rules rather the membership of this group changes over period of time. This is, therefore, "The humane climax of the elitist doctrine like Marx's classless society" whereas Pareto examines the psychological make-up of both elite and non-elite, Mosca and Robert Michaels emphasized organisational abilities of elites.

James Burnham and Milovan Djilas, were mostly concerned with socialist countries, Burnham emphasized control of economic resources where Djilas talked of the emergence of the new class in erstwhile USSR which became stronger at the cost of the Communist Party itself. C. Wright Mills — an American scholar — while describing the political process of a democracy, liberated the Elite Theory from its despotic association as depicted by Pareto and Mosca. He has also examined the position they hold, in a number of key institutions within a society. In other words the hierarchical organisation of societies allow the minority to capture and monopolise power.

H.D. Lasswell, however, emphasises that as politics is the study of influence and influentials, the elites (influentials) are those who get most of what there is to get.

## 8.4. ELITE AND DEMOCRACY

The critics of Elite Theories are of the view that the Elitists doctrine is opposed to, or critical of modern Democracy. They argue that upholding the idea of elitism simply means the denial of democratic ideal or the denial of democracy. The opposition between the idea of Elites and the idea of democracy may, however, be expressed in two forms.[91] Firstly, the insistence in the elite theories upon the inequality of individual endownment runs counter to a fundamental stand in democratic political thought the emphasis on underlying equality of individuals. The Elite theories are, therefore, critical of modern democracy and still more of socialism.[92] Secondly, the notion of a governing minority contradicts the democratic theory of majority rule.[93]

But the supporters of Elitism do not agree with this view. They believe that democracy is still compatible with elite theories. They argue that right from the day the representative democracy spread in Europe, there arose misgivings about its nature among intellectuals, conservatives and socialists. He further added that even Lincoln and J.S. Mills over emphasized the role of the people as they believe that all democratic governments tend to rule for the people and in the name of people. If democracy is regarded as being primarily a political system than in actual practice in modern mass society, government by the people (*i.e.*, the effective rule of the majority) is impossible in practice.[94] But the significance of political democracy is primarily that the positions of power in society are open in principle to everyone. There is competition for power, and that the holders of power at any time are accountable to the electorate. In other words the classical concept of democracy has, therefore, been revised. Sebumpeter, thus defines the democracy as "An institutional arrangement for arriving at political decisions in which individuals acquire the power to decide by means of a competitive struggle for the people's vote".[95] Other Elitist thinkers also point out that political Democracy envisages that the choice of personnel should be "open and subject to negotiation and bargaining", among the various elements of the population.[96] Democracy, therefore, provides an opportunity to the people to choose among competing elites. It needs to be emphasize at that political competition and of equality of opportunity can be presented as corollaries of liberal or laissez-faire economic theory.[97] Democracy will then be treated as a type of society in which the elites — economic, cultural, as well as political — are open in principle and are in fact recruited from different social strata on the basis of individual merit.[98]

## 8.5. CRITICISM

The political Elite doctrine has been criticised on several grounds, such as Elite theories are opposed to or critical of modern democracy, socialism and failed to explain the reality of the situation as it obtains in different societies.[99] The elitist theories are nothing but strong reactions against Marxian doctrine of class war. These theories though laid too much stress on elitist politics, yet they failed to offer any viable alternative to the Marxian doctrine of class war.[100] The elitist scholars believe that the elite group not only has ultimate political power but also controls all political activities. But in actual practice it is not so. Robert Dahl, on the other hands points outs that in society there are three notables or elites namely economic, social and political and each of them has its own sphere of influence.[101] As such political elites primarily influence politics and not to that extent other spheres of life.

The critics are also of the view that elitist doctrine did not provide any satisfactory alternative to the basic question of social change, which is vital for the health of a society in every form of government. They also challenged the elitist view that people become elite because of their control on means of production and distribution. That is the political power of elite flows from wealth. This is also not true. It is also not necessary that those who exercise political power are always wealthy people.

Critics do not agree with the view that whatever the Elites say and preach in the society becomes values.[102] Whereas each society has certain values of its own and the elites are supposed to uphold them.

The critics point out that it is not true to say that elite group when come in power try to defend the interests of the masses because elite group go on changing and masses have the potential to change the group. Whereas each elite group generally tries to protect and defend its own interest and not the collective interests of the masses.

The view that elite group being well united and remains in power as it has group consciousness, coherence and conspiracy is not acceptable to many. In reality there are not only rivalries and infighting in every elite group but keen competition for coming in power and joining core of the group.

So far as the view that elite group, being having ultimate authority in decision making process has no restrictions while taking decisions is concerned, the critics point out that there are several factors influencing decision making, such as taste and mood of the masses, social and political values, pressure groups, policies and programme of the rival group etc. etc. It may sometime difficult for the political elites to ignore them.

To believe the elites are the most capable persons and have all the qualities of their wisdom by which they convince the masses to obey them is also not correct. On the other hand the elitists rule because the masses have agreed to be ruled. Otherwise it will impossible for them to rule or to remain in power.[103]

## REFERENCES

1. Maheshwari, S.R. : *Comparative Government and Politics; op.cit.*, p. 141.
2. *Ibid.*
3. Ashraf, Ali; Sharma, L.N. : *Political Sociology; op.cit.*, p. 61.
4. Schumpeter : *Capitalism, Socialism and Democracy*; Harper; New York 1950, p. 269.
5. Ball, R, Alam : *Modern Politics And Government; op.cit.*
6. (i) Wiarda, Howard, J : *Directions In Comparative Politics*; West View Press — Boulder and London 1985, p. 156.
   (ii) Chilcote, Ronald H : *Theories of Comparative Politics*; West View Press, U.S.A., p. 350.
7. Chilcote, Ronald H : *Theories of Comparative Politics; op.cit.*, p. 351.
8. Bottomore, T.B : *Elites and Society*; Penguin Books Ltd. England 1970, p. 1.
9. *Ibid.*
10. Maheshwari, S.R. : *Comparative Government and Politics; op.cit.*, p. 142.
11. Buttomore, T.B : *Elites and Society; op.cit.*, p. 1.
12. Maheshwari, S.R : *Comparative Government and Politics; op.cit.*, p. 142.
13. Chilcote, Ronald H : *Theories of Comparative Politics; op.cit.*, p. 350.
14. Verma, S.P. : *Modern Political Theory*; Vikas Publishers, Delhi 1975 p. 145.
15. Hans Raj : *Comparative Politics; op.cit.*, p. 102.
16. *Ibid.*
17. Maheshwari, S.R. : *Comparative Government and Politics; op.cit.*, p. 141.
18. L.N. Sharma's article "*The Theories of Elites ; Impact and Relevance*", The Indian Journal of Political Science, Vol. XXXVIII, No. 1, January — March 1977, The Indian Political Science Association, p. 64.
19. Verma, S.P : *Modern Political Theory*; Vikas Publishers, Delhi, 1975, p. 143.
20. Maheshwari, S.R : *Comparative Government and Politics; op.cit.*, p. 142.
21. *Ibid.*

22. Ashraf, Ali; Sharma, L.N : *Political Sociology; op.cit.*, p. 62.
23. Vilfred Pareto's Theory of Elite is found in following of his works
    (a) A monograph written in Italian in 1901, published in English under the Title
    "The Rise And Fall of the Elites : An Application of Theoretical Society" New Jersey, The Bedmiton Press 1968.
    (b) 3000 pages Treaties written in Italian in 1916. Its English Translation was first called "Mind and Society" — 4 vols. Hascount Brace New York, 1935.
    (c) Two other works not translated — Les Systems Socialistes (Giard, Paris 1902- 03) and Manule di Economic Pelitica (1906).
24. Pareto, Vilfred : *The Mind and Society*; Jonathan Cape, London, Vol. III, 1935, p. 1423.
25. The Indian Journal of Political Science, Vol. XXXVIII, No. 1, January — March 1977, The Indian Political Science Association, p. 64.
26. Pareto, Vilfred : *The Mind And Society; op.cit.*, p. 27.
27. The Indian Journal of Political Science, Vol. XXXVIII, No. 1, January — March 1977, *op. cit.*, p. 65.
28. *Ibid.*
29. *Ibid.*, p. 64.
30. Wiarda, Howard J. : *Directions in Comparative Politics; op.cit.*, pp. 156 -57.
31. Pareto, Vilfred : *The Rise and Fall of Elites*; The Bedmiton Press, New Jersey, 1968, p. 36.
32. Ashraf, Ali; Sharma, L.N. : *Political Sociology; op.cit.*, p. 64.
33. *Ibid.*, p. 65.
34. Pareto, Vilfred : *The Rise and Fall of the Elites; op.cit.*, p. 59.
35. *Ibid.*, p. 36.
36. *Ibid.*, p. 86.
37. *Ibid.*
38. Maheshwari, S.R : *Comparative Government and Politics; op.cit.*, p. 143.
39. *Ibid.*
40. Mosca, Gaetano : *The Ruling Class*; First published in Italain in 1896, and its English edition was published by McGraw Hill Inclave, New York, and London in 1939.
41. Bottomore, T.B : *Elites and Soceity; op.cit.*, p. 9.
42. *The Indian Journal of Political Science; op.cit.*, p. 68.
43. *Ibid.*
44. *Ibid.*
45. *Ibid.*
46. Bottomore, T.B : *Elites and Society', op.cit.*, p. 9.

47. *Ibid.*
48. Mosca, Gaetano : *The Ruling Class; op.cit.*, pp. 57-60.
49. *The Indian Journal of Political Science; op.cit.*, p. 69.
50. *Ibid.*
51. *Ibid.*
52. *Ibid.*, p. 65.
53. Mosca, Gaetano : *The Ruling Class; op.cit.*, p. 64.
54. *Ibid.*
55. *The Indian Journal of Poltical Science; op.cit.*, p. 70.
56. *Ibid.*
57. Robert, Michaels: Political Parties: A Sociological Study of the Oligarchical Tendencies of Modern Democracy : The Fee Press Illinois 1915, p. 418.
58. Maheshwari, S.R : *Comparative Government and Politics; op. cit.*, p. 146.
59. *Ibid.*
60. *Ibid.*
61. *The Indian Journal of Political Science; op.cit.*, p. 70.
62. *Ibid.*, p. 71.
63. *Ibid.*
64. *Ibid.*
65. *Ibid.*
66. Ashraf, Ali; Sharma, L.N : *Political Sociology,; op.cit.*, p. 69.
67. *Ibid.*
68. *The Indian Journal of Political Science; op.cit.*, p. 73.
69. *Ibid.*
70. Bottomore, T.B : *Elites and Society; op.cit.*, p. 83.
71. *Ibid.*
72. *Ibid.*, p. 84.
73. *The Indian Journal of Political Science; op.cit.*, p. 73.
74. *Ibid.*
75. *Ibid.*
76. Mills, C. Wright : *The Power Elite*; Oxford University Press, London, 1959, p. 4.
77. Maheshwari, S.R. : *Comparative Government and Politics; op.cit.* p. 146.
78. Mills, C. Wright : *The Power Elite; op.cit.*, p. 4.
79. *The Indian Journal of Political Science*; *op.cit.*, pp. 73-74.
80. *Ibid.*
81. *Ibid.*
82. Maheshwari, S.R : *Comparative Government and Politics; op.cit.*, p. 147.

83. Lasswell, H.D : Politics, Who Gets What, When How, Collected in the Political Writings of H.D. Lasswell. The Free Press, Illinois, 1951, p. 295.
84. Hansraj : *Comparative Politics; op.cit.*, p. 112.
85. *Ibid.*
86. *Ibid.*
87. *The Indian Journal of Political Science; op.cit.*, p. 74.
88. *Ibid.*
89. Hansraj : *Comparative Politics; op.cit.*, p. 112.
90. *The Indian Journal of Political Science; op. cit.*; p. 75.
91. Bottomore, T.B : *Elites And Society; op. cit.*, p. 16.
92. *The Indian Journal of Political Science; op. cit.*, p. 76.
93. Bottomore, T.B : *Elites and Society; op.cit.*, p. 16.
94. *Ibid.*
95. *The Indian Journal of Political Science; op.cit.*, p. 77.
96. *Ibid.*
97. Bottomore, T.B : *Elites and Society; op.cit.* p. 17.
98. *Ibid.*
99. Hansraj : *Comparative Politics; op. cit.*, p. 116.
100. *Ibid.*
101. *Ibid.*
102. Hansraj : *Comparative Politics; op.cit.*, p. 116.
103. *Ibid.*, p. 117.

# 9

# Political Modernisation

The interest of the Western Capitalist nations in the poor nations in Post-World War Second era has been focused not only on profits, extraction of raw material, new markets but on the assumption that massive financial and technical assistance from the west would transform these agricultural subsistence societies into modern industrial societies.[1] They, therefore, pleaded that the newly emerging nations should adopt the European values along with assistance for their political development and modernisation.[2] They believe that the experience of the Western Europe of development and modernisation would modernize the less developed nations of the Third World also. Another view is that the need for the study of modernisation and its related problems has arisen simply because many of the emerging nations not only won political freedom but have developed a craze for economic development. In other words the urge for socio-political reforms and economic growth was the part of their movement of political freedom.[3] The aspiration for national dignity and development as well as independence, therefore, found a practical basis for the academic concern with political development and political modernisation.[4]

The political scientists who have worked in this field, however, failed to develop a universally accepted theory about Political Modernisation5

## 9.1. MODERNISATION AND POLITICAL MODERNISATION — CONCEPTS

The concept 'Political Modernisation,' like Political Development is very vague. Different scholars have defined it differently. Most of the western political scientists regarded modernisation as westernisation.[6]

The term 'Modernisation' is, however, said to be the current term for the old process, the process of social change, whereby less developed societies acquire characteristics common to more developed societies.[7] It is a process based upon the rational utilisation of resources and aimed at the establishment of a modern society.[8] For some persons, modernisation is a process of structural differentiation, functional specialisation and adaptive upgrading.[9] Modernisation in the evolutionary perspective refers to transition from primitive to traditional, to industrialised society; from religious to secular ideology, from particularism, ascription, diffuseness, self orientation to universalism, achievement, specificity, and collectively orientation from extended family to nuclear family and so on.[10] Maufred Halpern defines modernisation as the capacity to or control of rapid and continuous change.[11]

Modernisation is also defined by some scholars as the process by which individuals change from traditional way of life to a new complex, technologically advance, rapidly changing styles of life. In other words modernisation "is regarded as a comprehensive phenomenon which brings about radical changes in the field of economic development, mainly in the direction of industrialisation and material advancement, changes in the nature and content of political systems and also changes in the social and psychological spheres of life."[12] According to W.W. Rostow "Modernisation implies an intellectual, a technological and social revolution."[13] A.B. Smith points out "Modernisation is defined as man's increased knowledge and mastery of his environment. Benjamin Schwartz degines Political Modernisation as "The systematic, sustained and powerful application of human energies to the rational control of man's phyical and social environment for various human purposes."[14] C.E. Black defines "The process by which historically evolved institutions are adapted to the rapidly changing functions that represent the unprecedented increase in man's knowledge, pertaining to control over his environment that accompanied scientific revolution is called Modernisation."[15]

Gabriel A. Almond and G. Bingham Powell Jr. Say "The Political Modernisation refers to those processes of differentiation of political structures and secularisation of political culture which enhance the capacity of society's political system."[16] Michael Curtis points out that "Modernisation implies economic growth, the increase of gross national product and of per capita income, economic planning, greater industrialisation, the accumulation of capital, increasing urbanization and a reduction in the proportion of those engaged in agriculture, scientific advance, improved transport and a higher rate of literacy."[17] It signifies a move from a subsistence to an industrialized economy and a social change from an extended to a nuclear family."[18]

According to Huntington "Modernisation is a multifaceted process involving change in all areas of human thought and activity". He further points out that "the principal aspects of modernisation are urbanisation, industrialisation, secularisation, democratisation, education and media participation."[19] He further adds that "Modernisation implies industrialisation, economic growth, increasing social mobility and political participation."[20]

Davies and Lewis argue that Modernisation is the term stands for the transformation of the political culture in response to the changes in social and physical environments.[21] According to Yogendra Singh "Modernisation is "differentiation and rational organisation of rules and its aggregates at structural level and represents the historical evolution and synthesis of values of modernity at the fundamental or categorial levels with those at the instrumental or pragmatic level, on cultural plane."[22]

At the national level various processes such as industrialisation, economic growth, rationalisation, political development, social mobilization, structural differentialism, secularisation, democratisation and some other processes are conceptualized as modernisation.[23]

Marxist scholars define modernisation in terms of consciousness as ideology or superstructures. They see modernisation as the imposition of infrastructures of domination and exploitation and interpret elements of consciousness as dependent variable i.e. an appendage of infrastructures.[24]

In the words of Karl Deutch "Modernisation is a process by which major cultures of old social, economic and psychological commitments are eroaded or broken down and the people become available for new pattern of socialization and behaviour."[25] Modernisation, thus, involves a large varieties of inspirations, dynamism, change, mechanisation, industrialisation, urbanisation, increase in literacy, increase in mass media, economic growth, greater social and occupational mobility.

Since various meanings have been given to the Concepts of 'Modernisation.' There is hardly a universally accepted view as what exactly the term 'Modernisation' wants to convey. There is, thus, confusion and blur in the conceptualization of Modernisation.

The political aspects of modernisation however, refer to the ensemble of structural and cultural changes in the political systems of modernising societies.[26] Political Modernisation, therefore, refers to those processes of differentiation of Political structure and secularisation of political cultures which enhance the capability—the effectiveness and efficiency of performance — of a society's political system.[27]

Political Modernisation can also be viewed from a historical, a typological, and an evolutionary perspective.[28] Historical political modernisation refers to the totality of changes in political structure and culture which characteristically have affected or have been affected by those major transformative processes of modernisation which were first launched in Western Europe in the sixteenth century and which subsequently have spread, unevenly and incompletely, throughout the world.[29] These are secularisation, commercialization, industrialisation, accelerated social mobility, restratification, increased material standards of living, diffusion of literacy, education, and mass media, national unification, and the expansion of popular involvement and participation.[30]

Typological political modernisation, on the other hand, refers to the process of transmutation of a pre-modern traditional polity into a post-traditional modern polity.'[31] But evolutionary Political modernisation refers to that open-ended increase in the capacity of political man to develop structures to cope with or resolve problems, to absorb and adapt to continuous change, and to strive purposively and creatively for the attainment of new social goals.[32]

## 9.2. CHARACTERISTICS OF MODERNISATION

S.N. Eisenstadt sums up the characteristics of modernisation as follows:[33]

### 9.2.1. Social Mobilisation

The indices of social mobilization are exposure to aspects of modern life such as machinery and mass media; change of residence *i.e.*, urbanization; change from agricultural occupation and literacy and the growth of per capita income.

### 9.2.2. Social Differentiation

Which implies the specialisation of institutional, structures and recruitment based on universal achievement criteria and separatism between the different roles held by an individual and the disposal of rules;

### 9.2.3. Economic Change

Which means change with reference to technology and development of secondary and tertiary occupations and mass consumption;

### 9.2.4. Political Change

Which includes the extension of territorial scope and the intensification of the power of the centre; the continued spreading political power to wider groups; populistic and democratic politics and participation; fluidity of political support; interest oriented politics; and political institutions like political parties and pressure groups.

In other words the main characteristics of Modernisation are social mobility, economic development, rationalisation of authority, differentiation of structures, extention of political participation; democratisation of political institutions and secularisation of world culture.

## 9.3. PROBLEMS OF MODERNIZING SOCIETIES, PATHS TAKEN BY THEM AND THE MODELS OF POLITICAL MODERNISATIONS.

C.E. Black has identified the following four critical problems that all modernising societies must face:[34]

(a) A challenge to modernity;
(b) The consolidation of modernising leadership;
(c) Economic and social transformation; and
(d) Integration of society.

Barrington Moose has, on the other hand, suggested the following three different patterns taken by societies on the road of modernity:[35]

(a) A bourgeois revolution resulting in Western democracy.
(b) A conservative reaction leading to fascism.
(c) A peasant revolution leading to Communism.

As a result the models of Political Modernisation are Liberal; Democratic, Communistic and authoritarian-particularly military regimes.[36]

## 9.4. APPROACHES TO MODERNISATION

The approaches to Modernisation can be classified as Conservative and Modern. Conservative approaches are further classified as Fascism, Nazism, Apocalytic, Cyclical and Evolutionary. Whereas Modern approaches are classified into Revolutionary and Liberal or Laiseze faire. The approaches of modernisation are, therefore, presented in the following table.

**Approaches to Modernisation**

- Conservative
  - Fascism
  - Nazism
  - Apocalytic
  - Cyclical
  - Evolutionary
- Modern
  - Revolutionary or Dialectrical or progressive
  - Liberal or Laiseze Faire

### 9.4.1. Fascism

The term 'Fascism' or word 'Fascist', which was overused and misused, has been taken from the ancient Roman symbol of authority, a bundle of sticks bound around an ax (the fasces) most of all hated disorder and wanted strong leadership to end it.[37] Being reaction to the democracy, socialism and communism it not only opposes the rationalist traditions of the west, international organisations, rejects equality, repudiates individualism but also substitutes the principle of hierarchy culminating in a supreme leader or dictator whose will is law, and who asserts that all the values derive from the state, which is an end itself and man as an instrument, and relied upon military solution.[38] 'Fascism' believes the true liberty found only in subjucation to the state authority, peace to be corrosive and a cause of decadence, complete conformity, rigid discipline, unquestioned obedience, legitimate use of force, and reason and logic to be substituted by emotions and faith.[39] No organisation is allowed to complete the state for loyalty of individual, legislatures will be ratifying bodies, Courts lose independence, local governments controlled by the central authority, political power in the hands of dictator and single political party, which monopolised political power.[40] It strives to engender mass enthusiasm for its regime and policies. According to Fascists such a state will rapidly bring modernisation. For example in Fascist, Italy Fascism looked impressive. There was little crime, much monumental construction, stable prices, no unemployment and even trains ran on time. Fascism was, therefore, said to be wave of the future.[41]

### 9.4.2. Nazism

Nazism is a variety of Fascism which became wide-spread in Germany during Hitler. Nazism, therefore, means all the charactersitcs of Fascism plus superiority of race. All the Political Powers were monopolised by a single party, which is controlled by a dictater. For example in Germany under Hitler, The Nazis — members of the National Socialist German Workers Party — believed the Germans as a distinct and superior race. Though they were of a special branch of the white race yet Aryans — the bearers of all civilization.[42] In Germany, under Nazism, the economy and unemployment improved, production increased and a kind of prosperity appeared. Many working people felt that they were getting a good deal with the jobs, vacations and welfare. Its economic policies were designed to build a powerful military machine.[43]

### 9.4.3. Apocalytic

Apocalytic approach refers to the religious or divine revolution like the last book of the New Testament, a revelation of the end of the world. A revelation about the path followed by society moving forward. For example Christianity believes that society is moving towards a final judgement resulting in just social order. Hinduism, on the other hand, refers to the wheel of time *i.e.*, Satayuga — 4000 years; Thratayuga 3000 years, Dwapeiyuga — 2000 years and Kalyuga for 1000 years. The society, therefore, moves from one stage to another.

### 9.4.4. Cyclical

Cyclical approach refers to the evolution of a society from imperfection towards perfection. In other words the evolution of a society follows a well marked stages of progress and towards increasing perfection. Just like the Dasawan Theory of evolution of man.

### 9.4.5. Evolutionary

Evolutionary approach refers that all societies have period of rise and fall, growth and decline. For example Petrie's revolution of civilization, spengler's Decline of the West, Nixion's Rise of the Third World in 21st Century.

### 9.4.6. Revolutionary/Dialectical/Progressive

Modern approaches, are, however, Revolutionary or Dialectical or Progressive and Liberal or Laissez-faire. The Revolutionary or Dialectical or Progressive approach is a radical break from the past. It is future oriented. It believes in progress in a planned way *i.e.*, not to allow changes in haphazard manner. For example the interaction between capitalism and proleterates leads to communism. This happened in Russia, China, Vietnam, and other socialist countries.

### 9.4.7. Liberal or Laisseze-Faire

Liberal or Laisseze-Faire approach supports individualism. It lays stress on the freedom of individuals in all spheres of life in general and in economic sphere in particular. This approach does not support radical or revolutionary ways for a change in society but pleads for step by step change. For this approach the freedom of individuals is paramount and the democratic way of life is the only way for the progress of a society towards true or perfect social order.

## 9.5. POLITICAL MODERNISATION AND POLITICAL DEVELOPMENT

There are a few concepts in social sciences in general and in political science in particular which appear synonymous. These concepts generally used interchangeably giving false impression of being common. 'Political Modernisation' and 'Political Development' are also such concepts. These two terms are, however, qualitatively distinctive processes having strong value connotation. Change is the characteristic of a social system. But all the changes that take place are two types.[44] Firstly, some of them are automatic, involuntary not having the power of will or choice.[45] Secondly, the changes which are the product of the intervention of will or choice *i.e.*, desired, planned, directed and stimulated. The concepts of modernisation and development are, therefore, belong to the second category.[46] While distinguishing between 'Development' and 'Modernisation' David Apter points out

"Development, the most general, results from the proliferation and integration of functional roles in the Community Modernisation is a particular case of development. Modernisation implies three conditions — a social system that can constantly innovate without falling apart. ...; differentiated, flexible social structures, and a social framework to provide the skills and knowledge necessary for living in a technologically advanced world. Industrialisation, special aspect of modernisation, may be defined as the period in a society in which the strategic functional roles are related to manufacturing."[47]

The distinctions between two concepts are as under :

1. Modernisation is open ended and value free term. But as political development implies movement forward to some goal or preferred political order, it is value oriented term.
2. Political Modernisation provides both the possibilities of development as well as decay. Whereas Political development is a movement towards some higher order.
3. Political Modernisation is a narrow term. But Political Development is a broad term as it even covers Political Modernisation also.
4. Whereas Political Modernisation lays stress on the spreading of secular world culture and democratisation of Political

institution, the Political Development lays emphasis on the overall socio-economic development.

C.H. Dodd, however, points out that the problem of distinction between political modernisation and political development is full of ambiguity and theoretical difficulties. These two concepts are, therefore, complimentary and not contradictory.

## REFERENCES

1. Chilcote, Ronald H : *Theory of Comparative Politics*, West-View Press, U.S.A., p. 278.
2. *Ibid.*
3. Hans Raj : *Comparatice Politics, op.cit.*, p. 234.
4. Ashraf, Alia, Sharma, L.N. : *Political Sociology, op.cit.*, p. 120.
5. Hans Raj, *Comparative Politics, op.cit.*, p. 234.
6. Verma, S.P. : *Modern Political Theory, op.cit.*, p. 348.
7. Encylopaedia of Social Sciences.
8. *Ibid.*
9. Pandey, Rajendra: *Sociology of Development*, Mittal Publishers, Delhi, 1985, p. 175.
10. *Ibid.*, p. 175.
11. *Ibid.*
12. Varma, S.P. : *Modern Political Theory, op.cit.*, pp. 302-303.
13. Rostow, W.W.: *Politics and The Stages of Growth*, Cambridge University Press N. Y. 1971, pp. 58-60.
14. Johari, J.C. : *Comparative Politics, op.cit.*, p. 124.
15. Black, C.E. : *The Dynamics of Modernisation : A Study in Comparative History*, New York; Haper and Row, 1968.
16. Almond, Gabriel A: Powell, and Bingham G. *Comparative Politics: A Developmental Approach.*
17. Curtis, Michael : *Comparative Government and Politics, op.cit.*, p. 76.
18. *Ibid.*
19. Huntington, Sammal P. : *Political Order in Changing Societies*, New Haven Conn. Yale University Press, 1968.
20. Chilcote, Ronald H. : *Theory of Comparative Politics, op.cit.*, p. 280.
21. Davis, Morton R, Lewis, Vangham A. : *Models in Political Science.*
22. Pandey, Rajendra, *Sociology of Development, op.cit.*, p. 175.
23. *Ibid.*, p. 171.
24. *Ibid.*, p. 174.
25. Ashraf, Ali, Sharma, L.N. : *Political Sociology, op.cit.*, p. 123.
26. David & Sills : *International encyclopedia of the Social Sciences*, (Edt.), Vol. 10, The Macmillan Company and the Free Press, 1968, U.S.A., p. 395.
27. *Ibid.*

28. *Ibid.*
29. *Ibid.*
30. *Ibid.*
31. *Ibid.*
32. *Ibid.*
33. Eisentadt, S.N. : *Modernisation, Protest and Change*, Prentice-Hall of India, New Delhi, 1964, p. 11.
34. Ashraf, Ali, Sharma, L.N., : *Political Sociology, op. cit.*, p. 123.
35. Curtis, Michael : *Comparative Government and Politics, op. cit.*, p. 78.
36. Hans Raj : *Comparative Politics, op. cit.*, p. 235.
37. Cord, Robert L, Medeiros, James A., Jones, Walter S. Roskin, Michael G.: *Political Science —An Introduction* Prentice-Hall Inc., Engle Wood Cliffs, New Jersey, 1985, p. 116.
38. Dunner, Joseph (Ed.): *Dictionary of Political Science*, Vision Press Ltd., 74 A Regent Street, London, 1965, p. 179.
39. *Ibid.*
40. Carlton, Clymer Rodee, Anderson, Totton Jame : *Introduction to Political Science*, Mc-Graw-Hill Kogakusha Ltd; London, 1967, p. 110.
41. Cord, Robert L, Medilros, James A, Jones, Walters. S, Roskin, Michael, G.: *Political Science; An Introduction, op.cit.*, p. 116.
42. *Ibid.*, p. 116.
43. *Ibid.*
44. Pandey, Rajendra : *Sociology of Development, op.cit.*, p. 223.
45. *Ibid.*
46. *Ibid.*
47. Chilcote, Ronald H : *Theory of Comparative Politics, op.cit.*, pp. 281-282.

# BIBLIOGRAPHY


Almond, Gabriel A. and Coleman, James S., *Politics of Developing Areas* (edited), Princeton University Press, Princeton, 1970.

Almond, Gabriel A. and Verba, Sidney, *Civic Culture*, Princeton New Jersey, 1972.

Almond, Gabriel A. and Powell, G. Bingham Jr., *Comparative Politics — A Developmental Approach*, Oxford and IBH Publishing Co., New Delhi, 1978.

Apter, David E., *Introduction to Political Analysis*, Prentice-Hall of India Pvt. Ltd., New Delhi, 1978.

Atal, Yogesh, *Building A Nation*, Abhinave Publications, New Delhi, 1981.

Ashraf, Ali and Sharma, L.N., *Political Sociology —A New Grammar of Politics*, Universities Press Pvt. Ltd. Madras, 1983 .

Blondel, Jean, *An Introduction to Comparative Government*, Weidenfeld and Nicolson, London, 1969.

Ball, Alan R., *Modern Politics And Government*, The Macmillan Press Ltd., London, 1971.

Brown, Bernard E., *New Direction in Comparative Politics*, Asia Publishing House, New Delhi, 1961.

Bryce, *Modern Democracies*, The World Press Pvt. Ltd., Calcutta, 1962.

Blondel, Jean and Herman, Valentine, *Work Book For Comparative Politics*, Weiden Feld and Nicolson, London, 1972.

Bendix, Reinhard, *Nation-Building And Citizenship : Studies of Our Changing Social Order*, Wiley Eastern Ltd., New Delhi, 1969.

Binder, Leonard, *Crisis And Sequences In Political Development*, Princeton University Press, Princeton, 1971.

Bottomore, T.B., *Elites And Society*, Penguin Books Ltd; England, 1970.

Black, C.E., *The Dynamics of Modernisation*, Harper & Row, New York, 1968.

Cord, Robert L., Medeirous James A; Jones, Walters; Raskim, Michael G.: *Political Science An Introduction*, Prentice-Hall Inc., New Jersey, 1985.

Curtis, Michael, *Comparative Government and Politics*, Harper & Row Publishers, New York, 1968.

——, *Comparative Government and Politics*, (Second Edition), Harper and Row Publishers, New York, 1978.

Chilcote, Ronad H., *Theories of Comparative Politics*, West-View Press, U.S.A.

Deutsch, Karl, *Nation and World, Contemporary Political Science*, McGraw Hill Co., New York, 1967.

Davies, Morton R., Lewis, Vaugham A., *Models of Political System*, Vikas Publications, Delhi, 1971.

Dicey A.V., *Law of the Constitution*, Macmillan, London, 1959.

Duverger, Maurice, *Political Parties*, Methuen & Co. Ltd; London, 1954.

Dogan, Mattei; Rose, Richard, *European Politics*, Little Brown & Co., Boston, 1971.

Dunner, Joseph, *Dictionary of Political Science*, Vision Press Ltd., London, 1965.

Djilas, Milovan, *The New Class: An Analysis of the Communist System*, Frederick A. Praegar, New York, 1957.

Easton, David, *A System Analysis of Political Life*, The University of Chicago Press, Chicago, New York, 1965.

Encyclopaedia Brittanica. Vol. 14.

Eisenstadt, S.N., *Modernisation, Protest And Change*, Prentice-Hall of India, New Delhi, 1969.

Finer, S.E., *Comparative Government*, Allen Lane, The Penguin Press, London, 1970.

Finer, Herman, *The Theory and Practice of Modern Governments*, Methuen Co. Ltd., London, 1965.

Friendrich Carl, J. and Brazenzinski, Zbigniew, K., *Totalitarian, Dictatorship and Autocracy*, The Times of India Press, Bombay 1969.

Gamer, J.W. and Row, *Political Science And Government*, World Press, London, 1952.

Gandhi, Madan G., *Modern Political Analysis*, Rohtak University Press, Rohtak, 1976.

Greenstein, Fed I., Polsby, Nelson W., *Hand Book of Political Science* (edited), Vol. 3, Addison-Weslay Publishers Company, London, 1975.

Geetz, Clifford, *Old Societies and New States*, Amerind Publishing Co., New Delhi, 1971.

Grazia, Alfred de., *Political Behaviour*, Vol. I, The Freepress, New York, 1962.

Hans Raj, *Comparative Politics*, Surjeet Publications, Delhi, 1985.

Holt, Robert And Tunner, John, E., *The Political Basis of Economic Development*, East-West Press, New Delhi, 1970.

Hening, Stanley and Pinder, John, *European Political Parties*, (edited), George Allen & Unwin Ltd., Ruskin House, London, 1969.

Hunlinglon, Samuel, P., *Political Order in Changing Societies*, New Haven Coun. Yale University Press, U.S.A. 1968.

Hyman, Herbert, *Political Socialization*, The Free Press New York, 1959.

*International Encyclopaedia of the Social Science*, Vol. 14. *The Indian Journal of Political Science*, Vol. XXXVIII, No. 1, January-March, 1977. The Indian Political Science Association.

*International Encyclopaedia of the Social Sciences*, Vol. 11.

Johari, J.C., *Comparative Politics*, Sterling Publishers, New Delhi, 1980.

Kavangh, Dennis, *Political Culture*, London, 1972.

Kebschull, Harvey G., *Politics in Transitional Societies* Appleton- Century-Crafts Educational Division Meredith Corporation, New York, 1968.

Kothari, Rajni, *State And Nation Building*, (ed.), Allied Publishers Pvt. Ltd., New Delhi, 1971.

Lasswell, H.D., *Politics, Who Gets What, When, How*, The Free Press Ulinos, 1951.

Lasswell, H.D., and Kaplan A, *Power and Society*, London, 1952.

Larson, Allan L., *Comparative Political Analysis*, Nelson Hall, Chicago, 1980.

Lucian, W. Pye and Kay Ryland, *Committee on Comparative Politics*, Social Science Research Council, New York, 1971.

La Palombara, Joseph and Weiner, Myron, *Political Parties and Political Development* (edited), Princeton, New-Jersey, Princeton University Press, 1966.

Maheshwari, Sriram, *Comparative Government and Politics*, Lakshmi Narain Aggarwal, Educational Publishers, Agra, 1980.

Merkl, Peter H., *Political Continuity And Change*, Harper & Row, Evanster, London,

——, *Modern Comparative Politics*, Holt, Rinehart and Winston, New York, 1970.

Macridis, Roy C., *Political Parties Contemporary Trends, And Ideas* (edited), Harper Torch Book, New York, 1967.

Mosca, Gaeteno, *The Ruling Class*, McGraw Hill Inclave, New York, 1939.

Mills, C. Wright, *The Power Elites*, Oxford University Press, London, 1939.

Neumann, Sigmund, *Modern Political Parties* (edited), The University of Chicago Press, London, 1967.

——, *Towards Comparative Study of Political Parties*, New York, 1963.

Puri S., *Modern Political Analysis*, Publishing Company, Jullunder, 1977.

Pulparampil, John, K., *Models of National Building*: A Critical Appraisal Amarko Book Agency, B-12, Amer Coloney, New Delhi.

Pye, Lucian W., and Verba, Sidney : *Political Culture and Political Development*, Princeton University Press, 1965.

Pye, Lucian W., *Aspects of Political Development*, Boston, Little Brown, 1965.

Pareto, Vilfred : *The Mind And Society*, Jonathan Cape, London, 1935.

Pareto, Vilfred, *The Rise And Fall of Elites*, Bedmiton Press, New Jersey, 1968.

Pandey, Rajendra, *Sociology of Development*, Mittal Publishers, Delhi, 1985.

Ray, Amal; Bhattacharya, Mohit, *Political Theory*, The World Press Pvt. Ltd., Calcutta, 1983.

Robson, W.A., *The University Teaching of Political Science*, Political Science (Paris), UNESCO, 1954.

Rodee, Carlton Clymer; Anderson, Totton James; Christol, Carl Quimby and Greene, Thomas H.; : *Introduction to Political Science*, McGraw-Hill Kogakusha Ltd., London, 1957.

Rose, R., *Electoral Behaviour*, A Comparative Handbook, New York, 1974.

Rosenbaum, Walter A., *Political Culture.*

Robert, Michaels, *Political Parties*, Free Press, Illinos, 1975.

Rostow, W. W., *Politics and the Stages of Growth*, Cambridge University Press, New York, 1971.

Sabine, George H., Thorson, Thomas L.,A. *History of Political Theory*, Oxford & IBH Publishing Co., New Delhi, 1973.

Sartori, G., *Concept Misformation on Comparative Politics*, American Political Review, Vol. 54, 1970.

Schumpeter, *Capitalism, Socialism And Democracy*, Harper, New York, 1950.

Sibley, Mulford Q., *Political Ideas and Ideologies*, Harper and Row Publishers, New York, 1970.

Sprenger, Danald P., *Comparative State Politics*, Charless E. Merrill Publishing Company, Columbus OHIO, 1972.

Strong, C.F., *Modern Political Constitutions*, Sidgwick and Jackson Ltd., London, 1963.

Suda, Jyoti Prasad, *History of Political Thought*, Vol. I & II, Jai Prakash Nath and Co., 1958, Meerut.

*The Times of India* of 30th June, 1980.

Verma, S.P., *Modern Political Theory*, Vikas Publishing House Pvt. Ltd., New Delhi, 1975.

Wiarda, Howard J., *New Direction in Comparative Politics*, West-View Press, Boulder and London 1965.

Welsh, William A., *Studying Politics*, Praeger, New York, 1973.

Wheare, K.C., *Modern Constitutions*, Oxford University Press, London, 1966.

*World Encyclopeadia of Political Systems*, Vol. I & II, Edited by George E. Delury, Longman Burnt Hill, Harlow, Essex, U.K., 1983.

Young, Oran R., System of Political Science, Prentice-Hall Inc Englewood, Cliffs, New Jersey, 1966.